HIP-HOP
hitmakers

LANDMARK
HIP-HOP HITS

Carol Ellis

MC Mason Crest
Philadelphia

Mason Crest
370 Reed Road
Broomall, PA 19008
www.masoncrest.com

CPSIA Compliance Information: Batch #HHH040112-8.
For further information, contact Mason Crest at 1-866-MCP-Book

First printing
1 3 5 7 9 8 6 4 2

Library of Congress Cataloging-in-Publication Data

Ellis, Carol, 1945-
 Landmark hip-hop hits / Carol Ellis.
   p. cm. — (Hip-hop hitmakers)
 Includes bibliographical references and index.
 ISBN 978-1-4222-2121-1 (hc)
 ISBN 978-1-4222-2134-1 (pb)
 ISBN 978-1-4222-9461-1 (ebook)
 1. Rap (Music)—History and criticism—Juvenile literature. I. Title.
 ML3531.E46 2013
 782.421649—dc23
                                    2012016173

Photo credits: Getty Images: 6, 10; © 2012 Photos.com, a division of Getty Images: 4; PR Newswire: 30; Redferns: 12; Admedia / Shutterstock.com: 21; Arvzdix / Shutterstock.com: 53; Helga Esteb / Shutterstock.com: 18; Featureflash / Shutterstock.com: 8, 23, 36, 40, 41, 43, 45, 47, 50, 54, 55 (top); Left Eyed Photography / Shutterstock.com: 49; Randy Miramontez / Shutterstock.com: 44; Lev Radin / Shutterstock.com: 9, 25; Derrick Salters / Shutterstock.com: 22, 26; Tristan Scholze / Shutterstock.com: 29; Joe Seer / Shutterstock.com: 17; John Steel / Shutterstock.com: 55 (bottom); Stocklight / Shutterstock.com: 16.

Contents

Hip-hop music was born in the South Bronx, a New York City borough across the Harlem River from Manhattan, during the 1970s.

the early years

In October 1979, a disc jockey on station WESL-AM in St. Louis "dropped the needle" on a 12-inch vinyl record. A catchy, upbeat tune with rhymes spoken in time to a funky beat played across the airwaves. The station's phone lines lit up. *What's that music?* listeners wanted to know. *Who's doing it? Where can I buy the record?*

And even though the song was almost 15 minutes long—three times longer than most songs—callers begged for it to be played again … and again … and again.

The group was the Sugarhill Gang. Their song was called "Rapper's Delight," and it was the first hip-hop song to become a mainstream hit.

STREET MUSIC

Hip-hop was new to a lot of radio listeners, but it had been heard on the streets of Bronx, New

Members of the Sugarhill Gang (left to right) Michael "Wonder Mike" Wright, Guy "Master Gee" O'Brian, and Henry "Big Bank" Jackson perform on stage in New York during the late 1970s. Their hit "Rapper's Delight" is generally considered to be the song that drew national attention to hip-hop music.

York for years. "Hip-hop is street music!" explained rapper Busta Rhymes. "It ain't come from nobody's house! You know what I'm saying? It's something that we all gathered in the street to do."

In the 1970s, many people in this borough of New York City were poor. Most of the residents were African Americans. Their neighborhoods were run-down, with cracked sidewalks, piled-up garbage and burned-out apartment buildings. Drugs and street gangs led to crime and death. It was a tough place to grow up in and live in.

But there was always music to lighten things up. Most young people could not afford tickets to dance and music clubs. There were no mp3 players then, no downloading to a computer or an iPod. People got their music from the radio. They played vinyl records on a turntable or cassettes on a tape player. Someone was always playing music at neighborhood block parties, in the parks, on the street corners. These outdoor places became the "clubs" where people gathered to have a good time and dance to the music.

> ## FAST FACT
> "Rapper's Delight" hit number four on Billboard's R&B charts. It made it to number 36 on the pop charts. At the height of its popularity, it was selling 50,000 copies every day.

THE DJ, THE MC, THE B-BOYS, AND THE RAP

Hip-hop was born at these street parties. It started with the DJs who set up turntables and speakers and played soul, funk, R&B and disco at the parties and parks. But DJs didn't just put on a record and let it play. They experimented with the sound. One technique that DJs used became known as "scratching." This technique was developed by a DJ who called himself Grand Wizard Theodore. He would move a record back and forth against the needle to make a scratching sound that would add to the song's rhythm.

Another Bronx DJ, known as Kool Herc, liked to use two records of the same song on separate turntables. He would play the "break"—the instrumental section of a funk or R&B song—over and over again, making it last longer. The break was the most popular part of the music for dancing, and DJ Kool Herc's long breaks gave dancers a chance to perfect and show off their *intricate* footwork and spinning moves. Kool Herc called these dancers "break boys," because they danced during the song breaks. After a time, the term "b-boys" came to mean anyone who lived the hip-hop lifestyle.

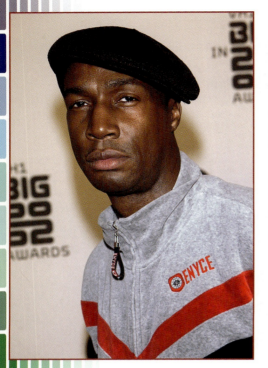

Grandmaster Flash was one of the leading figures in the early days of hip-hop. A talented DJ, his most influential hit was 1982's "The Message." It was different from the usual good-time party music of the early hip-hop days. "The Message" was one of the first hip-hop records to talk about the harshness of street life, and included the well-known refrain, "It's like a jungle sometimes/ it makes me wonder how I keep from goin' under."

Another important figure on the hip-hop scene was the MC—the master of ceremonies. While a DJ was busy playing records, the MC would grab the microphone and get the crowd involved. At first, they would simply encourage the audience to dance or clap to the beat. But many MCs didn't stop with simple *catchphrases*. They took their performances to a whole new level. They began speaking lyrics to accompany the beat of the music. These grew into complicated, poetic raps. Freestyle rhyming—in which an MC made up rhymes on the spot, without working out a rap ahead of time—became a hip-hop art form.

In the late 1970s, a DJ named Grandmaster Flash began working with five talented MCs. They became known as the Furious Five, and were famous for their intricate rhymes. By breaking up the phrases, they could make five MCs sound like one.

MCs soon became the stars of the hip-hop scene. And the hip-hop scene was fast becoming more than gatherings on the street or in

Fab 5 Freddy was another pioneer in the evolution of hip-hop culture. He was a well-known graffiti artist and rapper in the 1970s and early 1980s. His best-known song, "Change the Beat," was released in 1982. Freddy later hosted the first hip-hop music video show on television, Yo! MTV Raps, *from 1988 to 1995.*

apartment courtyards. Clubs like Harlem World and the T Connection packed in huge crowds. People recorded the sessions and traded or sold their tapes.

But until 1979, hip-hop was still a local music style. No one heard it on the radio, only at the clubs and parties. Then "Rapper's Delight" hit the airwaves and things started to change. "Rapper's Delight" used the base line from a song called "Good Times," repeating the instrumental over and over as the rapper performed. *Sampling* became a common element of hip-hop music.

BREAKTHROUGH

Christmas music fills the airwaves at holiday time. Some people love it. Others tune it out. But in late 1979, a holiday song came along that almost no one could ignore. Called "Christmas Rappin'," it was a hip-hop version of "The Night before Christmas."

"Bout a red-suited dude with a friendly attitude
And a sleigh full of goodies for the people on the bl
Got a long white beard, maybe looks kind a weird
And if you ever see him, he could give you quite a

Two of the early stars of hip-hop music were rapper Kurtis Blow (left) and DJ Kool Herc. This photo was taken in the early 1980s.

"Christmas Rappin'" put a modern, urban spin on a classic holiday poem. It was funky and funny and an instant hit for rapper Kurtis Blow. Born Curtis Walker, Kurtis Blow grew up in New York in the early days of hip-hop. He learned the ropes from other DJs and MCs and became a master at spinning and rapping. His talent convinced the two writers of "Christmas Rappin'" to record their song with him.

"Christmas Rappin'" was not just a huge it. It also led to a huge breakthrough for Kurtis Blow and for hip-hop itself. For the first time in hip-hop's history, a major record label signed a deal with a rapper. In 1980, Mercury Records released Blow's **single**, "The Breaks." It became an even bigger hit than "Christmas Rappin'." More than 500,000 copies of "The Breaks" were eventually sold, making it the first hip-hop single to be certified as a **gold record.**

===**FAST FACT**===

An album that has sold 500,000 copies is a certified gold record, a platinum album has sold 1,000,000 copies, and an album that sells over 1,000,000 copies has gone multi-platinum.

FEUDS AND RIVALRIES

Since the beginnings of hip-hop music, there have been rivalries between different MCs or rap groups. As MCs at street parties began to come up with more complex rhymes, they began to give "shout outs" to friends in the audience. The MCs would also brag about their rapping skills, often claiming to be the best. Sometimes, they would insult other rappers, who would then respond. This would create a rivalry, also called a feud or a beef.

In the early days of hip-hop, feuds were generally confined to lyrical insults. Although rappers would tease or put down their rivals, violence was unusual. Sometimes rival rappers would appear together in "battles," and exchange rhymes. The audience could then decide which rapper was the better MC.

An early rivalry began with the release of a song called "Roxanne Roxanne," by the group UTFO in 1984. The song was about a girl who does not pay attention to the group's members. Dozens of other performers created songs in response over the next few years. These included "Roxanne's Revenge," "The Real Roxanne," and "Sparky's Turn (Roxanne, You're Through)."

The groundbreaking group Run-DMC helped to shape the sound, and look, of hip-hop music in the 1980s.

a new age

In the late 1970s, when Curtis Walker started MCing under the name Kurtis Blow, his manager was an ambitious young man named Russell Simmons. Simmons spread the word about Kurtis Blow, booked him to perform at clubs, and helped make him famous. Simmons also supplied him with a DJ—his own teenage brother, Joseph Simmons. Joseph Simmons billed himself as DJ Run, the Son of Kurtis Blow.

THREE FRIENDS FROM QUEENS

Joseph Simmons grew up in a middle-class neighborhood in the Hollis, Queens, neighborhood of New York. He was a big fan of the new hip-hop music, and would practice DJ techniques late into the night. His brother, Russell, and Russell's friends started to notice. "I would be sitting there when they came home from the club, deejaying from the attic from what little knowledge I had, and they were like, 'Joey can deejay!'"

Run could rap as well as he could DJ. His comic-book and football-loving friend Darryl McDaniels, nicknamed "DMC," was a master at rhymes. A third friend, Jason Mizell, who called himself Jam Master J, could spin turntables like a wizard. Like hundreds of young guys from New York, they practiced their skills in hopes of one day making it in the world of hip-hop. Their chance came when Run's brother Russell persuaded Profile Records to sign them as an act. They called themselves Run-DMC.

DIFFERENT SOUND, DIFFERENT LOOK

Run-DMC released their first single in 1983. Their song "It's Like That," and the B-side "Sucker MCs," marked a change from the cheerful, funky sound of earlier hip-hop music. It had a hard electronic beat. Instead of trading off verses, the rappers finished each other's lines. And the lines were not about having fun and dancing:

> *"You can see a lot in this lifespan*
> *   Like a bum eating out of a garbage can*
> *You noticed one time he was your man*
> *   It's like that and that's the way it is"*

"It's Like That/Sucker MCs" became a top 20 R&B single. The group's first album, *Run DMC*, was certified gold in 1984. Their second album, *King of Rock* (1985), sold more than a million copies, making it the first hip-hop album to be certified as a *platinum record*. But

Run-DMC's greatest success came with the group's third album, 1986's *Raising Hell,* which included the song "Walk This Way." Recorded with the hard rock band Aerosmith, the song was one of the first to combine rap with rock music. It was a spectacular hit and

FAST FACT

In 1983, the Los Angeles radio station 1580 KDAY made history. It became the first radio station in the world to play hip-hop 24 hours a day, seven days a week.

became the first rap single to reach the top 10 on Billboard's music chart. It also helped the entire album go multi-platinum. Run-DMC was one of the first rap groups to have videos air on MTV, and was the first to appear on the cover of the magazine *Rolling Stone,* which is known for covering music and popular culture.

Fans of hip-hop loved Run-DMC, but they weren't the only ones. The group opened up the world of rap and hip-hop to a whole new

THE LOOK

Run-DMC pushed hip-hop in a new musical direction. They also changed its look. In the early days of hip-hop, DJs and MCs often dressed in flashy clothes. They wore tight leather pants, shirts and hats decorated with frills or rhinestones, and leather boots. The members of Run-DMC had other ideas. They put together a look that matched their music—streetwise and cool, with a bit of an edge. Jeans and leather jackets or black warm-up suits, gold rope chains, black *fedoras*, and Adidas sneakers without laces became the new b-boy look. Run-DMC's hit single "My Adidas" brought them a million-dollar endorsement deal with the athletic clothing company that made the shoes. Their style was part of the hip-hop culture for many years.

group of music lovers—the mostly white kids who lived in the sub-urbs. Hip-hop was becoming cool everywhere. And Run-DMC seemed to be everywhere, too—on MTV, on tours, at a Live Aid concert, on the cover of *Rolling Stone*.

Run-DMC may have been hip-hop's most popular act in the mid-1980s, but they weren't alone. That decade is sometimes called a "golden era" of hip-hop music. The sound, the look, the whole cul-ture of the music was spreading across the country and around the

WOMEN IN HIP-HOP

Male artists dominated the hip-hop world from the beginning, but women could rock the mic just as well, and they proved it. Lady B became the first female rap soloist when she recorded "To the Beat, Y'all," in 1980. She then went on to become a famous radio DJ in Philadelphia.

Sha Rock started as a break-dancer in the Bronx, New York. She then became part of a rap group by the name of the "Funky 4 + 1." Sha Rock was the "+1" and the first female MC.

Salt-n-Pepa was one of the first all-female rap crews. They released their first single in 1985. Their fourth album, *Very Necessary*, was a huge success, selling over five million copies in the U.S. and seven million copies worldwide.

MC Lyte (pictured) was born in Brooklyn, New York. Her first single was "I Cram to Understand You" in 1986. Two years later she became the first solo female performer to release a full-length album, with *Lyte as a Rock* in 1988. MC Lyte was one of the first female rappers to attack the sexist atti-tudes that dominated most hip-hop lyrics at the time.

From Lady B through Queen Latifah and Missy Elliott, right on up to Beyoncé, women's voices have made a strong sound in the world of hip-hop.

world. People heard it on the radio. They watched it on MTV and saw it live at concerts. They bought the records. They played it on their boom boxes when they walked down the street. And they weren't listening to just a few rappers anymore. There were plenty of rappers and hip-hop groups out there. And by the mid-1980s, there was a record label devoted solely to producing hip-hop music.

FROM THE STREET TO THE STUDIO

Def Jam Recordings was the brainchild of Russell Simmons and Rick Rubin. Russell Simmons was black and from a middle-class Queens neighborhood. He was heavily into hip-hop. He promoted it, staged jam sessions and parties, and managed the careers of musicians like Kurtis Blow and Run-DMC.

Rick Rubin was white and from a wealthy family who hoped he would become a doctor. But Rubin had a different goal. He was a huge fan of hip-hop music and wanted to produce records. Instead of hitting the books in college, he turned his New York University dorm room into a mini-recording studio. There, he made *demo tapes* of rappers, hoping to

Russell Simmons is one of the great entrepreneurs of hip-hop history. His Def Jam eventually expanded to include clothing lines, film production, comedy shows, and other businesses.

The first Def Jam star, LL Cool J, has spent his entire career with the label. Since 1985 the critically acclaimed rapper has released 13 studio albums and two greatest hits compilations.

help them land recording contracts with bigger record companies.

Getting contracts with record companies (along with a part of the profit from sales) was still the goal when Rubin and Simmons became partners. In 1984, they took the plunge: armed with a great demo by a 16-year-old rapper, they decided to make the record themselves and market it under their own label—Def Jam Recordings.

"I Need a Beat," Def Jam's first single, was released in 1984. It was a modest hit, selling more than 100,000 copies. Def Jam would go on to become one of the most successful and influential recording companies in the United States.

Def Jam was also a force behind the successful careers of many hip-hop musicians, including the handsome young 16-year-old who rapped "I Need a Beat." His name was James Todd Smith, but he became better known by the stage name LL Cool J.

LADIES LOVE COOL JAMES

After the success of "I Need a Beat," LL Cool J left school to make his first album, *Radio*. The sound, with its hard, drum-machine beat, and the streetwise attitude of the lyrics, became a Def Jam hallmark. Two of the singles on *Radio*, "I Can't Live Without My Radio" and "Rock the Bells," helped the album go platinum. Many top-selling albums followed over the next ten years.

Many people in the hip-hop community sneered when LL Cool J recorded the soft ballad "I Need Love" in 1987. But "I Need Love" was a huge hit, becoming the first hip-hop song to reach number one on Billboard's R&B chart. Hip-Hop was definitely going mainstream. So when LL Cool J released the harder-hitting album *Mama Said Knock You Out,* in 1990, mainstream and pop fans were right there with him. Even his critics agreed that the album was one of his best. The title song, "Mama Said Knock You Out," won LL Cool J a Grammy Award for Best Rap Solo Performance.

While LL Cool J *fused* hip-hop and pop, another group of Def Jam stars started out as punk rockers. Even when they switched to hip-hop, some thought they didn't belong there because they were white. But the Beastie Boys proved them wrong.

THE BEASTIE BOYS

In the early 1980s, most people thought of hip-hop as "black" music. The Beastie Boys—three young white guys from New York—showed that successful hip-hop music was about talent, not race or color.

The Beastie Boys' album *Licensed to Ill* was released by Def Jam in 1986. It became the best selling rap album of the 1980s and the first one to hit number one on the Billboard charts. One of the album's singles, "(You Gotta) Fight for Your Right (to Party)" was a huge crossover success and became a teen party anthem all across the country.

FAST FACT

Before Rick Rubin co-founded Def Jam Records, he had his own punk band. And for a while, as "DJ Double R," he spun the turntables for the Beastie Boys.

The Beastie Boys used street-beats, metal riffs and bratty, juvenile humor in their work. Their concerts were plagued with violence and arrests. Some people thought they gave hip-hop a bad name. Others believed they weren't true rappers at all. But the Beastie Boys endured. Albums like *Paul's Boutique* (1988), *Check Your Head* (1992), *Ill Communication* (1994), and *Hello Nasty* (1998) were all hits. The Beastie Boys helped widen the audience for rap and hip-hop.

In 2012, the Beastie Boys were ***inducted*** into the Rock and Roll Hall of Fame. At the ceremony, they were presented for induction by a rapper named Chuck D, who had become famous in the late 1980s as the leader of a rap group called Public Enemy.

A NEW MESSAGE

In 1982, Grandmaster Flash and the Furious Five's hit "The Message" related the harsh conditions of life in poverty-stricken African-American neighborhoods. In the late 1980s, Public Enemy took that message to another level. Led by Chuck D's smart, clever rhyming and backed with a driving beat, Public Enemy turned a spotlight on issues that concerned many African Americans—issues like drug addiction, media bias, and police prejudice.

It Takes a Nation of Millions to Hold Us Back, Public Enemy's second album, was released in 1988. It was wildly popular with both African Americans and whites. In 2003, *Rolling Stone* ranked it 43rd on its list of the 500 greatest albums of all time. It was the highest-ranking hip-hop album on the list.

*Public Enemy founders Chuck D (left) and Flavor Flav sign records
at an event in Las Vegas. The influential group's biggest hits include
"Don't Believe the Hype" (1988) and "Fight the Power" (1989).*

Public Enemy didn't just turn a spotlight on the issues—they demanded change. They rapped about political revolution and greater rights for African Americans. The group expressed the frustrations that many in the black community felt about the police, the media, and other aspects of American culture and society.

In 1989, a Public Enemy song called "Fight the Power" was used on the soundtrack to the Spike Lee film *Do the Right Thing*. The movie was a hit and helped introduce the group to new fans. "Fight the

During the late 1980s, rapper Big Daddy Kane was considered one of the most skilled MCs in hip-hop. His biggest hits included "Smooth Operator" and "I Get the Job Done," as well as "Back on the Block," a collaboration with music producer Quincy Jones that won a Grammy Award in 1991 for Best Rap Performance by a Duo or Group. In the late 1990s Kane also served as a mentor to an up-and-coming rapper from Brooklyn, Shawn "Jay-Z" Carter.

As the "Fresh Prince," rapper Will Smith (right) teamed up with his friend Jeffrey "DJ Jazzy Jeff" Townes on several mainstream hits. In 1989 they became the first act to win a Grammy Award for Best Rap Performance, for their song "Parents Just Don't Understand." Smith would eventually start a highly successful acting career, while continuing to release occasional albums.

Power" was released as a single off Public Enemy's third studio album, *Fear of a Black Planet* (1990). It reached number one on Billboard's Hot Rap Singles chart and number 20 on the Hot R&B Singles chart. Today, many people consider "Fight the Power" one of the greatest hip-hop songs of all time.

Public Enemy inspired many other rappers or hip-hop groups to perform music with political or social messages. Some of these included Kool Moe Dee, Eric B. & Rakim, Queen Latifah, and A Tribe Called Quest.

During the late 1980s and early 1990s, Public Enemy was a highly *controversial* group. But within a few years, even more controversy would emerge from the world of hip-hop.

Gangsta Rap

Compton is a city near Los Angeles, California. During the late 1980s, a hip-hop group called N.W.A. brought the city national attention—but not in a positive way. N.W.A.'s first album, *Straight Outta Compton*, was released in 1988. It turned a spotlight on the violent lifestyles of young black men living in inner cities on the West Coast, especially in the Los Angeles area.

Straight Outta Compton was a pioneering work in a new form of hip-hop music, known as *gangsta rap*. This hip-hop *genre* sought to describe the experience of young black men living in America's gang-infested inner cities. Gangsta rap featured graphic language and themes many people found disturbing. It appeared to glorify drug abuse, gang membership, violence, and the mistreatment of women. Without airplay or advance publicity, *Straight Outta Compton* became an underground phenomenon. It eventually sold more than 2 million copies.

ORIGINS OF GANGSTA RAP

The gangsta rap style of hip-hop originated in the mid-1980s. In 1985, a Philadelphia rapper known as Schoolly D released a song called "P.S.K.: What Does it Mean?" The **hardcore** song was written for his friends in a West Philadelphia gang called the Park Side Killers. It described their lives and the ways they made money.

"P.S.K." inspired a young rapper who lived on the West Coast, known as Ice-T. In 1986, Ice-T released the song "6 in the Mornin'," which is often called the first gangsta rap song. Beginning with the line "6 in the morning, police at my door," the song describes the hectic life of a drug dealer. Over a threatening drum-machine beat in the background, Ice-T raps about violence, attempts to avoid the police, time in jail—and later, being back on the street with his

Tracy "Ice-T" Marrow attracted attention with controversial songs. In 1992, his song "Cop Killer" was criticized by President George H.W. Bush as well as representatives of law enforcement agencies.

Former Boogie Down Productions rapper KRS-One has released many solo albums. In 2009 he received the Urban Music Living Legend Award.

friends. Ice-T's first album, *Rhyme Pays* (1987), painted an often-bloody picture of life on the streets of Los Angeles. *Rhyme Pays* was also the first hip-hop album to get a Parental Advisory Warning because of its explicit lyrics.

Another group that created songs credited with inspiring the gangsta rap genre was Boogie Down Productions. The New York group released its first album, *Criminal Minded*, in 1987. Songs like "9mm Goes Bang," "South Bronx," and "Criminal Minded" contained vivid descriptions of gangsta life in the Bronx. A few months after the album was released, DJ Scott La Rock of Boogie Down Productions was shot and killed by gangstas in the Highbridge Projects of the South Bronx. The other members of the group, rapper KRS-One and D-Nice,

FAST FACT

Schoolly D contributed songs to the soundtracks of several movies about drug dealers and gangstas, including *King of New York* (1990) and *Bad Lieutenant* (1992).

continued to perform. Much of their later music encouraged young people to avoid violence and find peaceful ways to solve problems. In 1989, KRS-One established the "Stop the Violence Movement" to address this issue in the hip hop community.

N.W.A. AND THE F.B.I.

In 1989, the F.B.I. sent a letter to Priority Records, the company that distributed N.W.A.'s records. "Advocating violence and assault is wrong," the letter said, "and we in the law enforcement community take exception to such action." The letter noted that in 1988, a total of 78 law enforcement officers had been killed in the line of duty. It said that "recordings such as the one from N.W.A. are both discouraging and degrading to these brave, dedicated officers." The letter did not mention a song, but almost everyone knew it was one that protested police brutality—and promised a "bloodbath" of L.A. cops.

The American Civil Liberties Union, as well as some members of Congress, said the F.B.I. had no right to try to curb artistic expression. The F.B.I. replied that they were not sending a threat or trying "to chill anyone's right to express themselves."

Neither N.W.A.'s members nor Priority Records spoke to the media about the letter. However, the publicity worked in the group's favor, by helping to create more interest in *Straight Outta Compton*.

The success of N.W.A.'s *Straight Outta Compton* provided even more attention to gangsta rap. The lyrics were exciting, and the beats got the listeners' adrenaline pumping. *Straight Outta Compton* attracted a lot of listeners. It also drew a lot of attention—not all of it positive.

A STORM OF CRITICISM

While many people liked the sound of N.W.A.'s music, the lyrics were another story. Almost every other word was R-rated. In N.W.A. songs, women were treated like trash and police were the enemy. Drugs and drive-by shootings were normal.

Mainstream critics said the music glorified violence. Many radio stations—even stations that only played rap music—would not play gangsta rap songs. MTV refused to air the group's first video.

N.W.A. refused to apologize. The group's members claimed that they were just reporting the things that really occurred in the inner cities. "Violence is reality," said rapper Ice Cube, a member of the group, to *Rolling Stone*. "You're supposed to picture life as a bowl of cherries, but it's not. So we don't do nothin' fake."

N.W.A.'s appeal went far beyond African Americans living in the ghettos of the inner cities. White teenagers from middle-class families became fans of the group. They helped make *Straight Outta Compton* a major hit. N.W.A.'s next album, released in 1991, was even more popular. It reached number one on the Billboard 200 album chart—without the benefit of N.W.A.'s songs being played on mainstream radio stations.

In spite of the criticism, *Straight Outta Compton* helped to establish gangsta rap as a legitimate form of hip-hop music. Whether anyone liked it or not, gangsta rap was here to stay. For a while, N.W.A. was

Ice Cube became a star with N.W.A., and enjoyed a successful solo career after leaving the group in 1989. His biggest solo hit was "It Was a Good Day," released in 1993.

the leading group of the gangsta rap genre. But soon other performers and groups would surpass N.W.A. in popularity.

DR. DRE AND *THE CHRONIC*

Andre "Dr. Dre" Young was an original member of N.W.A. He left the group in 1991 because of disagreements about money. In 1992, Death Row Records released Dr. Dre's first solo album, *The Chronic*. With songs like "Lyrical Gang Bang" and "Stranded on Death Row," *The Chronic* picked up where N.W.A. had left off. The music was still hardcore gangsta. Violence was not sugar-coated, and drug use and dealing were a part of everyday life.

But by the time *The Chronic* was released, the opposition to gangsta rap seemed to be fading. Mainstream radio stations and MTV were ready to accept the new genre. One reason was the quality of the music. Dr. Dre blended, or fused, elements of hip-hop, funk, soul, and jazz music to create an appealing new sound. He used synthesizers and saxophones and even flutes. The rapping—done in a laid-back, lazy drawl—was spellbinding. Dr. Dre called his sound G-funk (gangsta funk). In the mid-1990s, G-funk was the sound people thought of when they thought of gangsta rap.

With the release of The Chronic *in 1992, Dr. Dre (right) introduced the world to his protégé, rapper Snoop Dogg.*

The Chronic reached number three on the Billboard album charts. It went on to sell over three million copies. *The Chronic* also introduced a talented new rapper to the hip-hop world: Snoop Dogg.

SNOOP BECOMES A STAR

Snoop Dogg's first solo album, *Doggystyle*, was released in 1993 by Death Row Records. It sold over four million copies and did even better on the Billboard charts than *The Chronic*, reaching the number one spot in its first week of release.

Like other gangsta rappers, Snoop Dogg rapped about what he knew. "I can't rap about something I don't know," he said in an interview. "You'll never hear me rapping about no bachelor's degree. It's only what I know and that's that street life."

Snoop Dogg's rhymes were full of violence. But his smooth, soft vocal style made them easy to listen to. *Doggystyle* brought in a wide audience of new listeners. For a time, Snoop Dogg ruled as the king of rap.

Like N.W.A., Dr. Dre, and many other gangsta rappers, Snoop Dogg was from the West Coast. Hip-hop had gotten started on the East Coast. But by the mid-1990s, West Coast rappers and their gangsta sound were outselling the East Coast rappers. A rivalry began to develop between performers from the two areas.

THE EAST COAST–WEST COAST FEUD

The hip-hop rivalry that became known as the East Coast–West Coast

=== FAST FACT ===

Snoop Dogg's real name is Calvin Broadus. His mother nicknamed him Snoop because she thought he looked like the character in the Peanuts cartoon. He first called himself "Snoop Doggy Dogg," then shortened it to "Snoop Dogg."

Feud began at New York City's Paramount Theater on the night of August 3, 1995. The event was the second annual Source Hip-Hop Music Awards. In attendance were the biggest stars in the rap world, including many artists from two of the most powerful labels: Bad Boy Entertainment, headquartered in New York City, and L.A.-based Death Row Records.

Onstage to present one of the awards, Death Row Records president Marion "Suge" Knight told the assembled artists, "If you don't want the owner of your label on your album or in your video or on your tour, come sign with Death Row." Though he hadn't mentioned any names, everyone knew that Knight was referring to the founder of Bad Boy, Sean "Puff Daddy" Combs, who had a habit of sharing the spotlight with his artists. Knight was making fun of Combs while also issuing a business challenge. Many people interpreted the Death Row president's comments as an insult to Bad Boy's artists and to East Coast rappers in general.

Witnesses have said that Combs was visibly shaken by Suge Knight's remarks. Later, when it came time for him to present an award—as fate would have it, to Death Row's Snoop Dogg—Puff Daddy hugged Snoop and spoke of the need for "unity" in the hip-hop world. But there would be no unity.

On September 24, 1995, Suge Knight and Sean Combs, along with their *entourages*, were at a club in Atlanta for a party for rap producer Jermaine Dupri. During the course of the evening, Knight's close friend Jake Robles got into an argument that turned into a fistfight. Gunfire erupted, and Robles was fatally wounded. Police were never able to identify the shooter, but some witnesses blamed one of Puff Daddy's bodyguards.

Combs denied any knowledge of, or involvement in, the killing. He reached out to Suge Knight in an attempt to defuse the growing East Coast–West Coast feud. Combs sent the son of a prominent black minister to Los Angeles to try to make peace. But Suge Knight refused even to speak with Puff Daddy's representative. A friend of the Death Row CEO told a reporter that Suge would "settle the beef his way. On the street."

The entertainment media reported breathlessly about the "rap war." Fans took sides. Standing out as symbols of that rivalry were Death Row rapper Tupac Shakur and Bad Boy's biggest star, the Notorious B.I.G.

FRIENDS TURNED RIVALS

Although Tupac Shakur was born in New York, his family moved to California when he was young. As a teenager he joined the hip-hop group Digital Underground. In 1993, Tupac released his first solo album *2PacalypseNow* under the name 2Pac. One of the album's singles, "Brenda's Got a Baby," reached number three on the Billboard Hot Rap Singles chart. His second album went platinum.

Tupac received plenty of attention. He was praised for his musical talent, criticized for his violent lyrics, and spent time in prison for assault. In fact, he was in prison when his third album, *Me Against The World*, reached the number one spot on the Billboard 200 albums chart.

In the early 1990s Tupac had become friends with Christopher Wallace, another up-and-coming young rapper. Wallace, who performed under the names "Biggie Smalls" and "the Notorious B.I.G.," was from Brooklyn, New York. As a teenager, Wallace had made a demo tape that was noticed by Sean "Puff Daddy" Combs. In 1992 he signed a deal with Uptown Records, where Combs worked. When Combs started his own company, Bad Boy Records, Wallace moved to the new label.

As Biggie Smalls, he created a lot of buzz by performing guest raps on albums by other Bad Boy stars. In 1994, Biggie's first solo album, *Ready to Die*, was released. In a powerful voice, Biggie told stories of dangerous, tense situations like being on the run from police or pulling off a robbery. He put himself in those stories—he was the robber, he was the one being chased. *Ready to Die*'s first single, "Juicy," reached number three on Billboard's Hot Rap Singles chart. Many people consider this song about Wallace's childhood and his dreams of becoming a music star one of the greatest hip-hop songs of all time.

Ready to Die included several other hit songs, making Biggie Smalls a sensation—and a hero to East Coast rappers. Fans thought he would be the one to defeat the West Coast rappers and bring the East to the top of the hip-hop world again.

The friendship between Tupac and Biggie ended in November 1994. Tupac was visiting a recording studio in New York when he was confronted by two armed men. They robbed the rapper and shot him five times before fleeing. Tupac recovered from his wounds, but he was very angry. He believed the two men had been sent to kill him. And he believed that they had been sent by Combs and Biggie.

After this incident, Tupac entered the East Coast–West Coast feud in a big way. He repeatedly **dissed** Puff Daddy and Bad Boy's rappers. He threatened them with violence. Some of Tupac's nastiest insults were aimed at his former friend Biggie Smalls. Biggie—who by now was calling himself the Notorious B.I.G.—responded with angry and insulting raps of his own.

The East Coast–West Coast feud ended in tragedy. In September 1996, Tupac Shakur was shot and killed in Las Vegas. Six months later, in March 1997, the Notorious B.I.G. was shot and killed after leaving a party in Los Angeles. Both sides in the feud believed that the other had been responsible for the murder, but the cases were never conclusively solved.

The violent and tragic end of the rap feud made many people reconsider the gangsta rap genre. Some people argued that gangsta rap was doing more than just describing life on the streets—it was actually creating a culture that celebrated violence. No one could say for sure, but the popularity of gangsta rap began to decline in the late 1990s. It would soon be replaced by a new musical sound that would not come from the East Coast or West Coast, but from a different part of the country—the South.

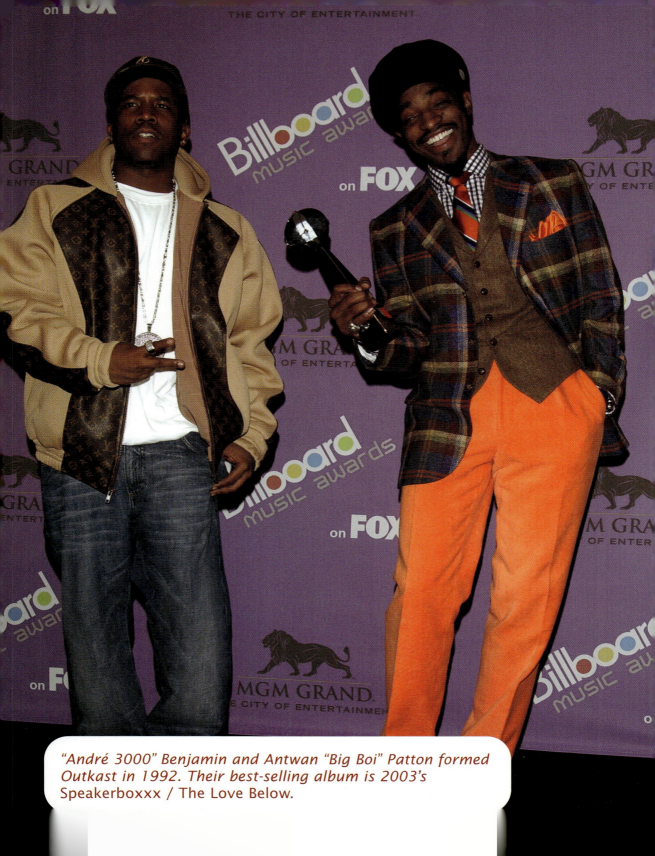

"André 3000" Benjamin and Antwan "Big Boi" Patton formed Outkast in 1992. Their best-selling album is 2003's Speakerboxxx / The Love Below.

the Rise of the South

Hip-hop started on the East Coast in the 1970s and early 1980s, and was revitalized on the West Coast in the late 1980s and early 1990s. Eventually, some record companies began looking elsewhere for a new hip-hop sound. They found it in the South. In cities such as Atlanta, Houston, New Orleans, and Memphis, artists were creating their own styles of hip-hop. They drew on local music styles for inspiration. In the mid-1990s, two friends from Atlanta helped set the stage for the rise of southern hip-hop.

OUTKAST

Andre "Andre 3000" Benjamin and Antwan "Big Boi" Patton were friends in high school. Both were big fans of hip-hop and both were talented rappers. They began writing their own raps and recorded them on cassette tapes. Then they looked for a way to break into the music business. Organized Noize, a production company in Atlanta, gave them that break.

"Player's Ball," Outkast's first single, was released in 1993. It made it to the number one spot on Billboard's rap singles chart and stayed there for six weeks. The next year, Outkast released their first album, *Southernplayalisticadillacmuzik*. It climbed to number three on Billboard's R&B/hip-hop albums chart.

Outkast didn't try to copy the sound of rappers from the East or the West coasts. They liked the G-funk sound that Dr. Dre had devel-

WORKING HARD TO GET NOTICED

Rappers in the South had as much talent and ambition as rappers from New York, Los Angeles, or other major cities on the East and West coasts. Their biggest problem was getting their music heard. The major record companies did not have offices in the South, and talent scouts mostly ignored the region. So many southern rappers did the next best thing—they made their own records and tapes, using inexpensive recording equipment and computers that had become available during the 1990s.

Some rappers started their own record companies. They tried to make a name for themselves by selling their records or tapes on the streets and to local record stores. If they got lucky, they would sign a deal with a distributor. This meant their music could be sold in stores throughout an entire region, rather than just in their hometown. Once that happened, the performer had a better shot at signing a contract with a major record label. And a major record label meant that their music would be heard nationwide.

oped, but added elements from other music. This included beats from electronic dance music popular in Miami and other places, as well as gospel, blues, jazz, and soul music.

The members of Outkast didn't try to copy the style of other rappers, either. They spoke about the things they knew from growing up in the South, rather than rapping about life in New York or Los Angeles. They used expressions commonly heard in the South in their raps. Southern slang and the Southern black experience were a big part of their music. Bubba Sparxxx, a rapper who grew up in rural Georgia, explained how as a young man he was inspired by *Southernplayalisticadillacmuzik*. "Those were Southern Black boys, the kind I went to school with," Sparxxx said. "The kind I knew, the kind my closest neighbor was. They were people that talked like me."

TIMBALAND

Southern accents are not all alike, and neither are southern hip-hop artists. Different sounds and musical expressions emerged from different areas. In Virginia, Tim "Timbaland" Mosley developed his own unique sound—a sound that would help him rise to the top as a record producer.

Timbaland began mixing records and creating tracks when he was about eleven. This gained him quite a reputation as a party DJ in high school. When he met Melvin Barcliff, the duo became a team and started rapping together.

In the early 1990s, Tim began working as a record producer. His first jobs were producing R&B records. He broke into the mainstream by producing the hit R&B/hip-hop album *Ginuwine … the Bachelor* in 1996.

"Things are more creative in the South," the influential music producer Timbaland once said. *"It's like southern cooking. You know how your grandmother will go to the kitchen and come up with some biscuits that you would never get from a store anywhere? Southern hip hop is like that."*

But even as he produced R&B records, Tim was creating his trademark sound: electronic, fast-paced, with a heavy bass, clear drum breaks—and original music. It was hip-hop sound applied to rhythm & blues. It was new and unique.

In 1997, Tim and Melvin—calling themselves Timbaland and Magoo—released their first album, *Welcome to Our World.* He and Magoo did a second album together, and Timbaland would go on to release three solo albums.

But it was his creativity as a producer that made Timbaland a force in the hip-hop world. His work helped propel other artists to fame. One of those artists was another Virginian—and a hometown friend.

MISSY ELLIOTT

"I'm going to be rich and famous," Melissa "Missy" Elliott used to tell Timbaland's mother. "We're going to keep working on it until we get to the very top." A lot of kids dream of the same thing. Missy Elliot made her dream come true.

Missy Elliott was born in 1971. She grew up loving music and wanting to sing. As a teenager, Missy joined with some girlfriends to form a group called Fayze. Missy rapped and was also the group's main songwriter. When Fayze put out an independent record, Timbaland's partner Magoo heard it and liked what he heard. He introduced the group to Timbaland. Missy and Timbaland soon began writing songs and producing records together.

In 1991 record producer DeVante Swing signed Fayze to a contract with Swing Mob Records. He changed the group's name to Sista and took them to New Jersey to work. Their big break turned out to be short-lived. Sista's **debut** album *4 All the Sistas Around da World* didn't sell many copies, even though music critics praised it. The group returned to Virginia and eventually broke up.

Missy and Timbaland kept writing and producing demo records. Motown Records asked Missy to perform a guest rap on an album by the group 702. She also wrote one of the tracks for their album.

Next came Atlantic Records, which gave Missy and Timbaland a shot at working on an album for R&B singer Aaliyah. Missy and Timbaland wrote seven tracks for Aaliyah's 1996 album *One in a Million*. Two of them,

Missy Elliott has released six platinum albums and has won five Grammy Awards. She has also written and produced songs and albums for stars like Janet Jackson, Mariah Carey, Justin Timberlake, Ludacris, and Beyoncé.

"If Your Girl Only Knew" and "One in a Million," were number one hits on Billboard's hip-hop charts. They helped the album sell more than 8 million copies worldwide.

In 1997, Missy released her first solo album. *Supa Dupa Fly* shot to number three in its first week on the charts. Singles like "The Rain (Supa Dupa Fly)" and "Sock it to Me" helped the album sell more than a million copies.

Missy Elliott's sound and attitude had a big impact on the world of hip-hop. Electro-funk music was backed by a strong beat. The lyrics could be playful as well as serious, and they often made the point that women were people, not objects. A line from one of her songs, "I got my own ride and gas in da tank/Thanks, but no thanks, I won't be needin' you," made it perfectly clear that women could make it on their own.

BEYOND RAPPING

Not all southern hip-hop artists made it big, but some who did—like Timbaland—didn't stop at rapping. They used their energy and smarts to create multi-million dollar businesses.

Born in New Orleans, Percy Miller moved to Oakland, California, in the late 1980s and opened his own record store. Its name was No Limit Records. In the early 1990s, Miller noticed that his customers were buying gangsta rap. But major record companies had not yet embraced that type of music. So under the name "Master P," he began to record albums himself under the label No Limit Records. He sold them in his store, as well as from the trunk of his car. The first albums did not sell very well, but they earned enough for him to make more albums.

Percy "Master P." Miller built No Limit Records into a hip-hop powerhouse. He even turned his son, Lil Romeo, into a rap star.

Master P began to receive national attention after his No Limit Records label signed a ***distribution deal*** with Priority Records. His 1996 album *Mr. Ice Cream Man* sold more than a million copies. The next year, he released *Ghetto D*, which included his most popular single, "Make 'Em Say Uhh!" The song reached number six on the Billboard Hot Rap Singles chart, and helped the album sell more than three million copies. Master P's best-selling album was released in 1998. *MP Da Last Don* sold over four million copies and hit number one on the Billboard album charts.

By 1998, No Limit was one of the biggest independent record labels in the music industry. In addition to Master P, the label released hits by other performers, such as Mystikal and Silkk the Shocker. *Forbes* maga-

Dwayne "Lil Wayne" Carter was one of the biggest Southern hip-hop stars of the 2000s. His biggest hits included "A Milli," "Swagga Like Us," and "Lollypop."

Music producer Jermaine Dupri poses with former protégé Lil Bow Wow, 2001.

zine ranked Master P among the highest-paid entertainers, with an estimated income of more than $50 million a year. However, the success didn't last. Master P became distracted by other interests. The stars left the label and No Limit Records filed for bankruptcy in 2003. Since then, Percy Miller has continued working in the music industry.

Jermaine Dupri from Atlanta is another "do-it-yourself" rapper and music producer. When he was in high school, he made and sold his own cassette tapes under his record label So So Def Recordings. The label scored a major success when Dupri discovered the teenage rappers Chris "Mac Daddy" Kelly and Chris "Daddy Mac" Smith. Performing under the name Kris Kross, their 1992 song "Jump" spent eight weeks at number one on the Billboard Hot 100 chart. Another young artist he discovered was Lil Bow Wow. Dupri had some success as a singer, but made his reputation as a talented record producer. He produced hits for dozens of artists, including Da Brat, Xscape, MC Lyte, TLC, Usher, and Mariah Carey.

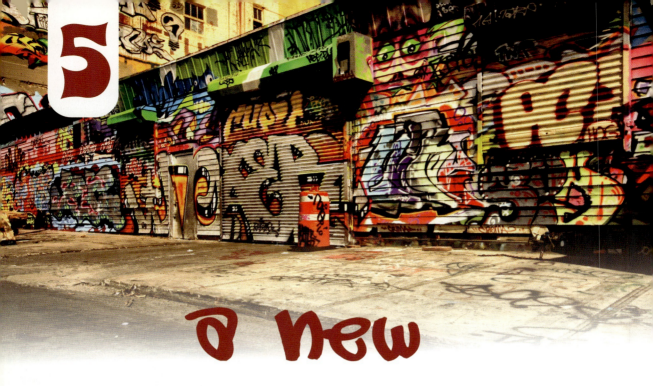

5

A New Millennium

By the late 1990s, hip-hop had moved into the mainstream. The music, the language, even the fashion became part of the world's culture. People by the millions bought the music and eagerly awaited the their favorite hip-hop star's next release. One of those stars burst onto the scene in 1999.

Eminem's second album, *The Slim Shady LP*, took the hip-hop world by surprise. The surprise was that Eminem (born Marshall Bruce Mathers III), was white. In spite of the success of the Beastie Boys, white rappers were definitely in the minority.

His lyrics created controversy. Many people thought Eminem's violent lyrics were dangerously twisted. Eminem said he was just play-

Eminem is known for his complex lyrics and careful phrasing. The rapper has sold nearly 90 million albums worldwide.

ing the role of his *alter ego*, Slim Shady.

Eminem was born in Missouri and grew up in Detroit, Michigan. He grew up poor, in a rough neighborhood and with a rough home life. Hip-hop was his escape. Two of his favorite rappers were LL Cool J and Tupac Shakur. "Me and my friends used to stand in front of the mirror and perform," Eminem said in an interview. "The kids from the neighborhood would come around to watch. We knew all the words."

Soon, Eminem was writing his own words. He released a record, won a freestyle hip-hop award, and started getting noticed. His second album caught the attention of Dr. Dre, who produced records under the label Aftermath Entertainment.

The Slim Shady LP climbed to number two on the U.S. album chart. His next album, *The Marshall Mathers LP*, debuted at number one. Several of the hits from that album, such as "The Real Slim Shady" and "Stan," are considered among the greatest hip-hop songs of all time. Other major hits by Eminem include "My Name Is," "Lose Yourself," and "Without Me."

In spite of his controversial lyrics and his skin color, Eminem has become one of the most successful rappers in hip-hop history. He has also helped to give talented young performers their first big break. For example, In 2002, Eminem heard a CD called *Guess Who's Back?* He liked what he heard and introduced the rapper to Dr. Dre. The rapper's name was Curtis Jackson, but he performed under the name 50 Cent.

"50 CENT IS THE FUTURE"

For a time, it looked like 50 Cent wouldn't have any future at all. He skipped school, sold drugs, and got arrested. In 2000, he was shot nine times at close range by a gunman outside his grandmother's house in Queens, New York. But by the time he was shot, he had already started on his career as a rapper. He had even signed a contract with Columbia Records. The record company dropped him from their label while he was recovering, so 50 Cent began releasing his work himself. First came a *mixtape* called "50 Cent Is The Future." It was followed by another, "Guess Who's Back?" Then Eminem came calling, and the buzz about 50 Cent became a roar.

Eminem and Dr. Dre produced 50 Cent's 2003 album *Get Rich or Die Tryin'*. The album went straight to number one on the Billboard charts. It included the hit singles "In da Club," "21 Questions," "P.I.M.P.," and "If I Can't." With more than 8 million copies sold, *Get Rich or Die Tryin'* is one of the best-selling albums in hip-hop history. His follow-up album, *The Massacre*, was another major success. It included the hits "Candy Shop," "Just a Lil Bit," and "Outta Control."

50 Cent used his fame as a rapper to launch a career as an actor. He started with a 2005 film loosely based on his life and called *Get

50 Cent has had a successful career as a rapper, actor, and music producer.

Jay-Z holds the Billboard Music Award for Rap Artist of the Year,
1999.

Rich or Die Tryin', then appeared in other films. 50 Cent also started his own record label, G-Unit Records. He continued to produce best-selling albums, including *Curtis* (2007) and *Before I Self-Destruct* (2009). Many people consider 50 Cent one of the best rappers of the 2000s.

FROM RAGS TO RICHES TO ROCAWEAR

Another rapper who made his way from a hard-knock life to the top of the heap is Shawn "Jay-Z" Carter. Born in Brooklyn, New York, he grew up in a housing project that was known for drugs and crime. Like Eminem, rap was Jay-Z's way to escape from violence and poverty. He began that escape by recording a song with another rapper. That got them an appearance on *Yo! MTV Raps*.

When Jay-Z couldn't interest a mainstream record company in releasing his music, he started his own label with two friends, Damon Dash and Kareem Biggs. They called their label Roc-a-Fella Records.

FAST FACT

Jay-Z attended the Westinghouse Career and Technical Education High School in Brooklyn, New York. One of his classmates was Christopher Wallace, who would eventually gain fame as rap star the Notorious B.I.G.

Roc-a-Fella Records released Jay-Z's first album, *Reasonable Doubt*, in 1996. His second album, *In My Lifetime, Vol. 1* (1997), was produced by Sean "Puffy" Combs. Both albums were fairly successful. However, it was Jay-Z's third album, *Vol. 2 ... Hard Knock Life* (1998), that made him a hip-hop superstar. It featured the single "Hard Knock Life (Ghetto Anthem)," which was Jay-Z's first big hit song. The album spent five weeks in the number-one spot on Billboard's chart, and eventually sold more than 5 million copies. Fans loved Jay-Z's lyrics and the way he rapped about cars, money, girls and guns. *Vol. 2 ... Hard Knock Life* also won the Grammy Award for Best Rap Album in 1999.

Like other best-selling artists, Jay-Z used his success to get into the business side of music. In the late 1990s Roc-a-Fella Records expanded from music into other areas, including a clothing line called Rocawear that featured cool, urban clothes. and a movie production company called ROC Films.

After releasing several other hit albums, including *Vol. 3 ... Life and Times of S. Carter* (1999), *The Dynasty: Roc La Familia* (2000), *The Blueprint* (2001), *The Blueprint^{2}: The Gift & The Curse* (2002), and *The Black Album* (2003), Jay-Z announced that he would be retiring as a performer. Def Jam Records purchased Roc-a-Fella Records, and Jay-Z became president of Def Jam in 2004. He signed artists like Rihanna, Young Jeezy, and Kanye West to the label.

Jay-Z ended his three-year "retirement" with the 2006 album *Kingdom Come.* He followed this success with more hit records, including *American Gangster* (2007) and *Blueprint 3* (2009). In 2011, Jay-Z and Kanye West **collaborated** on an album called *Rock the Throne.* In a single month, the album topped the rap, R&B and pop charts. As Jay-Z sang in one of the songs from that album, "I guess I got my swagger back."

"RUN THE WORLD (GIRLS)"

"Run the world (Girls)" is a the lead single on Beyoncé's 2011 album, *4.* The album hit the number one spot on Billboard's Top 200. It was no surprise. Beyoncé was a major star of the music world, appreciated and enjoyed by fans of R&B, hip-hop, and pop music.

Born in Texas, Beyoncé began singing when she was seven. When she was a teenager, she joined with a cousin and classmates to form a group called Destiny's Child. By 2000, it had become one of the most successful female R&B groups of all time.

In 2003, Beyoncé released her first solo album, *Dangerously in Love*. The album, which included collaborations with Missy Elliott, Jay-Z, and Outkast's Big Boi, went multi-platinum. Four of the songs were top-ten hits. Beyoncé won five Grammy Awards.

I Am … Sasha Fierce was released in 2008. Four of its singles, (including "Single Ladies (Put a Ring on It)" became major hits and helped Beyoncé win six more Grammy Awards. Some of Beyoncé's other major hits are "Crazy in Love," "Baby Boy," "Check on It," and "Irreplaceable."

Beyoncé is not only a singer. She's also a successful songwriter, record producer, and actress.

A STAR OF THE MIDWEST

Nelly shows off the American Music Award he received in 2002.

Most rappers came from the East Coast, the West Coast, or the South. One who came from the American heartland was Cornell "Nelly" Haynes Jr., who grew up in the state of Missouri. In high school, Nelly formed a hip-hop group called the St. Lunatics. After putting out a couple of records, they decided to try their luck in Atlanta, Georgia. There, Nelly got a record deal with Universal Records. His first album, *Country Grammar*, hit number one on the Billboard 200 albums chart. It sold more than 8 million copies.

Nelly's second album, *Nellyville* (2002), included two songs that were number-one hits: "Hot in Herre" and "Dilemma." Nelly continued to release hit songs and albums for the rest of the decade. In 2009, Billboard ranked Nelly as one of the top artists of the decade.

"MOMENT 4 LIFE"

"Moment 4 Life" is a song by American rapper Nicki Minaj. It features Canadian rapper, Drake. Both are up-and-coming hip-hop stars.

Nicki Minaj spent the first five years of her life in Trinidad and Tobago, in the Caribbean Ocean. Her family then moved to Queens, New York, where she went to a high school for music and the performing arts. *Pink Friday,* her first album, was released in 2010. It was a hit. Later that year, Minaj became the first artist to have seven songs on the Billboard Hot 100 chart at the same time.

Aubrey "Drake" Graham was born in Toronto, Canada. He first reached fame as an actor in the popular teen soap, *Degrassi: The Next Generation.* In 2006, Drake started making mixtapes. In 2009, his catchy single, "Best I Ever Had," reached number two on Billboard's hot 100 singles chart. In 2010, his album *Thank Me Later* hit number one in both the United States and Canada, eventually selling more than a million copies.

Nicki Minaj and Drake both wrote "Moment 4 Life." The song is based on a story by Minaj. It's about two kids sharing the dream of becoming famous rappers. It was the third single on *Pink Friday,* and topped Billboard's Hot R&B/Hip-Hop song chart.

Nicki Minaj and Drake collaborated on a big hit in 2011.

Chronology

1979 "Rapper's Delight" and "Christmas Rappin" are first heard on the radio.

1980 Kurtis Blow's "The Breaks" is released.

1982 Grandmaster Flash and the Furious Five release "The Message."

1983 Run-DMC releases its first single, "It's Like That/Sucker MCs." Los Angeles radio station 1580 KDAY becomes the first radio station to play only hip-hop music.

1984 Rick Rubin and Russell Simmons form Def Jam Recordings. The first Def Jam single, LL Cool J's "I Need A Beat," is released.

1986 Run-DMC's third album *Raising Hell* becomes the first hip-hop album to be certified multi-platinum. The Beastie Boys' album *Licensed to Ill* becomes the first hip-hop album to reach number one on Billboard's album charts. The two albums are credited with helping to broaden the appeal of rap music.

1988 Public Enemy releases *It Takes a Nation of Millions to Hold Us Back.* N.W.A. releases *Straight Outta Compton* and launches the gangsta rap genre.

1992 Death Row Records releases Dr. Dre's first solo album, *The Chronic.* It is praised by music critics for its innovative blending of musical styles, which Dr. Dre calls the "G-funk" sound.

1993 Snoop Dogg's first solo album *Doggystyle* is released.

1994 The Notorious B.I.G. releases *Ready to Die.* It becomes one of the best-selling albums in hip-hop history. Outkast releases *Southernplayalisticadillacmuzik.*

Chronology

1995   Tupac Shakur's third album, *Me Against the World,* debuts at number one on the Billboard 200. A feud between East Coast and West Coast rappers begins.

1996   In November, Tupac is murdered in Las Vegas.

1997   The Notorious B.I.G. is murdered in Las Angeles in March. His two-disc album *Life After Death* is released 15 days after the murder. It eventuallys sells over 10 million copies. Timbaland and Magoo release *Welcome to Our World.* Missy Elliott releases *Supa Dupa Fly.*

1998   Jay-Z's third album, *Vol. 2 ... Hard Knock Life,* is released, featuring his first major hit, "Hard Knock Life (Ghetto Anthem)."

1999   Eminem releases *The Slim Shady LP.* It wins a Grammy Award for Best Rap Album.

2003   50 Cent releases *Get Rich or Die Tryin'.* Beyoncé releases "Dangerously In Love."

2007   Grandmaster Flash and the Furious Five are inducted into the Rock and Roll Hall of Fame.

2009   Run-DMC is inducted into the Rock and Roll Hall of Fame.

2010   Nicki Minaj releases *Pink Friday,* which includes the single "Moment 4 Life" with Drake.

2012   The Beastie Boys are inducted into the Rock and Roll Hall of Fame.

Glossary

alter-ego—a second side of a person's personality.

catchphrases—words or expressions that are used over and over.

collaborate—to work with others on a project.

controversial—causing much discussion, argument, or disagreement.

debut—the first appearance by a performer; to make one's first appearance.

demo tape—a music recording produced to promote the talents or skills of an MC or DJ.

diss—to insult someone or put them down.

distribution deal—in music, an arrangement between an independent artist or record label and a larger organization, in which the latter handles the process of placing the artist's works into stores to be sold.

entourage—a group of people, often friends or assistants, who travel with a famous person

fedoras—low, soft felt hats with the crowns creased lengthwise.

fuse—in music, to unite or combine two or more musical styles to create a sound that is unique and innovative.

gangsta rap—a style of rap music that emphasizes violence, drug use, and hostility toward women and authority as it describes inner-city life.

genre—a category of artistic work, such as hip-hop music.

Glossary

gold record—a record that sells at least 500,000 copies.

hardcore—a form of rap music in which the lyrics are angry, aggressive, and confrontational. The hardcore rap of the 1980s evolved into the gangsta rap of the 1990s.

inducted—admitted.

intricate—complicated.

mixtape—a collection of songs recorded onto a tape cassette, CD, electronic music file, or any other audio format. Although some are recorded by amateurs for private use, DJs and MCs will often prepare high-quality mixtapes for sale to showcase a performer's talent.

platinum record—a record that sells a million copies.

sampling—a musical production technique, used especially in hip-hop, in which parts of other artists' recordings are incorporated into a new song.

single—a song that is released to the public for sale or for promotional use, such as commercial radio airplay.

Further Reading

Baker, Soren. *The History of Rap and Hip-Hop.* Detroit: Thomson-Gale, 2006.

Chang, Jeff. *Can't Stop, Won't Stop: A History of the Hip-hop Generation.* New York: St. Martin's Press, 2005.

Cornish, Melanie J. *The History of Hip Hop.* New York: Crabtree Publishing, 2009.

Higgins, Dalton. *Hip Hop World: A Groundwork Guide.* Groundwood Books, 2009.

Light, Alan, ed. *The Vibe History of Hip Hop.* New York: Three Rivers, 1999.

Internet Resources

http://www.kidzworld.com/article/5321-pioneers-of-hip-hop

Kidzworld offers an overview of hip-hop as well as biographies and facts about many of its stars, such as Drake, Nicki Minaj, Missy Elliot and more.

http://www.pbs.org/independentlens/hiphop/timeline_2000s.htm

PBS's *Independent Lens* explores hip-hop history, provides a timeline of the artists, their hits and their impact on the genre, and offers a video, "Beyond Beats and Rhymes," that explores hip-hop's attitudes toward women and violence.

http://digitaldreamdoor.com

Digtialdreamdoor provides rankings and a timeline of hip-hop artists and their major hits and awards.

http://rockhall.com

The Rock and Roll Hall of Fame site lists the hip-hop artists who have been inducted into the Hall of Fame and provides biographies and background on each of them.

http://www.rapworld.com/history

Rapworld offers a history of hip-hop from its beginnings to the present.

index

Entries in **_bold italic_** refer to captions

64

KV-622-130

Adoption of Children

Adoption of Children

Tenth Edition

J F Josling
Solicitor

and

Allan Levy LL B
*of the Inner Temple
and of The South Eastern Circuit
Barrister*

Longman Professional

© Longman Group Ltd 1985

Published by

Longman Professional and Business Communications Division
Longman Group Limited
21–27 Lamb's Conduit Street, London WC1N 3NJ

First Published 1947
Tenth edition 1985

Associated Offices

Australia   Longman Professional Publishing (Pty) Limited
130 Phillip Street, Sydney, NSW 2000

Hong Kong   Longman Group (Far East) Limited
Cornwall House, 18th Floor, Taikoo Trading Estate, Tong Chong
Street, Quarry Bay

Malaysia   Longman Malaysia Sdn Bhd
Wisma Damansara/Tingkat 2, 5 Jalan Semantan, Peti Surat 63,
Kuala Lumpur 01–02

Singapore   Longman Singapore Publishers (Pte) Ltd
25 First Lok Yang Road, Singapore 2262

USA   Longman Group (USA) Inc
500 North Dearborn Street, Chicago, Illinois 60610

ISBN 0 85120 8665

Printed in Great Britain by Biddles of Guildford Ltd.

Contents

Preface

This is the tenth edition of 'Adoption of Children', which first appeared in 1947. The latest edition is necessitated by the major changes in adoption law which have occurred over the last four years.

In particular, the implementation of parts of the CA 1975 in February 1982 and May 1984, and the introduction of new rules of court, have had far-reaching effects on both the law and the practice.

We are grateful for the valuable assistance given to us by the Honourable Mrs Justice Butler-Sloss, and the Deputy Official Solicitor, H J Baker Esq. In addition we are indebted to Miss Fiona Graham, barrister, who conscientiously read through the manuscript as it took shape, and to Tony Radevsky, barrister, for his contributions.

The law is stated as at 1 May 1985.

J F Josling
Allan Levy
Hastings and London, May 1985

Table of Cases

Table of Statutes

Table of Statutory Instruments

Abbreviations

AA followed by the year	Adoption Act of that year
CA or CYPA	Children Act, or Children and Young Persons Act of year mentioned
CCA 1980	Child Care Act 1980
CCR 1981	County Court Rules 1981
DPMCA 1978	Domestic Proceedings and Magistrates' Courts Act 1978
FCA 1980	Foster Children Act 1980
GMA 1971	Guardianship of Minors Act 1971
Hassassa 1983	Health and Social Services and Social Security Adjudications Act 1983
MCA 1980	Magistrates' Courts Act 1980
RSC	Rules of the Supreme Court 1965
Acts or Adoption Acts	AA 1958, 1960, 1964, 1968 and adoption provisions of CA 1975, or any two or more of these as the context requires
1958 Act or Act of 1958	AA 1958
1975 Act or Act of 1975	CA 1975
AAR 1983	Adoption Agencies Regulations 1983 (SI 1983 No 1964)
AR	Adoption Rules 1984 (SI 1984 No 265)
MC(A)R	Magistrates' Courts (Adoption) Rules 1984 (SI 1984 No 611)

Chapter 1

Introduction

1 History

It was not until 1926 that English law recognised the legal possibility of adoption. Roman law, however, was familiar with it, Indian civilisations have long permitted it, and some continental and American systems have acknowledged the transfer from one person to another of parental rights and obligations. The English common law did not allow such rights and liabilities to be transferred by voluntary act (*Humphrys* v *Polak* [1901] 2 KB 385); nor were there formerly any facilities for judicial transfer.

It was noted in the Houghton Committee Report in 1972 (Cmnd 5107) that 'informal adoption had long been practised as a means of helping relatives and friends who could not look after their own children. After the first world war, which left so many children fatherless, it was realised that these informal arrangements did not provide proper security for the child, who did not become a full member of his new family, or for the adopters, who feared that the mother might reclaim the child when he was old enough to earn; or for the mother, who might be called upon to resume the care of the child at any time if the adopters tired of their responsibility for him. This created a demand for legal adoption, which was already available in some other British territories, Australia, for example, having introduced [it] in the nineteenth century'. (para 10)

The Adoption of Children Act 1926 made general provision for the statutory adoption of children by means of a court order, vesting in the adopter the natural parents' rights and liabilities in a number of stated respects. Rights and interests in property were expressly left undisturbed.

By subsequent statutes more incidents, notably rights of inherit-

1

ance, were by degrees carved out of the natural relationship and added to the adoptive one. Provisions were introduced for translating dispositions of property so as to treat the adopted person as the child of the adopter and not of his natural parents.

The activities of adoption societies and agencies were first dealt with in the Adoption of Children (Regulations) Act 1939, which came into force in 1943.

The Acts were consolidated, with minor amendments, in the AA 1950. The AA 1958, which implemented most of the Hurst Committee's recommendations made in 1954, further insinuated, legally speaking, the adopted person into his new family, and shut him out from the old. Revocation of adoption orders in cases of legitimation was provided for by the AA 1960, and the recognition of adoption orders made in the Isle of Man, the Channel Islands or Northern Ireland by the AA 1964.

The principal purpose of the AA 1968 was to prepare for ratification of the Hague Convention on Adoption of 1965. The 1968 Act dealt with international aspects of adoption. It provided for the recognition of certain overseas adoption orders and for orders to be made under the Hague Convention. Some of the Act has been merged into the CA 1975. Convention and other proceedings affected by the 1968 and 1975 Acts form the subject-matter of Part II of the present book.

The CA 1975 amended the AA 1958 substantially, as well as introducing new provisions relating to, for example, freeing for adoption (see chap 20), and parental agreement (see chap 6). The 1975 Act gave a new structure to the status conferred by an adoption order. The Act placed the adopted person for nearly all purposes of law squarely into the adoptive family; in the case of an adoption before 1 January 1976, from that date, and in the case of any other adoption from the date of the adoption. At the same time it divorced him from the old family by a provision which treats him, not simply as the child of the adopter, but as if he *had been born* the child of the adopter in lawful wedlock, so giving him a place in the new family's history.

The CA 1975, however, was not designed to affect events that had already occurred, so that dates can still be material to the nature and incidents of a pre-1976 adoption (see chap 27, where some qualifications of the general position are also noted).

A fresh consolidation is in the offing.

The AA 1976, of which so far only s 58A (information concerning adoption), inserted by Sched 2, para 35 of Hassassa

1983, is in force, incorporates in logical order all the legislative provisions that survive. Until it is brought into effect, the surviving provisions of the AAs 1958 and 1968 dovetail with Part 1 of the CA 1975 to form one statutory code. A table translating section numbers from the present Acts into those of the AA 1976 is in Appendix 4.

2 Nature of adoption

In England and Wales a legal adoption is effected by an 'adoption order' made by an authorised court on an application by a person or persons wishing to adopt a child. An adoption order vests in the adopter the parental rights and duties relating to the child. The procedure for applying for an order is governed by rules of court (see chap 8).

It has been said that, 'although [adoption] is a formal legal procedure it deals with very human problems. It focusses primarily on the needs and well-being of individual children for whom this form of substitute care is considered appropriate. Nevertheless adoption has to be considered in a family context. It has important personal implications for several different sets of people: the natural and the adoptive parents, and their respective families, and the child himself. Parents, whether married or single, who are unable through adverse circumstances of one sort or another to bring up their child themselves in a stable family home can feel that in relinquishing their child they have secured for him a better future than they could offer. For some childless couples, adoption can satisfy the basic emotional need to create a family and to care for and rear children. It enables the child to achieve permanent security in a substitute home with a couple fully committed to fulfilling parental responsibilities. The child is the focal point in adoption; providing homes for children who need them is its primary purpose'. (Houghton Committee Report 1972 (Cmnd 5107), para 14)

3 Making of an adoption order

The court has a discretion whether or not to make an adoption order. The applicant is not entitled to an order merely because he has satisfied specified conditions.

'In reaching any decision relating to the adoption of a child, *a court or adoption agency* shall have regard to all the circumstances,

first consideration being given to the need to safeguard and
promote the welfare of the child throughout his childhood; and
shall so far as practicable ascertain the wishes and feelings of the
child regarding the decision and give due consideration to them,
having regard to his age and understanding' (CA 1975, s 3).

The Section, it should be noted, applies to all those in agencies
concerned with the placement of a child as well as to the courts
considering an application. The duty is to give first consideration
to the welfare of the child. This is in contrast to proceedings
affecting the legal custody or upbringing of a child where the
court must regard the child's welfare as the first and paramount
consideration (GMA 1971, s 1). The precise meaning of 'first
consideration' as opposed to 'first and paramount' is far from
certain. It may, however, be that in adoption the court must place
less importance on the child's welfare: it must be given greater
weight than other considerations, but it may not necessarily
prevail over those considerations because it is not a 'paramount'
consideration. It still, of course, leaves the court (and the agency)
with a wide discretion in its decision-making process.

Section 3 of the CA 1975 does not, however, apply to the
decision whether a parent or guardian is withholding his agreement to adoption unreasonably (see chap 6) (*In re P* [1977] Fam
25, CA).

In considering whether an adoption order is in the best interests
of the child, the court is likely to consider such matters as 'material
and financial prospects, education, general surroundings, happiness, stability of home and the like' (per Davies LJ, *Re B* [1971]
1 QB 437, at 443). The child's ties, if any, with the natural parents
are of great importance and the questions of possible access and
rehabilitation in respect of them are familiar ones to be
considered. Matters of religion, race and culture are also likely to
be of significance, particularly in so-called trans-racial adoption
applications.

Where the parent or guardian withholds agreement to the adoption, the court must first consider whether adoption is in the
interests of the child, applying s 3, and if it is, then go on to
decide upon the question of whether the agreement of the parent
or guardian should be dispensed with (see chap 6).

'Welfare' can be translated as 'benefit' and is not, of course,
confined to material benefit (*Re D* (No 2) [1959] 1 QB 229). It is
a benefit to a child to have the stigma of illegitimacy removed
(*Re E(P) (An Infant)* [1968] 1 WLR 1913). The court, however,

declined to treat an attempt to avoid 'the stigma' as *alone* justifying an adoption order (CD, Petitioners [1963] SLT (Sh Ct) 7).

The main benefit of adoption will be to give the child the
social, legal and psychological benefits of belonging to a family. In
contrast with the position formerly, the court is now much more
concerned with cases involving children who have been in the
long-term care of a local authority, than with the future of illegitimate babies. Where, however, the object of adoption is to acquire
British nationality rather than the true benefit of a family for the
child, an adoption order will be refused (see *In re A (An Infant)*
[1963] 1 WLR 231). For contrasting circumstances, where an order
was made, see *In re R* [1967] 1 WLR 34. In the more recent case
of *In re H (A Minor) (Adoption: Non-patrial)* [1982] Fam Law
121, an adoption order was made, overriding an immigration
decision made by the Secretary of State. Hollings J held that the
welfare of the child prevailed over the decision to refuse to extend
his stay in the United Kingdom.

In a Scottish case an adoption order was refused where the
sheriff thought that the purpose of the application was to make it
easier for a parent to marry (EO, Petitioner [1951] SLT (Sh Ct)
11). There have also been several judicial statements decrying the
use of the adoption process as a means of changing the child's
name to that of a stepparent (eg *In re D (Minors)* [1973] Fam
209).

It has been said to be a misuse of the adoption procedure, if
the object of the adoption application is to override an area of
administration granted to a local authority by a statute such as
the Child Care Act 1980 *(In re H (Minors)* [1984] *The Times*, 21
November, (CA)). In *In re H* the misuse of the procedure related
to an application launched by foster parents in an attempt to
frustrate the local authority removing from them children, in
respect of whom the local authority had assumed the parental
rights and duties under s 3 of the CCA 1980.

The solemnity and importance of an adoption order were
emphasised by Lord Greene MR in *Skinner v Carter* [1948] Ch
387, at 391, and again by Lord Goddard CJ in *Hitchcock v WB*
[1952] 2 QB 561, at 569. Vaisey J in *Re DX (An Infant)* [1949]
Ch 320 said that adoption normally 'presupposes a complete and
final separation between the child and its natural parents. The
child looks henceforth to the adopters as its parents, and the
natural parents, relinquishing all their parental rights and duties,
step, as it were, for ever out of the picture of the child's life'. The

likelihood of the natural parents being brought back into the picture after an adopted person has reached adulthood is now, perhaps, not so remote as when Vaisey J spoke (see chap 29), but the words 'for ever' will stand for the vast majority of cases. See also chap 12 for the possibility of access to the natural parents or others being made a condition of an adoption order in exceptional circumstances.

An adoption order will not, of course, always be an appropriate way of meeting the child's needs. In circumstances, for example, where the occasion for an adoption application has been associated with the breakdown of a marriage, the legislature has given a strong lead. In the case of a post-divorce adoption application by a parent and stepparent, in general the court must dismiss the application if it considers the matter would be better dealt with by an order regarding custody under s 42 of the Matrimonial Causes Act 1973 (see chap 2). In addition, where a relative of the child, a stepparent or others apply for an adoption order, the court may in certain circumstances treat the application as if it were an application for a custodianship order (see chap 22, the provisions on custodianship in the CA 1975 will come into force on 1 December 1985). Again, the marriage of a child's parents may legitimate him or her, and this may be more beneficial to the child than adoption (see chap 26).

4 Adoption services

Section 1 of the CA 1975, which establishes unified adoption services in England and Wales and in Scotland, as yet awaits implementation. In the meantime, as explained further in chap 4, the system is generally for placements of children to be made by local authorities and approved adoption societies. These bodies perform functions described in the Adoption Agencies Regulations 1983 which, with the schedules, are referred to in chap 4, and set out fully in Appendix 3 to this book. Guidance is also regularly given to them by way of circulars from the Children's Division of the DHSS, Alexander Fleming House, Elephant and Castle, London SE1 6BY.

To adoption agencies—until the coming into force of s 1 of the CA 1975 being described as 'approved adoption societies or local authorities', (SI 1983 No 1946, Sched 2, para 8)—falls the duty, in appropriate cases, of applying to a court for an order freeing a child for adoption, a process introduced from 27 May 1984 by

the implementation of ss 14–16 of the CA 1975 (see chap 20). The new freeing procedure allows for the giving of or dispensing with agreement to the making of an adoption order by a parent or guardian to be dealt with at an early stage in the adoption process.

For assistance in selecting suitable agencies, the British Agencies for Adoption and Fostering, 11 Southwark Street, London SE1 1RQ (tel: 01 407 8800) may be approached.

5 Statistics (from Second Report to Parliament under the CA 1975)

(a) *Number of adoption orders granted*

1975	21,299	1980	10,609
1976	17,621	1981	9,824
1977	12,748	1982	10,240
1978	12,121	1983	9,029
1979	10,870		

(b) *Children adopted from care 1979–83*

1979	1,488	1982	1,861
1980	1,621	1983	2,159
1981	1,650		

6 Adoption and immigration

There is no provision in the immigration rules for a child to be brought to the UK *for* adoption. A child may be allowed in for adoption at the discretion of the Home Secretary, and in exceptional cases. Such cases would only arise where the Home Secretary was satisfied that:

(*i*) there was a genuine intention to adopt;

(*ii*) the child's welfare here was assured;

(*iii*) the court here would be likely to grant an adoption order; and

(*iv*) one of the intending adopters was domiciled here.

In addition the Home Secretary would want to be satisfied that the adoption is not merely a device for gaining entry to this country. Overall the position is that the discretion will be exercised in favour of entry in exceptional cases and if it is appropriate in all the circumstances (unpublished guidelines in circular letter

from the Home Office, Croydon). For a case where the Home Secretary was held to have acted unreasonably in departing from the different terms of an earlier circular letter, when he refused entry clearance to a Pakistani child to come to England for adoption, see *R* v *Sec of State for the Home Dept, ex p Khan* (1984) 14 Fam Law 278, CA. See also *In re H (A Minor) (Adoption: Non-patrial)* [1982] Fam Law 121, where Hollings J made an adoption order, holding that the welfare of the child prevailed over the Home Secretary's decision to refuse to extend his stay in the UK. Hollings J also pointed out the importance in such a case of serving the Home Secretary with notice of the adoption proceedings so that he is given the opportunity of intervening if he wishes, especially so as to ensure that national security considerations are not overlooked. See further *In re A* [1963] 1 WLR 231 and *In re R* [1967] 1 WLR 34.

The Immigration Rules do specifically deal with the bringing of adopted children *into* the UK for settlement with their adoptive parents, where the adopted children are not British citizens or Commonwealth citizens. They may join their settled adoptive parents in the UK if there 'has been a genuine transfer of parental responsibility on the grounds of the original parents' incapacity to care for the child and the adoption is not one of convenience arranged to facilitate the child's admission' (HC 169, para 50). It is essential that there has been a transfer of the child's day to day care to the adoptive parents and that they have undertaken complete responsibility for the child.

7 Adoption and confidentiality

The thread of confidentiality runs throughout the adoption process. It is noted, as necessary, in the chapters that follow.

In particular, any person who obtains any information in the course of, or relating to, any proceedings under the AA 1958, or Part 1 of the CA 1975, (or in the High Court only under the AA 1968), must treat that information as confidential and may only disclose it if:

(*a*) the disclosure is necessary for the proper exercise of his duties, or
(*b*) the information is requested
  (*i*) by a court or public authority (whether in Great Britain or not) having power to determine adoptions and related matters, for the purpose of the discharge of its duties in that behalf, or
  (*ii*) by the Registrar General [see chap 29], or a person authorised

in writing by him, where the information requested relates only to the identity of any adoption agency which made the arrangements for placing the child for adoption in the actual custody of the applicants, and of any local authority which was notified of the applicant's intention to apply for an adoption order in respect of the child, or

(*iii*) by a person who is authorised in writing by the Secretary of State to obtain the information for the purposes of research. (AR, r 53(3); MC(A)R, r 32(5))

An important new provision is contained in the AR, r 53(2) and the MC(A)R, r 32(4): A party who is an individual and is referred to in a confidential report supplied to the court by an adoption agency, a local authority, a reporting officer (see chap 9) or a guardian ad litem may (in the High Court or a county court) inspect or (in the Magistrates' court) be supplied with a copy of, for the purposes of the hearing, that part of any such report which refers to him, subject to any direction given by the court that:

(*a*) no part of one or any of the reports shall be revealed to that party, or

(*b*) the part of one or any of the reports referring to that party shall be revealed only to that party's legal advisers, or

(*c*) the whole or any other part of one or any of the reports shall be revealed to that party.

Documents or orders held by or lodged with the court in adoption proceedings are not open to inspection save as authorised by any enactment or by the rules of court relating to adoption or with the leave of the court; nor may copies be taken or issued (AR, r 53(4); MC(A)R, r 32(6)).

All documents relating to proceedings under the Acts are to be kept in a place of special security while they are in the custody of the court (AR, r 53(1); MC(A)R, r 32(3)). That part of the register kept under r 54 of Magistrates' Courts Rules 1968, which relates to adoption proceedings, must be kept in a separate book (the Register of Adoptions) and must contain the particulars shown in FORM 14 (see Appendix 1) (MC(A)R, r 32(1)). The book also records any declaration under ss 14(7) or 15(4) of the CA 1975 disclaiming involvement in future adoption questions (see chap 20).

Regarding the restriction on the publication orally or in writing of information about proceedings relating to adoption (or wardship), where the Court sits in private, see s 12(1)(*a*), (2) and (4)

of the Administration of Justice Act 1960, and *In re F (A Minor)* [1977] Fam 58, CA. See also in respect of the Magistrates' court, s 71 of the MCA 1980. For the position where the adoption of a ward is involved, see p 118.

8 Adoption in the United Kingdom

The law and procedure described in the present book is the English law of adoption, applicable in the courts of England, Wales and Berwick-on-Tweed. Wales is included in the term 'England' in statutes passed before 22 July 1967, but requires separate mention in those passed subsequently (Wales and Berwick Act 1746, s 3; Welsh Language Act 1967, s 4). The present statutes dealing with adoption embrace Scottish law, pending the implementation of the consolidating Adoption (Scotland) Act 1978. Legal adoption in Northern Ireland is regulated by the Adoption Act (Northern Ireland) 1967.

In dealing with the *effects* of an adoption it is not now usually necessary to distinguish according to the part of the UK in which the order was made (see chap 27).

Part I

Non-Convention Applications

Chapter 2

Qualifications of Adopters

1 General

The Acts have always laid down qualifications and restrictions concerning the eligibility of a person or persons to adopt. The provisions are now contained in ss 10 (married couples), and 11 (one person), of the CA 1975. The main conditions relate to age, number, status and domicile.

(a) Age

The applicant or joint applicants must be at least twenty-one years of age (ss 10(1), 11(1), CA 1975).

(b) Number and status of applicants

An adoption order may not be made on the application of more than one person unless the applicants are a married couple (s 10(1)).

A sole applicant must not be married, or if he or she is married, the court must be satisfied that:

(*i*) his [or her] spouse cannot be found, or

(*ii*) the spouses have separated and are living apart, and the separation is likely to be permanent, or

(*iii*) his [or her] spouse is by reason of ill health, whether physical or mental, incapable of making an application for an adoption order. (s 11(1)(*b*))

for the meaning of 'cannot be found', also used in s 12(2)(*a*) of the CA 1975, see p 42. In condition (*iii*), physical ill health may make a person unsuitable as an adopter but it is not too apparent how it would render him or her 'incapable' of making an application, save perhaps if they were in a coma. Indeed, each of the conditions might well lead the court to question closely whether

13

the overall circumstances are such that the adoption is in the child's interests.

An adoption order granted to joint applicants in the mistaken belief that they were lawfully married is voidable and not void, and the court may decline to set it aside in the interests of justice (*Re F* [1977] Fam 165, CA).

The present legislation does not prohibit the adoption of a child by an unmarried man not related to it (see *The Times*, 5 July 1978, p 2, 'Bachelors' adoption applications').

For the position regarding an adoption application by the mother or father of a child, see below.

(c) *Domicile*

The applicant, or at least one of two applicants who are a married couple, must be domiciled in a part of the United Kingdom, or in the Channel Islands, or the Isle of Man (ss 10(2)(*a*), 11(2)(*a*), CA 1975).

Under s 25 of the CA 1975, it is now possible for persons domiciled outside Great Britain to apply for an order vesting in them the parental rights and duties relating to a child, if they can satisfy the court that they intend to adopt a child under the law of or within the country in which they are domiciled (see chap 16).

(d) *Relationship to child*

Adoption by the child's mother or father (ie the natural or putative father in the case of an illegitimate child) either alone or jointly with the parent's spouse was formerly not uncommon. There have also, of course, been many cases of adoption by grandparents, aunts or other relatives.

A body of social opinion, however, set itself against adoption by stepparents and by relatives, arguing that the probable continuation of old relationships along with new tends to confuse the child, and in any case contradicts the concept of 'transplanting' him from one family into a new one. In addition, it was feared that a stepparent adoption may be used to sever the child's relationship with the other natural parent after a divorce.

The CA 1975 accordingly introduced conditions which discourage such adoptions and, when the custodianship provisions (ss 33–46, CA 1975) (see chap 22) come into force, may render adoption virtually impossible in many circumstances in which it was at one time commonplace.

2 Applications by mother or father alone

Section 11(3) of the CA 1975 forbids the making of an adoption order on the application of the mother or father of the child alone unless the court is satisfied that the other natural parent is dead or cannot be found, or that there is some other reason justifying his or her exclusion. Where an order is made, the reason justifying the other natural parent's exclusion will be recorded by the court staff in the statistical return form referred to at p 79. For the meaning of 'cannot be found', see p 42.

The scope of s 11(3) is somewhat uncertain. It is apparent, though, that only in special circumstances will an order in favour of one parent be made. It is a moot point whether or not the provision applies to the father of an illegitimate child. In general in adoption legislation he is not a 'parent' (*Re M* [1955] 2 QB 479), but a 'relative' (see below, and s 107(1), CA 1975 incorporating s 57(1), AA 1958). Section 11(3), however, refers to 'the other *natural* parent', and the context may well reverse the usual presumption.

The child in a s 11(3) application may invariably be an illegitimate child as there would seem to be no good reason for an application by one natural parent of a legitimate child. If, for example, the mother is divorced from the father she may have, or should seek, a custody order under the Matrimonial Causes Act 1973. If the father is dead, she may have a custody order, or, in any event, she will have become guardian of the child, either alone or jointly on the death of the father (GMA 1971, s 3).

'Some other reason' in s 11(3) justifying the exclusion of the other natural parent will presumably relate directly to the child's welfare. The grounds for dispensing with a parent or guardian's agreement to the making of an adoption order in s 12(2)(c)–(f) of the CA 1975 (see p 41), appear to be the kind of reasons contemplated (eg persistent ill-treatment of the child).

In an application, however, where it is necessary to obtain or dispense with the agreement of the other parent, ss 12 and 11(3) may well overlap, and the latter may in effect be superfluous. Findings reached regarding the issue as to agreement may be the same required to cover s 11(3) and justify the severing of the link with the other natural parent.

3 Stepparent applications

(a) *Post divorce or annulment*

Where a stepparent of the child applies for an adoption order, whether jointly with a natural parent or alone, the court must dismiss the application if it considers that the matter would be better dealt with under s 42 of the Matrimonial Causes Act 1973 (custody orders in cases of divorce etc (ss 10(3), 11(4), CA 1975).

The usual case involves a joint application, eg by the mother and the stepfather who have married after the mother's earlier marriage has been dissolved or annulled. Sections 10(3) and 11(4) do not apply, of course, if the mother has not previously been married, or where her only previous marriage (whether to the child's father or not) ended not in divorce or annulment but in her husband's death. In addition the sections do not apply where the previous marriage was dissolved in a court other than an English one (eg Scotland, see *In re S (Infants) (Adoption by Parent* [1977] Fam 173, at 176G). This follows from the specific reference to s 42, MCA 1973. The court may, however, bear in mind the philosophy behind the provision (per Ormrod LJ, *In re S* (supra), at 177B).

In *In re S*, in 1977, it was held that even in a case where adoption would safeguard and promote the welfare of the child (CA 1975, s 3), the court must consider the specific question, 'will adoption safeguard and promote the welfare of the child better than either the existing arrangements or a joint custody order under s 42 ?' (per Ormrod LJ, at 178B). The Court of Appeal upheld the judge below who had refused to make an adoption order in favour of the mother and stepfather of three children whose ages ranged from six to eleven years. The natural father had consented to the adoption. Although he had a minimal interest in the children as opposed to the stepfather who had formed a close relationship, the children might derive an advantage from contact with him and might be able to 'reforge their links with him'. The advantages of adoption were 'vague and uncertain'. Ormrod LJ contrasted the case with *In re S (A Minor) (1974)* 5 Fam Law 88 where the stepfather had been 'the father figure in the child's life' from an early age, and adoption was 'a formal recognition' of the situation. The child had no recollection of the natural father.

Subsequently, however, in *Re D (Minors) (Adoption by Stepparent)* [1981] 2 FLR 102, the Court of Appeal, contrary to the earlier decision of *In re S* [1977] Fam 173, held that the 1975 Act

requires the court to dismiss an adoption application if it considers that the matter would be *better dealt with by means of a joint custody order*. It is *not* a question of showing that an adoption order is itself better (per Ormrod LJ, at 104H). This now appears to be the authoritative ruling.

In *Re D*, the mother and stepfather of two girls, aged ten and thirteen, applied to adopt them. The mother was divorced from the natural father in 1973 and was given custody of the children. The natural father was in contact with the eldest child until Christmas 1977, and with the youngest until September 1978. In 1976 the mother married the stepfather who himself had custody of the two children of his previous marriage. The adoption application, in respect of the two girls only, was made in 1980. The natural father consented to adoption, and both girls wished to be adopted by their stepfather. The guardian ad litem on balance came down against adoption. The judge at first instance refused the application because the two girls had a proper recollection of their natural father as their father, and because the mother was not applying to adopt the stepfather's children from his previous marriage. The Court of Appeal allowed the applicants' appeal and made an adoption order.

The Court of Appeal noted that in September 1976 the natural father had agreed to the children's surname being changed to that of the stepfather, the girls did not regard or call their natural father their father, they were anxious to be adopted, and indeed everyone but the guardian ad litem favoured adoption, the natural father had dropped out of their lives and the stepfather's first wife had dropped out of the lives of the children of his first marriage, and the mother, the stepfather and the children were proposing to emigrate to Australia.

The Court of Appeal, in addition to interpreting s 10(3) (see above) held that:

(1) On the evidence the matter would not be better dealt with under s 42, MCA 1973 (per Brandon LJ, at 107G: 'I am not even persuaded that it would be dealt with as well');

(2) Section 3 of the CA 1975, inter alia, requires the court to ascertain the wishes and feelings of the children and give due consideration to them. The two girls wanted to be adopted, and in view of their ages and understanding, there would have to be a clear reason before refusing an adoption order;

(3) The fact that a child remembers his natural father is not a

reason for refusing an adoption order if otherwise it was indicated;

(4) per Ormrod LJ: the mother and the stepfather were correct, on the face of it, to think that it was unnecessary to seek an adoption order in respect of the children of his previous marriage, because his first wife had completely disappeared from the children's lives.

The Court of Appeal's interpretation of s 10(3) applies equally to s 11(4), in respect of a sole applicant who is the stepparent.

In cases under s 10(3) or s 11(4), if an adoption application is dismissed, a fresh application under s 42, MCA 1973 will have to be made to the divorce court, as the court hearing the adoption application is not empowered to make a custody order under the 1973 Act.

During its decision-making process the court in a stepparent adoption application will necessarily have to weigh the respective merits of adoption and a custody order. One significant factor against a custody order is that it may give rise to further litigation in the future, particularly as it is far from certain which rights go with the order (see eg *Dipper* v *Dipper* [1981] Fam 31).

(b) *Other cases involving stepparents and relatives*

Some stepparent cases are, until the custodianship provisions (see chap 22) come into force, likely to be relatively straightforward, eg where no application could be made to the divorce court because the child is illegitimate or the other parent has died. There may, however, in the latter case be a relative or relatives with whom it would be in the child's interest to maintain contact. This might militate against an adoption order (see eg *Re LA (A Minor)* (1978) 122 SJ 417). As to the restricted possibility of access as a condition contained in the adoption order, see p 81. For the definition of a 'relative' in s 107(1) of the CA 1975, see p 131.

For a recent example of circumstances where adoption by grandparents was approved by the Court of Appeal, see *Re W (A Minor) (Adoption by Grandparents)* [1981] 2 FLR 161 (in the particular circumstances adoption was in the child's best interests, because the grandparents were ageing and should be put in a position to appoint a testamentary guardian to control the child's future as far as possible. This could be done under an adoption order but not a custody order).

The courts will in the normal way, it would seem, be inclined against adoption if the relationship with the relative can be secured

by other reasons, eg appointment of him or her as a guardian under the GMA 1971. Once custodianship is available the balance in general will tilt more strongly against adoption. For the circumstances in which a custodianship order can be made on an adoption application, see p 133.

Chapter 3

Eligibility of Children for Adoption

An adoption order may only be made in respect of a child (CA1975, s 8(1)). A child (except where used to express a relationship), means a person who has not attained the age of 18 (AA 1958, s 57(1), as amended; CA 1975, s 107(1)). A person attains the age of 18 at the commencement of the relevant anniversary of the date of his birth (Family Law Reform Act 1969, s 9(1)). An adoption order may not be made in relation to a child who is or has been married (CA 1975, s 8(5)), but may be made notwithstanding that the child is already an adopted child (ibid, s 8(8)).

There is now no express requirement for special circumstances to justify the making of an adoption order in respect of a female child in favour of a sole male applicant. In addition there is no requirement as to the domicile, residence or nationality of the child. When considering, however, whether or not to make an adoption order, the question of whether the order will be recognised by the courts of the child's country of domicile is of importance because of the disadvantages that may follow from non-recognition. Evidence on this aspect should be placed before the court in cases involving a foreign element (*Re B(S) (No 2)* [1968] Ch 204).

Where a child is a ward of court, the leave of the court will be required before the child may be placed for adoption and before adoption proceedings (see p 118), or proceedings for a freeing order (see p 126), may be commenced.

In a case where a Magistrates' court has jurisdiction to make an adoption order, and there is in existence a High Court or County Court custody or access order which is at variance with and would be superseded by an adoption order, it is undesirable that the magistrates' court should exercise that jurisdiction. The proper course is to apply to the High Court or County Court to

discharge that order before adoption proceedings are brought. In such a case, however, adoption proceedings will be better brought in the High Court or County Court (per Sir George Baker P, *In re B (Adoption by Parent)* [1975] Fam 127, at 133).

Chapter 4

Adoption Societies and Local Authorities

1 Adoption services

The CA 1975 envisages the compulsory establishment in due course of an adoption service operating within the area of every local authority. The service is to be designed to meet the needs, in relation to adoption, of children who have been or may be adopted, of their parents and guardians, and of adopters and prospective adopters. The local authority must provide the requisite facilities, or secure that approved adoption societies provide them.

The facilities in question include arrangements for assessing children and prospective adopters, placing children for adoption, and counselling those with adoption problems. They are to be provided in conjunction with the local authority's other social services, and with approved adoption societies in their area. The aim is for help to be given in a co-ordinated manner 'without duplication, omission or avoidable delay' (CA 1975, s 1(3)).

At present ss 1 and 2 of the 1975 Act, which lay down this requirement of a unified adoption service, are not yet in force, though in practice, of course, many local authorities do work in concert with approved adoption societies. When s 1 comes into force, a 'local authority or approved adoption society may be referred to as an adoption agency' (s 1(4)). Until s 1 is in force wherever the words 'adoption agency' occur in the CA 1975 in ss 9 (trial period), 14, 15, and 16 (freeing for adoption), 18 (notice to local authority), 20 (guardian ad litem etc), 22 (making of order) and 23 (transfer of parental rights etc), the words 'approved adoption society or local authority' are substituted (SI 1983 No 1946, Sched 2, para 8). See also SI 1981 No 1792 regarding the AA 1958. The Adoption Agencies Regulations 1983 (SI 1983 No

1964) (AAR; see below and Appendix 3), continue to include both bodies in the term 'adoption agency', and the practice is followed in this chapter and elsewhere in the book.

2 Approved adoption society

An adoption society is a body of persons whose functions consist of or include the making of arrangements for the adoption of children (AA 1958, s 57(1); CA 1975, s 107(1)). A body which is a voluntary organisation and desires to act as an adoption society may apply to the Secretary of State for his approval (CA 1975, s 4(1), as amended). A voluntary organisation is a non-profit-making body other than a public or local authority (AA 1958, s 57(1); CA 1975, s 107(1)). An application must be made in writing on a form supplied by the Secretary of State (AAR 1983, reg 2(1)). An unincorporated body of persons cannot apply (reg 2(2)).

On a first application or one for renewal of approval, the Secretary of State will consider the following, and any other relevant considerations (CA 1975, s 4(2)):

(a) the applicant's adoption programme, including, in particular, its ability to make provision for children who are free for adoption;
(b) the number and qualifications of its staff;
(c) its financial resources; and
(d) the organisation and control of its operations. (ibid, s 4(3))

Where the applicant is likely to operate extensively within the area of a particular local authority, the Secretary of State must ask the local authority whether they support the application and must take into account any views they put to him (s 4(4)). The Secretary of State must, where appropriate, also consider the applicant's record and reputation in the adoption field, and the areas within which and the scale on which it is operating or has operated (s 4(5)). Approval lasts for a period of three years from a date specified in the notice, or in the case of renewal, from the date of the notice (s 4(7), and (2)).

Before notifying an applicant for approval that the application is refused because he is not satisfied that it is likely to make or is making an effective contribution the Adoption Service, the Secretary of State must serve on it written notice of the reasons why he proposes to refuse the application, and informing it that it may make representations to him within twenty-eight days of the date of service of the notice (s 4(6), and s 6(1), CA 1975). If

any representations are made, he must consider them before reaching a final decision (ibid. s 6(2)).

For the provisions as to withdrawal of approval, see CA 1975, s 5 and s 6(3) and (4), and for the provisions in respect of inactive or defunct societies, see s 7.

There is no right of appeal against a refusal to approve or a withdrawal of approval. Judicial review may be sought in an appropriate case.

A society approved only as respects Scotland must not act as an adoption society in England or Wales, except to the extent that it considers it is necessary to do so in the interests of children who have been or may be adopted, of parents and guardians of such children, or of adopters or prospective adopters (AA 1958, s 29(2A), inserted by CA 1975, s 28).

3 Local authorities

The authorities for the purposes of both the AA 1958, and the CA 1975 are, in England and Wales, the councils of non-metropolitan counties, of metropolitan districts and of the London Boroughs, and the Common Council of the City of London (AA 1958, s 28(1) as amended; CA 1975 (s 107(1)). Every such authority has power to make and participate in arrangements for the adoption of children (AA 1958, s 28(2)).

The local authority's functions regarding matters relating to adoption must be discharged through its social services committee (see the Local Authorities Social Services Act 1970, ss 2 and 6, and Sched 1). A councillor who is not a member of that committee is entitled to have access to its documents however, if he can establish that the information is needed by him to enable him to discharge his duties as a councillor properly. The 'need to know' test involves the application of a screening process which should be administered with great strictness in the case of a sphere as delicate and confidential as that of child care and adoption. The utmost care must be taken to prevent the unnecessary dissemination within the council of details relating to the child, to its natural parents, to any foster or adoptive parents, and of sources of information (*R* v *Birmingham City District Council Ex p O* [1983] AC 578). The decision whether the outside councillor has a good reason for access to confidential information may, in respect of adoption, be made, in the absence of express directions from the council, by the director and deputy director of social

services. In the event of a continued difference of opinion, the decision would ultimately lie with the councillors meeting in council (per Lord Brightman, at p 594). See also *R* v *Hackney LBC, ex p Gamper* (1984) 128 SJ 874.

4 Restrictions on making arrangements for adoption

(a) Private placements

A person other than an adoption agency (ie an approved adoption society or local authority), cannot lawfully make arrangements for the adoption of a child or place a child for adoption, unless:

(a) the proposed adopter is a relative of the child; or
(b) he is acting in pursuance of a High Court order.
(AA 1958, s 29(1), inserted by CA 1975, s 28(a)).

For the definition of 'relative', see p 131.

A person must be deemed to make arrangements for the adoption of a child, or to take part in arrangements for the placing of a child in the actual custody of another person if, as the case may be:

(a) he enters into or makes any agreement or arrangement for, or for facilitating, the adoption of the child by any other person, whether the adoption is effected, or is intended to be effected, in pursuance of an adoption order or otherwise; or
(b) he enters into or makes any agreement or arrangement for, or facilitates, the placing of the child in the actual custody of that other person;

or if he initiates or takes part in any negotiations of which the purpose or effect is the conclusion of any agreement or the making of any arrangement therefor, or if he causes another to do so. (AA 1958, s 57(2), as amended)

For the criminal offences under s 29, see chap 30. They include *receiving* a child placed in contravention of s 29(1), and so the prospective adopters are at risk.

If there has been a breach of s 29, any adoption application must be heard in the High Court, (*In re S (A Minor)* (1984) *The Times*, 2 November (CA)). For the circumstances in which wardship may be appropriate, see p 124.

Apart from the two exceptions in s 29(1), the general restrictions will not totally prevent 'private' or 'independent' placements. A child may have been placed with private *foster* parents, who,

after twelve months, then seek an adoption order (see CA 1975, s 9(2), (p 34)).

If the child was originally genuinely placed for fostering, and the foster parents afterwards formed an intention to apply for adoption, there would be no breach of s 29(1). However, the circumstances of the original placement may have prima facie been in breach of s 29(1). In *In re S* (supra), Slade LJ, whilst leaving the point open for future argument, expressed the view that he was not yet persuaded that s 9(2) of the 1975 Act eliminated the prohibitions of s 29 of the 1958 Act. Where there is a non-agency placement, the local authority must, for the purposes of its report to the court under s 18(2) of the CA 1975 (see p 35), investigate whether the child was placed with the applicant in contravention of s 29 of the AA 1958.

Where a person is convicted of a contravention of s 29(1), the court convicting (a magistrates' court) may, in exceptional circumstances, make a supervision order in respect of the child, or commit the child to the care of a local authority, as if it had refused an adoption application, using the powers in s 17 of the CA 1975, (see chap 14) (AA 1958, s 29(5)).

(*b*) *Certain payments*

As to payments, rewards and allowances in connection with adoption and placement, see chap 30. Section 50 of the AA 1958, (prohibition of certain payments in relation to adoption; see p 185), is of particular importance because the court must not make an adoption order in relation to a child unless it is satisfied that the applicants have not, as respects the child, contravened s 50 (CA 1975, s 22(5).

5 Arrangements to be made by adoption agencies

The Adoption Agencies Regulations 1983 set out in detail inter alia the adoption agencies' duties in respect of a child, his parents or guardian, a prospective adopter, and a proposed placement. They provide for the establishment of an adoption panel and its functions, and for the agency's arrangements for adoption work. They are reproduced in full in Appendix 3. An outline of some of the main points contained in them is set out below. The regulations are considerably more detailed than those they replaced.

Where an adoption agency operates only for the purpose of putting persons in contact with other adoption agencies, and for

the purpose of putting such agencies into contact with each other, or for either of such purposes, it is not required to follow all the steps laid down by the regulations nor set up an adoption panel as explained below (reg 4).

(a) Adoption panels (regs 5 and 10)

An adoption agency, unless exempt under reg 4, must establish at least one adoption panel, appointing not more than ten members to a panel. The function of a panel is to consider cases put before it by the agency and make recommendations. It is for the agency to make the decisions. The Chairman of the panel must be a person of appropriate experience in adoption work. For the other members, see reg 5(3). The panel must consider the case of every child, prospective adopter, and proposed placement referred to it by the agency, and make any one or more recommendations as to:

(a) whether adoption is in the best interests of a child and, if the panel recommends that it is, whether an application . . . should be made to free the child for adoption,

(b) whether a prospective adopter is suitable to be an adoptive parent, and

(c) whether a prospective adopter would be a suitable adoptive parent for a particular child. (see the terms of reg 10(1) and (2))

The panel must have regard to ss 3 (duty to promote welfare of the child,) and 13 (religious upbringing of adopted child,) of the CA 1975, obtain appropriate legal advice, and all necessary information (reg 10(3)).

(b) Agency arrangements for adoption work (reg 6)

An adoption agency must, in consultation with its adoption panel (if any), and medical adviser, make written arrangements to govern the exercise of the agency's and the panel's functions, and such arrangements must be reviewed by the agency not less than once every three years. Provisions that must be included in the arrangements are set out in reg 6(2). Adoption agencies and their caseworkers are affected by s 58A of the AA 1976 (added by Hassassa 1983), which introduced from May 1984 a new system for transmitting information to the Secretary of State by way of the Registrar General's office.

(c) *Duties of agency in particular cases (regs 7 and 8)*

Regulation 7 sets out the duties of the agency when it is considering adoption for a child, and reg 8 its duties when it is considering whether a person may be suitable to be an adoptive parent. The duties in respect of a child, his parents or guardian, and a prospective adopter, (which do not arise when the agency is satisfied that the relevant requirements have been carried out by another agency), may generally be described as the provision of a counselling service and of explanations, backed up by written information, of the legal implications of adoption and the relevant procedures. The duties also arise in respect of the father of an illegitimate child where his identity is known (see reg 7(3)). Subsequently written reports on medical and other matters are required. It is at this point that case records are to be set up (regs 7(2), and 8(2)).

(d) *Placement (regs 9, 11 and 12)*

When an agency proposes to place a particular child with a prospective adopter it must refer its proposal, together with a written report containing its observations on the proposal and any relevant information, to its adoption panel (see (a) above) (reg 9(1)), only after consultation with:

(1) any other agency which has decided that adoption is in the best interests of the child, or that the prospective adopter is suitable to be an adoptive parent; and

(2) any local authority or voluntary organisation which has parental rights and duties in respect of the child as a result of a freeing order or a transfer of those rights and duties (CA 1975, s 23, see p 109), or in whose care the child is, and which agrees with the proposal. (reg 9(2))

The adoption agency must only make a decision on any of the relevant matters after taking into account the recommendation of the adoption panel (reg 11(1)). Regulation 11(2) provides for notification of an agency's decision.

The duties of an agency, when a placement is decided upon, are the subject of reg 12, which contains detailed requirements for notification, monitoring and supervision, reporting and review.

(e) *Review of unplaced freed children (reg 13)*

The agency must review the case of a child who has been freed for adoption, but who does not have his home with a prospective adopter after six months have elapsed since the making of the

freeing order. The review must be undertaken by the agency in which the parental rights and duties are vested, and must be repeated at intervals of not more than six months (reg 13(1), and (2)).

For the agency's duty after a year has elapsed since freeing, to supply progress reports to a 'former parent' under s 15 of the CA 1975, see p 106 and reg 15.

(f) Records etc (regs 14–17)

Regulations 14 to 17 contain provisions as to the confidentiality, disclosure, preservation and transfer of case records and information. In general, an agency must preserve the indexes to all its case records and the case records themselves in respect of those cases in which an adoption order is made in a place of special security for at least seventy-five years (reg 14(3), and see reg 16(2)). Other case records must be preserved in a place of special security for as long as the agency considers appropriate.

(g) Post-placement

While a person who does not have the legal custody of a child has its actual custody, he has the like duties under the AA 1958 in relation to the child as if he had legal custody (AA 1958, s 57A(1), added by Hassassa 1983). For 'actual custody', see chap 5. In certain circumstances a child may be returned to the agency after placement and before an adoption order is made.

At any time after a child has been delivered into the actual custody of any person in pursuance of arrangements made by an agency for the adoption of the child by that person, and before an adoption order has been made in favour of that person:

(1) that person may give written notice to the agency of his intention not to retain the actual custody of the child; or

(2) the agency may give that person written notice of their intention not to allow the child to remain in his custody.
    (AA 1958, s 35(1))

After an adoption application has been made, however, the agency may only give notice under (2) above with the court's leave (s 35(2)).

Where notice is given, under either (1) or (2) above, or if an adoption application by a person in whose actual custody the child has been placed by an agency is refused or withdrawn, the prospective adopter must cause the child to be returned to the agency which must receive the child, or to a suitable person

nominated by it (s 35(3), and (5)). He must do this within seven days after the date on which the notice was given or the application refused or withdrawn, as the case may be (s 35(3)). The court may, however, where an application for an adoption order is refused, at any time before the expiry of the seven days, order the period to be extended for a specified duration, not exceeding six weeks (s 35(5A)).

The requirement to return the child cannot be stayed pending an appeal (per Roxburgh J, *Re CSC (An Infant)* [1960] 1 All ER 711). For the possible use of wardship, see p 122.

The same obligation to return the child within seven days arises if an interim order (see chap 15) expires, or if a permitted extension of it expires, without a full adoption order having been made (s 35(4)).

For the offence of contravening s 35, see chap 30. The convicting court may order the child to be returned to his parents or guardian or to the agency (s 35(6)).

6 Children in local authority care: special provisions

In the case of a child who, not having been placed for adoption by an agency, is nevertheless for the time being in the care of a local authority, and in the actual custody of a person who then gives notice of his intention to adopt, the provisions of s 35 of the AA 1958 (see above) apply, except that where the adoption application is refused or withdrawn the child need not be returned to the local authority unless the authority so require (AA 1958, s 36(1)).

Where notice of intention to adopt has been given in the circumstances set out in s 36(1), then until the adoption application has been disposed of, any right of the local authority to require the child's return *otherwise* than pursuant to s 35 is suspended (s 36(2)). In addition, whilst the child remains in the actual custody of the person who gave notice of intention to adopt, no contributions shall be payable to the local authority under s 45 of the CCA 1980 by the natural parents or the child, (without prejudice to recovery of any arrears due when the notice was given) unless twelve weeks have elapsed since the notice and the application has not been made, or the application has been refused by the court or withdrawn (s 36(2)(*a*)).

A proposing adopter may number the child he proposes to adopt amongst his family for the purposes of child benefit, since

having the child living with him renders him responsible within the meaning of the Child Benefit Act 1975. The regulation (SI 1955 No 1377, reg 1(2)), which disentitles a person to child benefit in respect of a child boarded out with him, does not apply to a prospective adopter, (*Simpson* v *DHSS* (1984) *The Times*, 9 October).

7 Supervision of protected children by local authority

A child is a protected child while he is in the actual custody of the applicant for adoption who has given the local authority notice of his intention to apply to adopt under s 18 of the CA 1975 (see chap 5) (AA 1958, s 37(1), as amended)). A child will therefore be a protected child where there has been a non-agency placement for adoption. This may now be a child who is to be adopted by a parent or a relative, by a person acting in pursuance of a High Court order, or by foster parents, for example, who have had the child living with them, or one of them, continuously for at least twelve months (see AA 1958, s 29, and CA 1975, s 9(2)).

While, however, the child is in the care of any person in any such school as is mentioned in s 2(2) of the FCA 1980, or in a home for the mentally disordered pursuant to s 1(3) of the Residential Homes Act 1980, or liable to be detained under the Mental Health Act 1983, he is not, simply by reason of a notice of intention to apply to adopt, a protected child (AA 1958, s 37(3)).

Protection of a child ceases on his attaining the age of eighteen, or before then:

(1) on the appointment of a guardian for him under the GMA 1971;

(2) on notification to the local authority that the adoption application has been withdrawn, or

(3) on the making of an adoption order, or a supervision or care order on dismissal of the adoption application (CA 1975, s 17, see chap 14), or a custodianship order under Part 11 of the CA 1975, when it is in force, or an order under ss 42, 43, or 44 of the Matrimonial Causes Act 1973. (AA 1958, s 37(4), as amended)

Whilst a child is a protected child, Part IV of the AA 1958 applies to him, and the local authority must supervise him as set out below.

(*a*) *General supervision*

Every local authority must ensure that protected children within their area are visited from time to time by its officers who must satisfy themselves as to the well-being of the children, and give advice about their care and maintenance (AA 1958, s 38). The officers may, on production, if it is requested, of their written authority, inspect any premises in the authority's area in which protected children are kept or are to be kept (s 39). Inspection may also be authorised by the Secretary of State (CCA 1980, ss 74 and 75, and Sched 4, para 8).

(*b*) *Change of address*

Where a person having the actual custody of a protected child changes his permanent address, he must give the local authority in whose area he has been living, written notice specifying the new address. The notice must be given not less than two weeks before the change, or if the change is made in an emergency, not later than one week after the change. If the new address is in the area of another local authority, the authority receiving the notice must inform the other authority of the change, and give them (so far as is known to them) details of the name, sex and date, and place of birth of the child, and the name and address of every person who is a parent or guardian, or acts as a guardian of the child, or from whom the child has been or is to be received (s 40(4), and (6)).

(*c*) *Death of child*

If a protected child dies, the person in whose actual custody he was at his death must, within forty-eight hours of the death, give written notice of the death to the local authority (s 40(5)).

(*d*) *Unsuitable premises and persons*

If satisfied, on the complaint of a local authority, that a protected child is being kept or is about to be received:
　(*i*) in any premises or any environment detrimental or likely to be detrimental to him; or
　(*ii*) by any person who is unfit to have his care,
the *juvenile* court may make an order for the removal of the child to a place of safety until he can be restored to a parent, relative or guardian, or until other arrangements can be made (AA 1958, s 43(1)). A single justice may make an order on the application of a person authorised to visit protected children, if it is proved

that the health or well-being of the child is in imminent danger (ibid).

Where Part IV of the AA 1958 involves an order of a juvenile court or any other magistrates' court, including a case where a single justice may make an order, an appeal lies to a Crown Court (s 48).

For criminal offences and penalties under Part IV of the AA 1958, see chap 30.

(e) Insurance

A person who maintains a protected child is deemed to have no interest in the child's life for the purposes of the Life Assurance Act 1774 (AA 1958, s 46), and a policy on that life for the use and benefit of the person in question is therefore void. Certain other policies (eg for personal accident) may also be affected by this provision (see *Halsbury's Laws of England*, 4th ed (Butterworths 1978), *25*, para 558).

Chapter 5

Trial Period

Beginning with the Adoption of Children (Regulations) Act 1939, progressively more stringent conditions have been enacted to ensure that the adoptive parents and the child have 'tried each other out' before the adoption becomes effective. Where proceedings are commenced after the 27 May 1984 the relevant provisions in the CA 1975 are ss 9 (child to live with adopters before order made, and minimum age), and 18 (need to notify local authority where *non-agency* placement), which are aimed at providing the court with sufficient material from which the suitability of the placement can be assessed.

1 Living together (s 9)

Where the applicant, or one of them, is a parent, stepparent or relative of the child, or the child was placed with the applicants by an adoption agency, or in pursuance of a High Court order, an adoption order cannot be made unless the child is at least nineteen weeks old, and at all times during the preceding thirteen weeks had his home with the applicants or one of them (CA 1975, s 9(1)). (For the position regarding the adoption of children abroad, see s 25(2), and chap 16.)

In all other cases an adoption order cannot be made unless the child is at least twelve months old, and at all times during the preceding twelve months had his home with the applicants or one of them (s 9(2)).

The reference to a placement in pursuance of a High Court order in s 9(1) presumably refers to the wardship or statutory jurisdiction (eg divorce or guardianship). In cases not within s 9(1), the longer period of twelve months is thought necessary for evaluating the suitability of adoption, because there will not

have been an investigation of the kind which precedes a placement by an adoption agency. An application by a foster parent is an example of such a case, where the original placement was not for adoption.

Section 9(2) may appear to offer a means of circumventing the restriction on private placements made by s 29 of the AA 1958 (see p 25). In *re S (A Minor* (1984) *The Times*, 2 November, (CA), Slade LJ, whilst leaving the point open for full argument in a future case, said that he was not yet persuaded that s 9(2) eliminated the prohibitions of s 29 of the 1958 Act. Section 29 would not, in any event, be contravened if the child was genuinely placed privately for fostering and the foster parents afterwards decided to make an adoption application.

A child *has his home with* the person who, disregarding absence of the child at a hospital or boarding school and any other temporary absence, has *actual* custody of the child (CA 1975 s 87(3)). A person has actual custody of a child if he has actual possession of his person, whether or not that possession is shared with one or more other persons (s 87(1)).

It is clear from s 9(1) and (2) that in the case of a joint application it is sufficient if the child has had his home with one of the two applicants. This will, of course, cover the situation where one of the prospective adopters is, for example, away on business for extended periods. The danger that the child may not get on sufficiently well with this applicant is covered by the provision that an adoption order cannot be made unless the court is satisfied that the agency which placed the child (or in a non-agency case, the local authority within whose area the applicants have their home), has had sufficient opportunities to see the child with both applicants together in the home environment (s 9(3)). The provision also applies in the case of an application by one person.

2 Notice to local authority (s 18)

An adoption order cannot be made in respect of a child who was *not* placed with the applicant by an adoption agency unless the applicant has, at least three months before the date of the order, given notice in writing to the local authority within whose area he has his home, of his intention to apply for the adoption order (s 18(1)), and s 107(1)).

On receipt of such notice from the applicant the child becomes a protected child (AA 1958, s 37(1)(*b*) and see p 31), and the

local authority must investigate the matter and submit a report to the court (s 18(2)). The local authority must, in particular, investigate:

(1) so far as is practicable, the suitability of the applicant, and any other matters relevant to the operation of s 3 of the CA 1975 (promotion of the child's welfare, see p 3), in relation to the application, and

(2) whether the child was placed with the applicant in contravention of s 29 of the AA 1958, (see p 25 and 186). (s 18(3))

Rule 21(4) of the AR and the MC(A)R, provides for the hearing to be timed to allow the authority to submit its report (see p 70).

Where a local authority receives a s 18(1) notice in respect of a child whom the authority know to be in the care of another local authority, it must inform that authority in writing within seven days (AA 1958 s 36(3)).

For the effect of a s 18(1) notice, given in respect of a child who is in the care of a local authority, in regard to the possible return of the child, and to the making of contributions under s 45, CCA 1980, see s 36(1) and (2) of the AA 1958.

It would seem that if an applicant lives abroad and has not got a home in England and Wales (and therefore cannot give notice to a local authority), an adoption order cannot be made.

Chapter 6

Agreement to Adoption Orders

1 From whom required

In the absence of an order freeing the child for adoption (see chap 20), the court cannot make an adoption order unless it is satisfied either:

(1) that each parent or guardian of the child freely, and with full understanding of what is involved, agrees unconditionally to the making of an order, (whether or not he knows the identity of the applicants); or

(2) that his agreement should be dispensed with on a ground specified in the Act (see p 41). (CA 1975, s 12(1))

'Parent', which is not defined in the Act, means by ordinary construction, the mother and father of a legitimate child, and the mother of an illegitimate child (see *Re M* [1955] 2 QB 479, and *In re Adoption Application (No 41 of 1961)* [1963] Ch 315). The adopter of an adopted child is included. The husband of the child's mother, if married to her at the time of the child's birth, is presumed to be a 'parent', although evidence may be put in to rebut the presumption, and demonstrate that his agreement is not required.

The putative father of an illegitimate child is not a 'parent' for the purposes of s 12(1) (*Re M* [1955] 2 QB 479, and see *R v Immigration Appeals Adjudicator, ex p Crew* (1982) *The Times*, 26 November). If, however, he has legal custody of the child by virtue of an order under s 9 of the GMA 1971 he comes within the definition of a 'guardian' (see below), and his agreement to the making of an adoption order must be obtained or dispensed with. The putative father may apply for a custody or access order under s 9 of the 1971 Act prior to the commencement of adoption proceedings. In *Re Adoption Application (No 41 of 1961)* [1963]

Ch 315, the putative father applied for custody to a magistrates' court before adoption proceedings were commenced in the High Court. It was held that the proper course was to adjourn the adoption application so that the putative father could bring a concurrent application for custody before the High Court. If an application by the putative father for custody or access is made during the currency of adoption proceedings, it may be convenient for arrangements to be made for both applications to be heard together. The adoption application in principle, however, need not be delayed by the putative father's application because there is no reason why he should not put his case in the adoption proceedings, (per Wilberforce J in *Re Adoption Application (No 41 of 1961) (no 2)* [1964] Ch 48). For the relevant Rules providing for a putative father to be made a respondent to the adoption application, and therefore to be entitled to attend the hearing and be heard on the question of whether an adoption order should be made, see p 58. He may, for example, be liable by order or agreement to contribute to the child's maintenance.

If the putative father's application for custody or access and the adoption application come on at the same time, the applications should, so far as possible, be heard together, and the judge should defer any decision until he has heard all the evidence (*Re O* [1965] Ch 23). In *C v H* (1979) 123 SJ 537, Balcombe J said that it was proper for magistrates to hear an access application and one for adoption by another applicant at the same time if the evidence was the same for both. If this was done the justices should bear both possibilities in mind and decide the two applications together on a 'balancing test'. They should not grant one first and then treat their decision on that as barring the second.

The parental rights and duties assumed by a local authority under s 3 of the CCA 1980, or the powers and duties of a parent vested in the authority under a care order do not give the authority the right to agree or to refuse to agree to the making of an adoption order (ss 3(10) and 10(5) of the CCA 1980, the latter added by Hassassa 1983, Sched 2, para 47). Similarly a voluntary organisation having the parental rights and duties in relation to a child under s 64 of the CCA 1980 is restricted in the same manner.

A custodian (see chap 22) is neither a 'parent' nor a 'guardian' and his agreement is not therefore required (see s 33, CA 1975).

A 'guardian' in s 12(1) of the 1975 Act means:

(1) a person appointed by deed or will pursuant to the provisions of the GMA 1971, or previously under the

Guardianship of Infants Acts 1886 and 1925, or by a court of competent jurisdiction, and

(2) in the case of an illegitimate child includes the putative father where he has legal custody of the child by virtue of an order under s 9 of the GMA 1971. (s 107(1), CA 1975)

By s 104 of the CA 1975 nothing in the Act restricts or affects the jurisdiction of the High Court to appoint or remove guardians.

2 Nature of agreement

It is apparent from s 12(1)(*b*) of the CA 1975, and FORM 7 in Sched 1 of each set of Adoption Rules (Agreement to an Adoption Order, see Appendix 1), that the agreement given must refer to a specific application for adoption already made or intended to be made by a specific applicant identifiable by name or by a serial number, (see also *Re Carroll* [1931] 1 KB 317, at 329, per Scrutton LJ, and for a contrasting situation in the freeing for adoption procedure, see chap 20). As noted above a valid agreement may be given by a parent or guardian whether or not he knows the identity of the applicants (for the serial number procedure, see p 61).

Agreement may be withdrawn up to the last moment before the adoption order has been made, even if it was given by deed (*Re F (An Infant)* [1957] 1 All ER 819, and see *Re Hollyman* [1945] 1 All ER 290 (CA)). The court may then, of course, in appropriate circumstances, dispense with the agreement on one of the grounds specified in s 12(2) of the CA 1975, see p 41.

The parent or guardian's agreement must be given freely and will full understanding of what is involved and must be unconditional (CA 1975, s 12(1)(*b*)(i)). For the reporting officer's duties regarding these requirements, see p 65, and for the adoption agency's duties in respect of providing information, see p 28. In *Re P* (1954) 118 JP 139, a children's officer told the natural mother that she would be subject to a claim for maintenance if she did not consent to the making of the adoption order. The Court of Appeal found the statement to be unjustifiable and regrettable, but held on the facts that it had not affected the free nature of the mother's consent.

As the agreement must now be unconditional, the parent or guardian cannot, for example, as formerly stipulate the religious upbringing of the child as a condition of his agreement. By s 13 of the CA 1975, however, an adoption agency when placing a

child for adoption must have regard (so far as is practicable), to any wishes of the child's parents and guardians as to its religious upbringing.

A mother's agreement is ineffective for the purposes of s 12(1)(*b*)(i) if it is given less than six weeks after the child's birth (CA 1975, s 12(4)). This protects the mother from being unduly influenced by anyone before she has recovered from the birth.

3 Form and evidence of agreement

The agreement of the parent or guardian may be given by him if and when he attends the hearing (see s 22(1) and (2), CA 1975). His attendance, however, is not normally obligatory and it is usual for the procedure for giving agreement in writing to be used. For the reporting officer's relevant duties including witnessing the parent or guardian's signature, see Rule 17(4) of each set of Rules, and p 65. A written agreement is authorised by s 102 of the CA 1975, and Rule 20(1) of each set of Rules provides that it may be in FORM 7, see Appendix 1, (it is the same form for all courts). Although the use of FORM 7 is optional, it is suggested, for obvious reasons, that it should be used.

Rule 20(1) of each set of Rules further provides that any document signifying the agreement to the making of the adoption order, if executed by a person outside England and Wales before the commencement of the proceedings, must be filed with the originating process.

If the document is executed outside England and Wales it must be witnessed as follows (see Rule 20(2)):

Place executed	*Witness*
Scotland	Justice of the Peace or a Sheriff
Northern Ireland	Justice of the Peace
Outside the United Kingdom	(1) Any person for the time being authorised by law in the place where the document is executed to administer an oath for any judicial or other legal purpose, or (2) a British consular officer, or (3) a notary public, or (4) if the person executing the document is serving in any of the regular armed forces of the Crown, a commissioned officer in any of those forces.

If executed in England and Wales the document will, of course, be witnessed by the reporting officer.

Section 102 of the CA 1975 deals with documentary evidence of agreement. If the document signifying the agreement to the making of an adoption order is properly witnessed, it is admissible in evidence without further proof of the signature of the person by whom it was executed (s 102(1)). A document signifying agreement which purports to be properly witnessed is presumed to be so witnessed, and to have been executed and witnessed on the date and at the place specified in the document, unless the contrary is proved (s 102(2)).

4 Dispensing with agreement

As already noted the court may dispense with the agreement of a parent or guardian to the making of the adoption order on a ground specified in the CA 1975. Section 12(2) sets out the available grounds which are considered below individually. They are that the parent or guardian:

(a) cannot be found or is incapable of giving agreement;
(b) is withholding his agreement unreasonably;
(c) has persistently failed without reasonable cause to discharge the parental duties in relation to the child;
(d) has abandoned or neglected the child;
(e) has persistently ill-treated the child;
(f) has seriously ill-treated the child, and the rehabilitation of the child within the household of the parent or guardian is unlikely either because of the ill–treatment or for other reasons. (The qualification as to rehabilitation is added by s 12(5).)

As the court has to be satisfied that the ground has been proved, it is for the applicant to prove it by admissible evidence on the balance of probabilities (see *Re B (an Infant)* (1960) *The Times*, 25 March, and *Re C (Adoption Application: hearing)* [1982] FLR 95, CA). The Court should not decide the issue on affidavit evidence: it is vital to see and hear the prospective adoptive parents, and the natural parent who is refusing to agree (see *Re F(R) (An Infant)* [1970] 1 QB 385, (CA)). Opportunities for cross-examination must be provided and a reasoned judgment delivered (see *Re C (A Minor)* (1981) *The Times*, 23 June, and *In re M* [1973] 1 QB 108).

So that the natural parent who is contesting the application

knows of the case he has to meet and in addition so that the issues are clarified, the respective Rules provide for the applicant who is requesting agreement to be dispensed with, to file three copies of the statement of facts on which he intends to rely (for the precedure see Rule 19 and p 70). A copy of the statement will be served on the natural parent and a copy supplied to the guardian ad litem, and to the reporting officer, if a different person.

For the status of and practice regarding the guardian ad litem's report, see p 68.

A natural parent should, if practicable, be legally represented at the hearing especially in serial number cases, and should be expressly advised by the court to consider applying for legal aid (per Sachs LJ, in *Re M* [1973] 1 QB 108, at 120, see also p 57).

(a) *Parent or guardian cannot be found or is incapable of giving agreement (s 12(2)(a))*

A parent or guardian cannot be found if all reasonable steps by reasonable means have failed to trace him (see *Re C (An Infant)* (1957) *The Times*, 2 April). Enquiries should be very thorough indeed and assistance should, if necessary, be sought, from, for example, the DHSS, the National Health Service Register, the Passport Department of the Home Office, and the Ministry of Defence. In *Re F(R) (An Infant)* [1970] 1 QB 385, the applicant's enquiries had not included approaching the father of the child's mother although they knew his address. The mother became aware of the adoption order two months after it was made. The Court of Appeal allowed her appeal out of time and sent the application back for a re-hearing. In *Re B (An Infant)* [1958] 1 QB 12 (CA), the adoption order was set aside because, although the applicants knew the mother's address, they failed to serve her (for service see Rule 9 of the respective Rules, and p 62).

If, however, there are no practical means of communicating with the parent or guardian, then he cannot be found for the purposes of s 12(2)(a), even if his whereabouts are in fact known. Where parents lived in a totalitarian country and any attempt to communicate with them would have been embarrassing and dangerous for them, it was held that they were persons who 'cannot be found', *and* who were incapable of giving (their) agreement. The latter finding was based on the fact that even if a request for them to give their agreement reached them, it was

probable that they would not be freely permitted to give such agreement (*Re R (Adoption)* [1967] 1 WLR 34).

In order to demonstrate that a person is incapable of giving agreement, for example, by reason of mental illness, admissible evidence of the nature and extent of the condition will be essential. The Court may well conclude that a guardian ad litem should be appointed to act on behalf of the parent or guardian.

(b) Parent or guardian is withholding his agreement unreasonably (s 12(2)(b))

This ground produces more case law at first instance and on appeal and more contested cases than any other area of adoption law. In the leading authority of *In re W* [1971] AC 682, it was held that the question is whether at the time of the hearing the parent or guardian is withholding his agreement unreasonably. The test is reasonableness and not anything else. It is not culpability or indifference or failure to discharge parental duties. It is reasonableness in the context of the totality of the circumstances (see Lord Hailsham at 699B). It is an objective test: the court must look and see whether it is reasonable or unreasonable according to what a reasonable parent in the parent's place would do in all the circumstances (per Lord Denning MR in *In re L* (1962) 106 SJ 611 (CA), approved as authoritative in *In re W*). In the later House of Lords' case of *In re D (An Infant) (Adoption: Parent's Consent)* [1977] AC 602, at 625G, Lord Wilberforce said that this involved considering how a parent in the circumstances of the actual parent but (hypothetically) endowed with a mind and temperament capable of making reasonable decisions would approach a complex question involving a judgment as to the present and the future, and the probable impact of these on the child. In this case the question whether one should postulate a reasonable homosexual or a reasonable heterosexual parent was considered to be an unreal one. It was meaningless to make any hypothesis about any sexual element in the act of judgment.

The court must be extremely careful not to substitute its own view for that of the parent: 'two reasonable parents can perfectly reasonably come to opposite conclusions on the same set of facts without forfeiting their title to be regarded as reasonable. The question in any given case is whether a parental veto comes within the band of possible reasonable decisions and not whether it is right or mistaken. Not every reasonable exercise of judgment is right, and not every mistaken exercise of judgment is unreason-

able. There is a band of decisions within which no court should seek to replace the individual's judgment with its own', per Lord Hailsham, in *Re W* [1971] AC 682, at 700 D.

In a further House of Lords' case, *O'Connor* v *A and B* [1971] 1 WLR 1227 at 1229, Lord Reid thought that a reasonable parent would have in mind the interests or claims of all three parties concerned—the child whose adoption is in question, the natural parents, and the adopting family.

Child's welfare In considering whether the agreement is being withheld unreasonably the welfare of the child is not the sole consideration, but it must be taken into account: great weight is given to what is better for the child by a reasonable parent. The child's welfare is relevant in all cases if and to the extent that a reasonable parent would take it into account. It is decisive in those cases where a reasonable parent must so regard it, per Lord Hailsham, *In re W* [1971] A C 682, at 698E, and 699B. In *In re P (An Infant)* [1977] Fam 25, it was held by a majority that s 3 of the CA 1975 ('in reaching any decision relating to the adoption of a child a court or adoption agency shall have regard to all the circumstances, first consideration being given to the need to safeguard and promote the welfare of the child throughout his childhood . . .'), does not apply to the question of whether or not agreement is being withheld unreasonably. Ormrod LJ doubted whether the section, in any event, materially altered the law as set out in *In re W*. This view was shared by Lord Simon in *In re D* [1977] AC 602, at 641 (see also *Re M (A Minor)* [1980] CLYB 1801, in which the House of Lords refused leave to appeal on the point). As a reasonable parent no doubt gives first consideration to the child's welfare, the point may not affect many decisions. In the recent case of *Re H and Re W* [1983] FLR 617 (CA), it was said that within the parameters set by the House of Lords, the Court of Appeal had moved towards a greater emphasis upon the welfare of the child as one of the factors to be considered when deciding whether a parent was withholding agreement unreasonably, but short of amending legislation or further consideration in the House of Lords, there must be a limit to this shift (per Purchas LJ at 624).

Lord Reid in *O'Connor* v *A and B* [1971] 1 WLR 1227, at 1230 put the child's welfare in perspective:

No doubt the child's interests come first and in some cases they may be paramount. But I see no reason why the claims of the natural parents

should be ignored. If the mother were deeply attached to the child and had only consented in the first place to adoption because of adverse circumstances it would seem to me unjust that on a change of circumstances her affection for the child and her natural claim as a parent should be ignored. And the adopting family cannot be ignored either. If it was the mother's action that brought them in, in the first place, they ought not to be displaced without good reason. So to balance these claims is no easy task. Often no ideal solution is possible. We are dealing largely with future probabilities for the decision once made is irrevocable. So we cannot be certain what will be in the child's best interests in the long run. That seems to me to be an additional reason for giving considerable weight in proper cases to the claims of the natural parents and of the adopting family.

In *Re H* and *Re W* [1983] FLR 617, at 624, it was pointed out that the local authority's representatives rightly consider solely the welfare of the child pursuant to their statutory duties. Their opinion, however, is concentrated on only one of the three interests involved. In particular there is room for the reasonable withholding of agreement by the natural parent even though those responsible for the child's welfare hold an acceptable view that the child's welfare demands adoption.

A parent in considering whether or not to refuse agreement is entitled to consider not only the welfare of the child but other factors such as his or her own wishes and welfare, the welfare of other children and the wishes and welfare of grandparents of the child (*Re El-G (Minors)* [1983] FLR 589 at 598).

Finally, on the welfare aspect it should be noted that s 1 of the GMA 1971 (welfare is the first and *paramount* consideration), has, of course, no application on the reasonableness question but relates in general to matters of custody and access.

The proper approach of the court when it is sought to dispense with agreement as being unreasonably withheld is first of all after hearing all the evidence to decide whether the adoption is in the child's best interests. If it is, then the question of dispensing with agreement should be considered (see *In re B* [1975] Fam 127, at 142 F, *In re P* [1977] Fam 25, at 28E, *In re F* [1982] 1 WLR 102 and *Re C (Wardship and Adoption)* [1981] FLR 177, at 191; a contrary view, however, was expressed in *Re D* [1976] Fam 185 where Stephenson LJ said that the two questions should be considered together). In deciding whether adoption is in the child's best interests, the court has to apply s 3 of the CA 1975 (see above, p 3, and see *Re W* [1984] FLR 402). If the order is not in the child's interests the application will fail. Even if the

answer is in the affirmative, however, it does not, of course, follow that an order will be made because different criteria apply to whether or not agreement is being unreasonably withheld by the parent or guardian.

As noted on p 39, agreement once given may be withdrawn before the hearing. Ormrod LJ, however, pointed out in *In re H (Infants)* [1977] 1 WLR 471, at 472 that:

Once the formal consent has been given . . . or perhaps once the child has been placed with adopters, time begins to run against the mother and, as time goes on, it gets progressively more and more difficult for her to show that the withdrawal of her consent is reasonable. (See also *Re W (Adoption: Parental agreement)* [1982] FLR 75.)

In *In re P* (1984) *The Times*, 19 May, the Court of Appeal noted that while a mother's vacillation over whether or not to agree to the adoption of her child could not be conclusively held against her as evidence that she was being unreasonable, it was a factor which could show that she did not possess the insight to enable her to make the judgment of a reasonable parent which was the test the judge ultimately had to apply. Griffiths LJ added on the facts that, 'the material benefit a child whose mother lived in poor circumstances would be likely to enjoy if adopted by middle class parents was not an element that should be allowed to weigh too heavily in the scales given that affluence and happiness were not necessarily synonymous'.

In deciding the question of reasonableness some relevant factors are the child's security, finances, and, 'education, general surroundings, happiness, stability of home and the like' (per Davies LJ, *Re B* [1971] 1 QB 437, at 443). In *In re F (A Minor) (Adoption: Parental Consent)* [1982] 1 WLR 102, the Court of Appeal said that in applying the objective test regarding reasonableness, the court had to have regard to the practical consequences of making or refusing to make the order. In this case it was held that the interests of a child aged five were that he should have a secure home with foster parents who had looked after him for three years, in a situation where they also felt secure in looking after him without the fear that the mother would bring proceedings in the future for care and control or access. Since the mother had no access and would have none in the foreseeable future, a reasonable parent would agree to the child's adoption and therefore her agreement was dispensed with and an adoption order made. Where, however, a parent has retained links with the child

the position may well be quite different. Indeed, the question of whether or not there should be access in the future is likely to be decisive in the outcome of the case.

In *Re H and Re W* [1983] FLR 614, the Court of Appeal laid down important guidelines (regarding the child's welfare, see above pp 44 and 45). There were a number of features common to both appeals: each was an application to adopt a long-standing foster child; each child was quite old (ten and eleven respectively); each child was integrated into the foster family and had a strongly held wish to be adopted; each child was old enough to have some degree of understanding; both children had maintained some degree of contact with their natural families, either with a parent or with siblings; in each case there was a question mark from past history over the suitability of the natural parent who was withholding agreement; each parent claimed to have put the past behind her; and each case raised the important issue of law as to the degree to which the welfare of the child is to be taken into account in deciding whether the natural parent is withholding agreement unreasonably.

It was emphasised that the court must look to the attitude of the natural parent as one of the potentially relevant factors when assessing the attitude of the hypothetical, reasonable natural parent. The key factors to be considered are:

(*i*) Where the natural parent presents himself or herself at the time of the hearing as someone capable of caring for the child, this is a factor which even the hypothetical reasonable parent should take into account together with the other circumstances of the case including, of course, the ultimate welfare of the child;

(*ii*) An important factor is whether there is an inherent defect likely to persist in the natural parent;

(*iii*) If the unsuitability of the natural parent can only be related to past history, it should carry little weight in the mind of the hypothetical reasonable parent, unless the past history is likely to influence the future position;

(*iv*) The chances of a successful re-introduction to, or continuance of contact with, the natural parent is a critical factor in assessing the reaction of the hypothetical reasonable parent.

It is important to note that in the *In re H* appeal, the Court of Appeal, because of insufficiency of evidence, ordered a re-trial before a different judge after the re-introduction of access by the

natural parent. It is clear in this type of case that it is essential to put in evidence dealing with access decisions and previous access and its effect, rehabilitation decisions and attempts, and the possibility of future contact and its relation to the security of the foster home (see also the recent House of Lords decision of *Re E (A Minor)* [1984] FLR 457, a wardship case, in which the lower courts had considered there were only two possible courses, adoption or the parent resuming control, but the House of Lords directed there should be a period of access before a final decision could be made).

In *Re B (Adoption by Parent)* [1975] Fam 127 (CA), it was said that, 'it is quite wrong to use the adoption law to extinguish the relationship between the protesting [parent] and the child unless there is some really serious factor which justifies the use of the statutory guillotine (per Cumming-Bruce J at 143, and see also *Hitchcock* v *W B and F E B* [1952] 2 QB 561, at 568, per Lord Goddard CJ).

In a proper case the court will dispense with agreement even though the parent or guardian is in no sense responsible for the situation giving rise to the adoption application. In *Re El-G (Minors)* [1983] FLR 589 (CA), for example, the natural mother had been 'struck down by a series of terrible blows which . . . for a long time destroyed her health and rendered her personally, in spite of her eagerness to be a mother to all her children, from fulfilling her maternal role' (*sic*). The children had a history of character disturbance; a number of changes in their care had adversely affected them, and they were at the date of the hearing settled with the foster parents and doing well. The success of long-term fostering would be imperilled if the children had to adjust themselves to a continuing relationship with the mother. The Court of Appeal therefore upheld the judge who had decided that the mother's agreement was being withheld unreasonably and that an adoption order should be made.

Where, however, the parent or guardian is not blameless, unreasonableness can include 'culpability or callous indifference . . . [and] . . . where carried to excess, sentimentality, romanticism, bigotry, wild prejudice, caprice, fatuousness or excessive lack of common sense' (per Lord Hailsham LC, *In re W* [1971] AC 682, at 700).

In *Re M (A Child)* (1984), 11 October (unreported) (CA), Ormrod LJ said that the custodianship procedure (see chap 22), when it comes into force, should be used in preference to adoption

proceedings in long-term fostering cases, unless the case for dispensing with parental agreement is strong, which means cases where the future of the children lies, so far as can be sensibly foreseen, with the foster parents, and access is no more than a remote possibility.

(c) *Parent or guardian has persistently failed without reasonable cause to discharge the parental duties in relation to the child (s 12(2)(c))*

Two conditions must be fulfilled: the failure must be persistent and must be without reasonable cause. 'Persistently' is to be understood in the sense of 'permanently' (per Sir George Baker P, *In re D (Minors) (Adoption by Parent)* [1973] Fam 209 (DC), at 214). The parent or guardian must be shown to have washed his hands of the child (see *In re B(S) (An Infant)* [1968] Ch 204, at 214). For the difference between persistent failure and consistent failure, see *M v Wigan MBC* [1980] Fam 36.

The failure envisaged by the subsection must be 'of such gravity, so complete, so convincingly proved, that there can be no advantage to the child in keeping continuous contact with the natural parent, who has so abrogated his duties that he for his part should be deprived of his own child against his wishes.' The failure must be culpable and culpable to a high degree (*In re D* (supra)).

In *In re D* the father had temporarily drifted apart and withdrawn from the children whilst the marriage was breaking up and during the subsequent divorce and ancillary proceedings. He saw the children irregularly, sent them presents and some clothes, but did not provide maintenance for them. It was held that persistent failure had not been made out. In *Re P (An Infant)* [1962] 1 WLR 1296, the ground was proved: the mother had parted with her children shortly after they were born, visited them infrequently, supported them only insignificantly, and could show no reasonable cause for her behaviour. In addition for a substantial period of time she had accommodation where she could have had the children with her.

In *Re M (An Infant)* (1965) 109 SJ 574 (CA), an unmarried mother's wish to hide the child's birth from her parents was held to be a reasonable cause for her failure.

In *Re P* (supra) it was said that the obligations of a parent 'must include first the natural and moral duty of a parent to show affection, care and interest towards his child; and second, as well, the common law or statutory duty of a parent to maintain his

child in the financial or economic sense' (per Pennycuick J at 1302). The words 'parental duties' in s 12(2)(*c*) will also, of course, cover any other parental legal duty.

(*d*) *Parent or guardian has abandoned or neglected the child (s 12(2)(d))*

In *Watson* v *Nikolaisen* [1955] 2 QB 286 (DC), a mother handed over her illegitimate daughter to prospective adopters. She signed a form consenting to adoption and mistakenly believed, as she intended, that by doing so she had given up all her rights to the child. She did not contribute to the child's maintenance but drew the children's allowance and kept it herself. By the time of the adoption hearing some two years later the mother had discovered that she could withdraw her consent. She did so, as she no longer wanted the child to be adopted. It was held by the justices and upheld on appeal that the mother had not 'abandoned' the child within the meaning of the section. She had not left the child to its fate, but had given it over to people who wished to adopt it and in whom she had confidence. Abandonment in the context was held to mean abandonment giving rise to criminal liability (see s 1, CYPA 1933, and s 27, Offences against the Person Act 1861). See also *Wheatley* v *Waltham Forest LBC* [1980] AC 311.

For criminal cases on the construction of 'abandoning', see *R* v *Whibley* [1938] 3 All ER 777 (in a moment of passion leaving five children at court—not abandonment); *R* v *Boulden* (1957) 41 Cr App R 105 (to abandon means to leave child to its fate); *R* v *White* (1871) LR I CCR 311 (example of abandoning: leaving child on a doorstep); and *R* v *Falkingham* (1870) LR I CCR 222 (sending child in a box by rail).

Clearly on the restricted meaning given to 'abandoned' the condition will be a difficult one to satisfy.

It is suggested that 'neglected' has the same restricted meaning (see *Re W* (1962) unreported, cited in *Re P* [1962] 1 WLR 1296). The conduct must be such as to make the parent or guardian criminally liable. For criminal cases, see for example *R* v *Senior* [1899] 1 QB 283, and *Oakley* v *Jackson* [1914] 1 KB 216 (refusal to allow operation).

(*e*) *Parent or guardian has persistently ill-treated the child (s 12(2)(e))*

It would seem probable that the conduct referred to in the subsection involves criminal ill-treatment or neglect. Because of

the word 'persistently' a single act will not suffice. In *Re A (A Minor) (Adoption: Dispensing with Agreement)* [1981] FLR 173 (CA), severe and repeated assaults over a period of some three weeks were held to amount to persistent ill-treatment. The ill-treatment, it would appear, must have been inflicted on the child who is the subject of the application and not, for example, on another child in the family.

(f) Parent or guardian has seriously ill-treated the child (s 12(2)(f))

Agreement may be dispensed with as a result of a single act of ill-treatment. It must, however, be sufficiently serious and therefore it may well also amount to criminal conduct.

The ground, however, does not apply unless because of the ill-treatment or for other reasons, the rehabilitation of the child within the household of the parent or guardian is unlikely (CA 1975, s 12(5)). 'Other reasons' may include for example, the parent or guardian's mental or physical condition, or inability to provide adequate accommodation.

Chapter 7

Jurisdiction and Venue

1 Courts

(a) *Venue generally*

An adoption order, or an order freeing a child for adoption (see chap 20) may be made by an authorised court (CA 1975, s 8(1)). In a case where the child is in England or Wales when the application is made, the following are authorised courts and have concurrent jurisdiction except as noted (ibid, s 100(2)):

(1) The High Court: ie in practice the Family Division (Supreme Court Act 1981 s 61(1), and Sched 1, para 3(*b*)(iii)) (CA 1975, s 100(2)(*a*));

(2) the county court within whose district the child is (ibid, s 100(2)(*b*));

(3) any other county court prescribed by rules made under s 75 of the County Courts Act 1984 (see below) (ibid, s 100(2)(*c*)); and

(4) a magistrates' court within whose area the child is (ibid, s 100(2)(*d*).

In addition in the case of a freeing order 'an authorised court' includes any county court within whose district, or any magistrates' court within whose area, a parent or guardian of the child is (CA 1975, s 100(2)(*b*), and (*d*)).

If the child is not in Great Britain when the application for an adoption order or a freeing order is made, only the High Court is an authorised court (s 100(4)).

The authorised courts in applications for the return of a child (see chap 13) are:

(1) if there is a pending application for adoption or freeing, the court in which that application is pending;

(2) in any other case, the High Court, the county court within

whose district the applicant lives, and the magistrates' court within whose area the applicant lives (CA 1975, s 100(8)).

Only the High Court or the county court within whose district the child is, may make a parental rights order under s 25 of the CA 1975 (see chap 16) (s 100(6)).

Where there has been a breach of s 29 of the AA 1958 (see p 25), any adoption application must be heard in the High Court (*In re S* (1984) *The Times*, 2 November (CA)).

(*b*) *County courts*

As well as a court within whose district the child is when the application is made, a further authorised court is any divorce county court in which a declaration has been made under s 41(1)(*b*), or (*c*) of the Matrimonial Causes Act 1973 in respect of the child (s 100(2)(*c*) and County Courts Rules 1981, Ord 47, r 7). This may be of particular relevance in stepparent cases (see chap 2).

(*c*) *Magistrates' courts*

'Area' in the CA 1975, s 100(2)(*d*), in relation to a magistrates' court, means the commission area (within the meaning of s 1 of the Justices of the Peace Act 1979) for which the court is appointed (CA 1975, s 107(1)). The applicant for an adoption order need not therefore be confined to a court within a particular petty sessions area.

All proceedings before a magistrates' court under the AA 1958, or Part 1 of the CA 1975 are included in the definition of 'domestic proceedings' in the MCA 1980, s 65(1), with the exception of proceedings under s 43 of the AA 1958, (removal of protected children from unsuitable surroundings) (see p 32), which are retained by the juvenile court (which now only plays a small part in adoption matters).

Domestic proceedings come before 'domestic courts' which consist entirely of justices qualified by membership of a domestic court panel (see MCA 1980, ss 66 and 67, and SI 1979 No 757).

Where an application is made to a magistrates' court in any adoption proceedings, the court must refuse to make an order if it considers that the matter is one which would more conveniently be dealt with by the High Court (CA 1975, s 101(3)). No appeal lies to the High Court against the decision. If the magistrates' court refuses to exercise jurisdiction, a fresh application should

be commenced in the High Court, for there is no provision for a transfer of proceedings.

(d) *Choice of court*

In practice the most common forum for adoption proceedings is the county court, with the magistrates' court substantially ahead of the High Court. The choice of court may well be affected by considerations of expense. If a novel or difficult point of law is involved, or a contested case is likely to take a number of days to be heard, the High Court is likely to be the most appropriate forum and the magistrates' court the least appropriate forum (see the comments of Sheldon J in *In re Adoption Application 118/ 1984* (1985) *The Times*, 15 February, in particular, about the difficulty of arranging for the same panel of justices to sit without a break). The lack of a reasoned judgment in the Magistrates' court is also a serious drawback. The attitude of the legal aid authorities in favouring the inferior courts in the interests of economy is also, of course, influential.

For the position where there is an order in existence which is at variance with and would be superseded by an adoption order, see p 20.

(e) *No jurisdication*

For cases which come to light on the preliminary examination of the application where there may be no jurisdiction to make an adoption order, see p 61.

2 Transfer of proceedings

For the possibility of transfer between county courts, see CCR 1981, Ord 16. By r 3, however, there cannot be a transfer to a county court which is not an authorised court.

The High Court may order the removal to the High Court of any proceedings taken in a county court under the AA 1958 or the CA 1975. The application for removal may be made by any party, and if granted, the order will be on such terms as to costs as the High Court thinks proper (CA 1975, s 101(1)). See RSC, Ord 90, r 10, and *Practice Direction* [1978] 1 WLR 1456.

Section 101(1) of the CA 1975 will be repealed when Part V of the Matrimonial and Family Proceedings Act 1984 comes into force. A flexible system of transfer between the High Court and the county court will then be available.

Section 38 of the 1984 Act provides that at any stage in any family proceedings in the High Court, the High Court may, either of its own motion or on the application of any party, order the transfer of the whole or any part of the proceedings to such county court or divorce county court as the High Court directs. 'Family proceedings' include any adoption proceedings within the jurisdiction of a county court or divorce county court (ss 38(1) and (2)(a), and 32);

Similarly by s 39 of the 1984 Act, any adoption proceedings commenced in a county court or a divorce county court may be transferred in the same manner by that court to the High Court (s 39(1)). The High Court may transfer those proceedings back to the county court, or to any other county court (s 38(2)(c)). A county court may transfer proceedings to the High Court even though they may previously have been transferred *from* the High Court under s 38 (s 39(2)(b)).

The magistrates' court is not included in the system of transfer in the 1984 Act, referred to above. It must, however, refuse to make an order if it considers that a matter is one which would more conveniently be dealt with by the High Court. A fresh application to the High Court would then be necessary (see above, and the CA 1975, s 101(3)).

3 Exercise of courts' powers

Unless the contrary intention appears, any power which by the AR may be exercised by the court, may be exercised by the proper officer. In the High Court this will be a registrar of the Principal Registry of the Family Division, and in the county court the registrar or, as regards formal and administrative acts, the chief clerk (see CCR 1981, Ord 1, r 3).

In the magistrates' court some preliminary and auxiliary powers (noted where appropriate below) are specifically made exercisable by a single justice, or by the justices' clerk.

Chapter 8

Procedure: Applications for an Adoption Order

1 Rules of court

The Adoption Rules 1984 (SI 1984 No 265), which are referred to in the text as 'AR', apply to both High Court and county court proceedings. The Magistrates' Court (Adoption) Rules 1984 (SI 1984 No 611), referred to as 'MC(A)R', govern the procedure in the domestic court. Both sets of Rules came into force on 27 May 1984. The previous Rules (1976, as amended) continue to apply only to applications made prior to that date, which had not been determined by 27 May 1984 (AR, r 54; MC(A)R, r 1(2)).

The full texts of the Rules are to be found in *The Supreme Court Practice, The County Court Practice*, and *Stone's Justices' Manual*. Each set of Rules appends schedules of forms for use at the various stages of an adoption matter (see Appendix 1).

Subject to these special sets of Adoption Rules, the Rules of the Supreme Court, and the County Court Rules 1981 respectively, apply with necessary modifications in the relevant courts to proceedings under the AA 1958, and the CA 1975 (AR, r 3(2), and (3)). Similarly the MC(A)R, provide that, save in so far as special provision is made in those Rules, adoption proceedings are to be regulated in the same manner as proceedings on complaint (ie under the Magistrates' Courts Rules 1981), the application being deemed to be a complaint, the applicant to be a complainant, the respondents to be defendants, and any notice served under the Rules to be a summons. No warrant of arrest, however, can be issued for failure to appear in answer to any such notice (r 33).

2 Legal aid

Legal aid is available, subject to the means of the party and there being reasonable grounds for being involved, in any adoption proceedings in the county court, the High Court, the Court of Appeal or the House of Lords, and also in a magistrates' court in which the making of an order under Part 1 of the CA 1975 is opposed by any party to the proceedings, or in which proceedings relate to an application for the removal of a child under ss 34 or 34A of the AA 1958 (Legal Aid Act 1974, s 7, and Sched 1, Part 1, as amended).

In contested adoption cases, legal aid must be regarded as something essential for safeguarding the interests of a person concerned, who is eligible for it, who may be someone unable to present his or her case adequately, and for ensuring that justice both is done and appears to be done (per Sachs LJ, *In re M* [1973] 1 QB 108, at 120). A rehearing might have to be ordered simply because a party was not made aware in appropriate terms of the availability of legal aid. Sachs L J further observed that special difficulties can arise in the course of serial number cases (see p 61), which make such legal aid essential.

In *In re Adoption Application 125/1983* (1985) *The Times*, 15 February, the refusal of legal aid on the merits to the natural parents who were contesting an adoption application in order to keep or have access to their children, caused concern to Sheldon J. Supporting the approach in *In re M* (supra), Sheldon J pointed out that the case before him demonstrated a pragmatic reason for granting legal aid; the substantial saving of time and public money.

Where there is a choice of court, an applicant for legal aid may have to satisfy the Committee that there is a good reason to apply in the High Court or county court rather than the domestic court. Sheldon J in *In re Adoption Application 118/1984* (1985) *The Times*, 15 February, for example, said that the magistrates' court was the least suitable forum for hearing an application by a local authority for a freeing order under s 14 of the CA 1975, (see chap 20), because the hearing of an opposed application could last several days and it was difficult to arrange for the same panel of justices to sit without a break. Another good reason may be that a difficult point of law has to be argued in, for example, a step-parent case (see *Legal Aid Handbook 1984* (HMSO) Notes for Guidance, para 30 'Adoption').

3 Commencement of adoption proceedings

(*a*) *Initiating process*

Proceedings for an adoption order are to be commenced as follows:

(1) *High Court*: by filing an originating summons in FORM 6 (see Appendix 1), issued out of the Principal Registry of the Family Division (AR, r 15(1)(*a*)). The Registry is at Somerset House, Strand, London;

(2) *County court*: by filing in the appropriate county court an originating application in FORM 6 (see Appendix 1) (AR, r 15(1)(*b*));

(3) *Magistrates' court*: by an application in FORM 6 (see Appendix 1), which is deemed to be a complaint (MC(A)R, r 15(1), and r 33).

The appropriate fees will have to be paid by the applicant:

High Court   £55 (as at 1 May 1985)
County Court   £20 (as at 1 May 1985)
Magistrates' Court   See Sched 6 of the MCA 1980, but they are often waived.

In the county court or the magistrates' court the application may be delivered to or sent by post to the appropriate court (CCR 1981, Ord 3, r 5(1), and MC(A)R, r 15(1)).

(*b*) *Parties*

The applicant for an adoption order is the proposed adopter (r 15(2) of the respective rules).

Rule 15(2) also sets out who are to be the respondents.

The child is only to be a respondent in the High Court (AR, r 15(2)(*k*)).

The following are respondents in *all* courts:

(*i*) each parent or guardian (not being an applicant) of the child, unless the child is free for adoption (see chap 20) (r 15(2)(*a*));

(*ii*) any adoption agency in whom the parental rights and duties relating to the child are vested by virtue of s 14 or s 23 of the CA 1975 (see chap 20) (r 15(2)(*b*));

(*iii*) any adoption agency named in the application, or in any form of agreement to the making of the adoption order as having taken part in the arrangements for the adoption of the child (r 15(2)(*c*);

(*iv*) any local authority to whom the applicant has given notice

under s 18 of the CA 1975 of his intention to apply for an adoption order (see chap 5) (r 15(2)(*d*);

(*v*) any local authority having the powers and duties of a parent or guardian by virtue of s 10 of the Child Care Act 1980 (r 15(2)(*e*));

(*vi*) any local authority in whom the parental rights and duties in respect of the child are vested, whether jointly or not, by virtue of s 3 of the Child Care Act 1980 (s 15(2)(*f*));

(*vii*) any voluntary organisation (see p 23) in whom the parental rights and duties in respect of the child are vested whether jointly or not, by virtue of s 64 of the CCA 1980 (s 15(2)(*g*));

(*viii*) any person liable by virtue of any order or agreement to contribute to the maintenance of the child (s 15(2)(*h*));

(*ix*) any local authority or voluntary organisation in whose care the child is under s 2 of the CCA 1980, or under or within the meaning of any other enactment (r 15(2)(*i*)); and

(*x*) where the applicant proposes to rely on s 11(1)(*b*)(*ii*) of the CA 1975, the spouse of the applicant (see p 13) (r 15(2)(*j*)).

The court may at any time direct that any other person or body (but not in the county court or the magistrates' court, the child) be made a respondent to the process (r 15(3)). A putative father, for example, therefore might become a respondent if he was not already one under (*i*) or (*viii*) above. He could not be a 'parent' within (*i*) but in certain circumstances could be a 'guardian', see p 38. Other potential respondents might be a mother's husband at the time of the child's birth, where someone else is in fact the father, or a close relative who is known to have sought custody of the child (per Lord Parker CJ, in *R* v *Liverpool City JJ* [1959] 1 All ER 337, at 340).

(*c*) *Contents of application and documents required*

The forms, like all those required in cases under the relevant adoption legislation, are scheduled to the respective rules, and are set out in Appendix 1 to this book, abbreviated where possible for reasons of space. The full and instructive notes to them repay careful study. The information required from the proposed adopter or adopters can be seen from FORM 6 for the High Court and county court (see Appendix 1), and FORM 6 for the magistrates' court (see Appendix 1).

The proposed adopter or adopters must, in particular, state that they understand that the parents or guardians will agree to the making of an adoption order, or alternatively request the court to dispense with the agreement of one or more of them on stated grounds. If the child has been previously adopted, the adoptive parentage is the relevant one.

If the date or country of the child's birth is uncertain, any relevant information should be entered in para 6 of the respective FORM 6.

FORM 6 allows the proposed adopter to elect the surname and other names by which the child is to be known if an adoption order is made. The heading, however, must show the child's first name(s) and surname as shown in his or her birth certificate (or if applicable adoption certificate); otherwise the names by which the child was known *before* being placed for adoption must be entered. The court may have a discretion in the interests of the child to control the names put forward.

Documents. On filing the originating process three copies of FORM 6 must be supplied by the applicant, and three copies of the following other documents (r 15(4)(*a*)):

- (*i*) the child's birth certificate, or, in the case of a child who has been previously adopted, a certified copy of the relevant entry in the Adopted Children Register (see chap 28);
- (*ii*) evidence of the applicant's marital status and, if applicable, evidence justifying the exclusion of the spouse of a married applicant applying alone (see p 13);
- (*iii*) any document signifying agreement to the adoption, if executed outside England and Wales before the proceedings (r 20(1)). This may be in FORM 7 (see Appendix 1));
- (*iv*) a statement of facts, if applicable, supporting the applicant's request for a parent or guardian's agreement to be dispensed with;
- (*v*) separate reports, if required, on the health of each applicant and of the child (see p 72);
- (*vi*) if the child has been freed for adoption, the freeing order (see chap 20), or any order under s 23 of the CA 1975 (see p 109);
- (*vii*) a copy of any maintenance order in force regarding the child;
- (*viii*) if the child is a ward of court, a copy of the order granting

leave for the commencement of adoption proceedings (see p 118).

The rules no longer require the application to be substantiated on oath.

(d) Confidential serial number applications

If any person who proposes to apply for an adoption order wishes his identity to be kept confidential, he may, *before* commencing proceedings, apply to the court for a serial number to be assigned to him for the purposes of the proposed application (r 14).

The application for a serial number should be made as follows:

(1) *High Court*: to a registrar of the Principal Registry of the Family division;

(2) *County court*: to the registrar or chief clerk;

(3) *Magistrates' court*: to the clerk to the justices.

A serial number will be assigned to the applicant accordingly. It will then be referred to, instead of the applicant's name being given on notices and documents supplied to respondents who are not already aware of the applicant's identity. The proceedings must be conducted with a view to securing that the applicant is not seen by or made known to any relevant respondent, except with the applicant's consent (r 23(3)).

Some courts, at present, unfortunately, show a certain laxity and lack of awareness in the arrangements made. See also chap 11.

4 Preliminary examination of application

If it appears to the registrar or justices' clerk on receipt of the application in FORM 6 that the court:

(a) *may* be precluded by s 22(4) of the CA 1975 from proceeding to hear the application, it being a second application by the same person(s) in respect of the same child, the previous application having been refused (see chap 19); or

(b) may, for any other reason appearing in the application, have no jurisdiction to make an adoption order,

he must refer it to the judge for directions or, as the case may be, bring the relevant matter to the attention of the magistrates' court, and the application must not be proceeded with unless the court gives directions as to its further conduct (r 16).

An example of a reason falling within (*b*) might be a stepparent case where it appears that the matter would be better dealt with under s 42 of the Matrimonial Causes Act 1973 (see p 16). The specific reference to this situation in the various 1976 Rules, however, has not been repeated in the AR 1984, or in the MC(A)R 1984.

5 Mode of service

Any notice or information under the AA 1958 or under Part 1 of the CA 1975 may be given by post (AA 1958, s 55 as amended).

Unless otherwise directed, any document under the rules may be served:

    (*a*) on a corporation or body of persons by deliving it at, or sending it by post to, its registered or principal office;

    (*b*) on any other person by delivering it to him, or by sending it by post to him at his usual or last known address. (AR, r 50(1); MC(A)R, r 29(1))

Notice of an adjourned hearing should be similarly served (see *Unitt* v *Unitt* (1979) 124 SJ 80).

In the High Court or county court, the person effecting service of any document must make, sign and file a certificate showing the date, place and mode of service or, as the case may be, of the fact of non-service with the reason why service has not been effected (AR, r 50(2)). The magistrates' court rule requires that a note of service or non-service must be endorsed on a copy of FORM 8 (Notice of Hearing) (MC(A)R, r 29(2)), and allows the court to treat service by post to a person's usual or last known address as good service, notwithstanding that the document has been returned undelivered (r 29(3)).

6 Directions

If at any stage before the hearing of the application it appears to the High Court or the county court, as the case may be, that directions for the hearing are required, the court concerned may give such directions as it considers necessary. In any event it must, not less than four weeks before the date fixed for the hearing, consider the documents relating to the application with a view to giving such further directions for the hearing as appear to it to be necessary (AR, r 21(5)).

Directions in a contested case might, for example, relate to:

(*i*) the filing of affidavits;

(*ii*) the obtaining of expert evidence;

(*iii*) in a confidential serial number case, the mechanics of keeping the parties apart;

(*iv*) the disclosure to the parties or their legal advisers of the contents (or parts of the contents) of any confidential reports supplied in the course of the proceedings by an adoption agency, a local authority, the reporting officer, or the guardian ad litem;

(*v*) ensuring that all concerned are ready for trial on the date fixed.

There is no corresponding provision as to directions in the magistrates' court.

Chapter 9

Procedure: Reporting Officer and Guardian ad Litem

Basically a reporting officer will be appointed when it appears that a parent or guardian of the child is willing to agree to the making of an adoption order, and a guardian ad litem when it appears that a parent or guardian is unwilling to agree. Each has a number of specific duties and one person may be appointed to carry out both roles, where one parent or guardian appears willing to agree but the other appears unwilling, or where a parent who at first agreed changes his or her mind, or vice versa. A guardian ad litem of the child may also be appointed in the special circumstances noted below.

1 Reporting officer

(a) Appointment

A reporting officer must be appointed as soon as practicable after the originating process has been filed, or at any stage thereafter, if the child is not free for adoption, and if it appears that a parent or guardian is willing to agree to the making of an adoption order and is in England and Wales (r 17(1) of the respective rules).

As to agreement generally, see chap 6. Rule 17(1) does not require the appointment of a reporting officer for a natural parent seeking to adopt his or her own child.

The reporting officer is appointed by the registrar, or as the case may be, the justices' clerk or a single justice (MC(A)R, r 17(5)), from a panel established under the Guardians Ad Litem and Reporting Officers (Panels) Regulations 1983 (SI 1983 No 1908), but he or she must not (with one exception) be a member or employee of a respondent body, or have been involved in the

making of any arrangements for the adoption of the child, or be an employee of the adoption agency which has placed the child for adoption (r 17(3), and CA 1975, s 20(2)). The exception referred to is that where a local authority is only a respondent because the applicant has given it notice under s 18 of the CA 1975 (see chap 5), a member or employee of it can be a reporting officer. On appointment the reporting officer will receive from the court a copy of the originating process and any documents attached, and a copy of the statement of facts in a dispensation case (rr 17(1), and 19(4)). The reporting officer is appointed *in respect of* a named person or guardian (r 17(1)), but the same person may be appointed in respect of two or more parents or guardians of the child (r 17(2)).

(b) Duties of the reporting officer

The reporting officer must:

   (*i*) ensure so far as reasonably practicable that any agreement to the making of an adoption order is given freely and unconditionally, and with full understanding of what is involved;

  (*ii*) witness the signature by the parent or guardian of the written agreement to the making of the adoption order (which may be in FORM 7 (see Appendix 1) (r 20(1));

 (*iii*) investigate all the circumstances relevant to that agreement; and

 (*iv*) on completing his investigations make a written report to the court drawing attention to any matters which, in his opinion, may be of assistance to the court in considering the application. (r 17(4))

The reporting officer may consider it necessary to make an interim report to the court with a view to obtaining the court's directions. He must report, in particular, if a parent or guardian is unwilling to agree to adoption, and the registrar or justices' clerk must then notify the applicant and appoint a guardian ad litem. Any report made to the court is confidential. The court may before the final determination of the application require the reporting officer to perform such further duties as it considers necessary. If required by the court, the reporting officer must attend the hearing (r 17(5) applying r 5(5)–(8)).

2 Guardian ad litem

(a) Appointment

As soon as practicable after the originating process has been filed, or after receipt of the statement of facts in a dispensation case (see p 70), if the child is not free for adoption, a guardian ad litem of the child must be appointed if it appears that a parent or guardian is *unwilling* to agree to adoption (r 18(1)).

If the proceedings are in the High Court, the Official Solicitor must be appointed as guardian ad litem if he consents, unless the applicant desires some other person to act (r 18(4)).

Where someone other than the Official Solicitor is required in the High Court, and also in the county court and the magistrates' court, the appointment must be made from a panel established by the Guardians Ad Litem and Reporting Officers (Panels) Regulations 1983 (SI 1983 No 1908), and the panel member must not be disqualified as described above under 'Reporting Officer' (AR, r 18(5); MC(A)R, r 18(4)).

There is also an additional and discretionary power for the court to appoint a guardian ad litem at any time, if there are special circumstances, and it appears to the court that the welfare of the child requires it (r 18(2)). Where such an appointment is made the court must indicate any particular matters which it requires the guardian ad litem to investigate.

The appointments are made by the registrar or, as the case may be, the justices' clerk or a single justice (AR, r 18(1); MC(A)R, r 18(6)). On appointment the guardian ad litem is sent a copy of the originating process by the registrar or clerk, any documents attached to it, a copy of the order appointing him, and, in dispensation cases, a copy of the statement of facts (rr 18(1), and 19(4)).

As noted above, an application may call for both a reporting officer and a guardian ad litem, and one person may carry out both roles. One parent may consent and the other oppose, or a parent who at first agreed might change his or her mind or vice versa (r 17(5), and r 18(3)).

(b) The Official Solicitor in the Family Division

If the Official Solicitor is to be appointed (see above), after the originating process has been filed, the Principal Registry at Somerset House will appoint the Official Solicitor to act as guardian ad litem of the child, subject to his consent. He will be sent a copy of the order appointing him, a copy of the originating

process and any documents attached to it and, in dispensation cases, the statement of facts. The Official Solicitor's consent to act will usually be given in consideration of an undertaking by the applicant to pay his proper costs in the matter. An appropriate form of undertaking will be prepared in the Official Solicitor's department if the case is approved for consent, and sent to the applicant's solicitor for completion by his client, or to the applicant if acting in person. An undertaking is not normally asked for where the adoption application relates to a ward of court and is made pursuant to leave granted in the wardship proceedings. In such cases the Official Solicitor always reserves the question of his costs to the judge who hears the application.

As already noted, r 18 of the AR envisages a guardian ad litem only being appointed when it appears the parent or guardian is unwilling to agree to adoption. Rule 15(2)(k), however, makes the child a party in the High Court in all applications, and the child, therefore, as a minor, requires a guardian ad litem to act for him. The practice is in fact to appoint the Official Solicitor both as reporting officer *and* as guardian ad litem, where a parent appears *willing* to agree to adoption.

(c) Duties of the guardian ad litem

With a view to safeguarding the interests of the child before the court the guardian ad litem must, so far as is reasonably practicable:

(*i*) investigate, so far as he considers necessary, the matters alleged in the originating process, the report supplied by the adoption agency, (or the local authority receiving notice under s 18 of the CA 1975), the statement of facts if it is a dispensation case, and any other matters which appear to him to be relevant to the making of an adoption order;

(*ii*) advise whether, in his opinion, the child should be present at the hearing of the application; and

(*iii*) perform any other duties as appear to him to be necessary or as the court may direct. (AR, r 18(6); MC(A)R, r 18(5)).

As in the case of the reporting officer, the guardian ad litem may, at any time, make an interim report with a view to obtaining the court's directions on any matter. On completing his investigations, the guardian ad litem must make a written report to the court, drawing attention to any matters which, in his opinion, may be

of assistance to the court in considering the application. His reports are confidential. Before the final determination of the application the court may, at any time, require him to perform such further duties as the court considers necessary. He must attend the hearing of the application unless the court otherwise orders. (AR, r 18(7), applying r 6(7)–(11); MC(A)R, r 18(6) applying r 6(6)–(10)).

In an application by a parent and a stepparent, it will be the duty of the guardian ad litem to draw the court's attention to the disadvantages as well as the advantages of adoption as compared to the other courses which the court must consider (per Ormrod LJ, *In re S (Infants) (Adoption by Parent)* [1977] Fam 173, at 179). Where there is agreement to adoption, this duty is likely to devolve onto the reporting officer (see r 17(4)(*d*)). These cases will require considerably more investigation and information than in 'normal' adoption cases, in which a satisfactory report from the guardian ad litem is usually sufficient.

It would be 'a grave irregularity' resulting in the ordering of a rehearing if a guardian ad litem retired with the justices or the judge (per Sir George Baker P, *In re B (Adoption by Parent)* [1975] Fam 127, at 137). It may be, however, that in exceptional circumstances, for example, to avoid harm occurring to the child, a private conversation might not offend the principle that justice had to be seen to be done (see *Official Solicitor* v *K* [1965] AC 201 (HL), at 219).

(d) The guardian ad litem's report

The report is confidential. Whether or not the report is disclosed to a party to the litigation is a matter of judicial discretion (per Lord Denning MR, *In re PA (An Infant)* [1971] 1 WLR 1530, at 1534). In general, and subject always to considerations of the well-being of the infant, a party should be allowed to see, or should be informed of the substance and effect of, any facts or matters in such a report which might weigh against that party in the judge's decision (per Megaw LJ, *In re M (An Infant)* [1973] QB 108, at 123, and see also *Re E (An Infant)* (1960) *The Times*, 24 March; *Re G (TJ) (An Infant)* [1963] 2 QB 73; *Re C (Adoption Application: Hearing* [1982] FLR 95; *Re T (Adoption) (Confidential Report: Disclosure)* [1982] FLR 183. It is important, therefore, that a party is given an opportunity to rebut any adverse matters, and has the fullest opportunity of putting his or her case. Subject to the above safeguards, the judge is entitled to take into account

the contents of a confidential report (per Sachs LJ, *In re M (supra)*, at 117).

The 1984 Rules now provide that a party who is an individual and is referred to in the guardian ad litem's report may, for the purposes of the hearing, be supplied with a copy of that part of the report which refers to him, unless the court directs that it is not to be revealed to him, or that it is only to be revealed to his legal advisers. The court may direct that he should receive the whole or any part of the report (AR, r 53(2); MC(A)R, r 32(4)). The rules also apply in respect of reports supplied to the court by a reporting officer, an adoption agency or a local authority.

Where the adoption proceedings relate to a ward of court, two reports will be filed by the guardian ad litem. The report in the adoption proceedings will in general be confidential to the court, whereas the one in the wardship proceedings will be disclosed to the parties.

Chapter 10

Procedure: Further Matters after Application

1 Statement of facts in dispensation cases

Where the applicant for an adoption order, in respect of a child who is not free for adoption, intends to ask the court to dispense with the agreement of a parent or guardian on any of the grounds specified in s 12(2) of the CA 1975 (see p 41), the request must, unless otherwise directed, be made:

(a) in the originating process; or

(b) if subsequently, by notice to the registrar or justices' clerk (r 19(1)).

In either case there must be attached to the application or notice three copies of a statement of *facts* on which the applicant intends to rely. If the request is made in the originating process the *grounds* must also be stated in the application.

Where it is a confidential serial number case (see p 61), the statement of facts must be framed in such a way as not to disclose the identity of the applicant (r 19(2)).

The parent or guardian in question is given notice by the registrar or justices' clerk of the dispensation request and sent a copy of the statement of facts (r 19(3)). A copy of the statement of facts is also sent to the guardian ad litem and to the reporting officer, if a different person (r 19(4)).

The statement of facts is in effect a pleading and not evidence in itself. The facts contained in it will have to be proved at the hearing by admissible evidence.

2 Listing and notice of hearing

As soon as practicable after the originating process has been filed, the registrar or justices' clerk must list the case for hearing

by a judge or by the domestic court (r 21(1)). This, of course, will be subject to the application not having been excluded on the preliminary examination under r 16 (see p 61). In a non-agency case, where the applicant has been required to give notice to a local authority under s 18 of the CA 1975 (see chap 5), the date fixed for the hearing must be not less than three months from the date of that notice (r 21(4)).

The registrar or justices' clerk then serves notice of the hearing (FORM 8, see Appendix 1) on all the parties, the reporting officer and, if appointed, the guardian ad litem. He also serves any local authority concerned under s 18 with a copy of the originating process and of the health reports (if any) (r 21(2)).

No other person, except the reporting officer, the guardian ad litem (if appointed) and, in cases where s 18 applies, the local authority receiving notice under that section, must be served with a copy of the originating process (r 21(3)).

If FORM 8 is addressed to any respondent from whom the applicant does not wish his identity to be concealed, the notice will show the time and place of the hearing, and will give the respondent an opportunity of attending and being heard. Where, however, it is a confidential serial number application, and the notice is addressed to an individual other than the applicant's spouse, the day and time of the hearing will not be disclosed. The respondent will be invited, if he wishes to be heard, to notify the registrar or justices' clerk before a named day, so that a special time can be fixed for his or her appearance.

3 Reports by adoption agency or local authority

In the case of an agency placement, the agency must supply to the court (CA 1975, s 22(3)) within six weeks of receipt of the notice of hearing, three copies of a report in writing covering the matters specified in Sched 2 to the respective sets of rules (see Appendix 2) (r 22(1)).

In a non-agency case, the local authority receiving notice under s 18 of the CA 1975 is under a similar obligation (CA 1975, s 18(2), and r 22(2)).

In either case the court may request further reports (r 22(3)).

The agency or local authority will lodge with the reports the ADOPTION PROCEEDINGS UNIT RETURN (see p 27) with sections A to E completed by the caseworker (see AA 1976, s 58A, added by Hassassa 1983).

The registrar or justices' clerk must send copies of the report to the reporting officer and to the guardian ad litem (if appointed) (r 22(4)). No other person must be supplied with a copy of any report and any such report is confidential (r 22(5)); but see AR, r 53(2), and MC(A)R, r 32(4) referred to on p 9.

4 Evidence

(a) Medical

Reports on the health of the applicant or applicants and of the child, required where the child was not placed for adoption with the applicant by an adoption agency, (save where the applicant or one of the applicants is a parent of the child), must be made by a registered medical practitioner and must cover the matters specified in Sched 3 to the respective rules (see Appendix 2). The reports must have been made not more than three months before the date of the application (r 15(4)(b)). A separate report is required in respect of each applicant.

(b) Identity of the child

It will be necessary, of course, to establish that the child referred to in the documents before the court is the same child to whom the order is to relate. This may be proved by oral or affidavit evidence. Where the child who is the subject of the proceedings is identified in the originating process by reference to a birth certificate which is the same, or relates to the same entry in the Registers of Births, as a birth certificate exhibited to a form of agreement, the child so identified is to be deemed, unless the contrary appears, to be the child to whom the form of agreement refers (AR, r 24(1)). This provision has the same effect in respect of a child who has been previously adopted, as if the references to a birth certificate and to the Registers of Births were references to a certified copy of an entry in the Adopted Children Register and to that Register (r 24(2)).

In the magistrates' court, where proof of the identity of the child is required for any purpose, any fact tending to establish his identity with a child to whom a document relates may be proved by affidavit (MC(A)R, r 24(1)). Where any such fact is proved by affidavit, it will not be necessary to call a witness to prove that fact at the hearing unless the fact is disputed, or for some special reason the court requires his or her attendance (ibid, r 24(2)).

(c) *Rehabilitation of offenders*

The admissibility of evidence which refers to a conviction which is 'spent' within the meaning of the Rehabilitation of Offenders Act 1974 is generally curtailed in most judicial proceedings. The restrictions, however, do not apply to the determination of any issue, nor prevent the admission or requirement of any evidence as to a person's previous convictions, or to circumstances ancillary thereto, in any proceedings relating to adoption (Rehabilitation of Offenders Act 1974, s 7(2)(c)).

(d) *Foreign element in adoption applications*

Whether a country where a child is domiciled will recognise an adoption order made in England and Wales is important because of the considerable disadvantages that may arise from non-recognition. Evidence on this aspect should be placed before the court in cases involving a foreign element (*Re B(S) (An Infant) (no 2)* [1968] Ch 204).

Chapter 11

Procedure: The Hearing

1 Confidentiality

Where a serial number has been assigned to the applicant and his identity is therefore to be kept confidential, the proceedings must be conducted so as to protect the confidentiality by, for example, ensuring that he is not seen by or made known to any respondent who is not already aware of his identity, except with his consent (r 23(3) of the respective rules). In a contested case, great care will be needed in the arrangements for the arrival and departure of parties and witnesses. In the High Court in London the facilities allow one party to be placed in a room away from the courtroom, whilst still being able to listen to the evidence by way of headphones. It is essential that parties are represented as, for instance, the natural parents may well wish to cross-examine the applicants for the adoption order. As to the importance of granting legal aid, see p 57.

In the High Court adoption proceedings are heard in chambers (CA 1975, s 21(1). The normal venue is the Royal Courts of Justice in the Strand in London. On application to a registrar at Somerset House, the hearing can in appropriate circumstances be transferred to a Crown Court outside London where a Family Division judge sits.

Adoption proceedings in the county court must be heard and determined *in camera* (CA 1975, s 21(2)). The situation is the same in a magistrates' court where they are heard before a domestic court (see p 53).

'Adoption proceedings' in s 21 of the CA 1975 include all those under the 1958, 1960, and 1975 Acts and so cover for example, besides applications for an adoption order, applications for a freeing order (chap 20), for an interim order (chap 15), for the

74

removal or return of a child (chap 13), for an order facilitating adoption abroad (in the county court or the High Court only) (chap 16), or for a Convention adoption order (in the High Court only) (chap 24).

2 Audience

At the hearing, or at any further appointment, any person entitled to notice under r 21 (see p 70) may attend and be heard on the question whether an adoption order should be made (r 23(1)).

Any member or employee of a party which is a local authority, adoption agency or other body may address the court if he is duly authorised to do so (r 23(2)).

In the High Court, where the guardian ad litem is almost invariably the Official Solicitor, he will be represented by counsel. It is the usual practice for his counsel to cross-examine last, present any evidence after the other parties, and address the court last.

Even in an uncontested application the court will usually want to hear a little oral evidence from the applicant but, particularly in some county courts, such applications may be dealt with with complete informality.

3 Attendance

The court must not make an adoption order except after the personal attendance before the court of the applicant and the child (r 23(4)) unless:

(a) if there are special circumstances which, having regard to the report of the guardian ad litem (if any), appear to the court to make the attendance of the child unnecessary, the court may direct that the child need not attend (r 23(5)); or

(b) if the application is a joint one under s 10 of the CA 1975 (see p 13), an adoption order may in special circumstances be made after the personal attendance of one only of the applicants, if the originating process is verified by an affidavit sworn by the other applicant, or if he is outside the United Kingdom, by a declaration made by him and witnessed by anyone competent to witness a document executed abroad signifying agreement to the making of an adoption order (see p 40). In the magistrates' court a

declaration witnessed by a justice of the peace or a justices'
clerk is required instead of an affidavit (r 23(7)).
If there are special circumstances which appear to the court to
make the attendance of any other party necessary, the court may
direct that that party must attend (r 23(6)).
A guardian ad litem must attend the hearing unless the court
otherwise orders (AR, r 18(7), applying r 6(10); MC(A)R,
r 18(6), applying r 6(9)). A reporting officer must attend if the
court so requires (r 17(5) applying r 5(7), of each set of rules).
Non-attendance of the child does not invalidate a refusal to
make an order (*In re G(TJ) (An Infant)* [1963] 2 QB 73).
If any party fails to attend, the court may proceed in his
absence, if it thinks it expedient, after being satisfied as to service
(see RSC, Ord 32, r 5, and CCR, Ord 21, r 3). In a proper case
a court could dispense with service (see, for example, *Re R* [1967]
1 WLR 34).

4 Dispensation cases

Where the issue of dispensing with consent arises and there is
a potential controversy about it, then the matter must be dealt
with in a proper judicial hearing; that is, everything must be on
oath, with opportunities for cross-examination and a proper note
made of the proceedings' (per Ormrod LJ, *Re C (Adoption Application: Hearing)* [1982] FLR 95, at 96, and see also *In re M (An
Infant) (Adoption: Parental Consent)* [1973] QB 108, CA).

5 Adoption applications and duplication of proceedings

For the relationship to adoption applications of access applications in the juvenile court under s 12C of the CCA 1980
regarding children in care, and also of applications to revoke care
orders or parental rights resolutions, see the discussion and cases
on p 112.

Chapter 12

The Order

1 The forms of order

Adoption orders (including, in the High Court or county court, authorisations for foreign adoption and, in the High Court only, Convention adoptions), orders freeing a child for adoption (see chap 20) or revoking such an order, and interim orders, are to be made in the respective forms scheduled to the Rules as specified in AR, r 52(1), or MC(A)R, r 31(1) (see Appendix 1).

Only full adoption orders made in non-convention cases, as a result of the steps described in previous chapters, are dealt with below. Cross-references are made in later chapters, when other variants of the forms are noted.

Between 1976 and 1984 the form of adoption order was furnished with an appendix recording in appropriate cases the grounds on which the court had dispensed with parental agreement, or the grounds on which it had been satisfied that a sole married adopter, or a parent who was a sole adopter, fulfilled the terms of s 11(1)(b), or (3) of the CA 1975. Rules of court secured that this appendix was excluded from abridgements of the order supplied to any person other than the Registrar General.

In cases commenced after the 27 May 1984 the above matters will not be part of the order, but will be included in the statistical form, devised to implement s 58A of the AA 1976, which the case worker in the adoption society or local authority will have provided (see p 27) and lodged, partly filled in, at the court with the originating process, and which the court staff will complete and send to the Registrar General, who alone receives the information as before.

2 Copies and notices

The former system of abridgements and other means of refraining from disclosing particular parts of an order to some of the parties has been discarded. The new rules (AR, r 52, and MC(A)R, r 31) specify to whom copies or notices of an order are to be sent or supplied. Except as so specified or pursuant to the provision of any enactment, or with the leave of the court, no order may be inspected by anyone and no copy of it or an extract of it may be taken by or issued to any person (AR, r 53(4); MC(A)R, r 32(6)).

Within 7 days of the making of an order in proceedings under the Adoption Acts, the registrar or clerk must send a copy to the applicant (r 52(3); r 31(3)). A copy of *any* order may be supplied to the applicant (r 52(a); r 31(9)), or to any other person with the leave of the court (r 52(10); r 31(10)).

Where an adoption order is made or refused, the registrar or clerk must serve notice to that effect on every respondent (r 52(5); r 31(5)).

The registrar or clerk must serve notice of the making of an adoption order on any court in Great Britain which appears to him to have made any such order as is referred to in s 8(3) of the CA 1975 in respect of any parental rights and duties, or maintenance payments relating to the child (eg an affiliation order).

3 Welsh cases

Where an adoption order is made by a court sitting in Wales in respect of a child who was born in Wales (or who is treated under r 24(4) of the respective rules (see p 79) as having been born in the district in which that court sits), the registrar or clerk must obtain a translation into Welsh of the particulars set out in the order, if the adopter requests it before the order is drawn up (AR, r 52(2); MC(A)R, r 31(2)). Within 7 days of the making of the order, a copy of it and of the translation must be sent to the adopter (r 52(3); r 31(31)). The English text prevails (r 52(4); r 31(4)).

4 The Registrar General

Every adoption order must direct the Registrar General to make an entry in the Adopted Children Register (see chap 28) (AA

1958, s 21(1) as amended). The Forms of Adoption Entry Regulations 1975 (SI 1975 no 1959) set out schedules of particulars which go to make up an entry in the Register.

The particulars are included in the forms of adoption order scheduled to the AR as FORM 15, and to the MC(A)R as FORM 13 (see Appendix 1). The court determines the details of a particular entry.

The English form requires (inter alia):

(*i*) Date and country of child's birth with the registration district and sub-district if the birth was in England or Wales. Both sets of rules provide that where the precise date is not proved to the satisfaction of the court, the court must 'give the child a birthday' by determining the probable date of his birth, and may specify it in the order (r 24(3)). The country may be omitted if not proved to the court's satisfaction. If however, it appears probable that the child was born within the United Kingdom, the Channel Islands or the Isle of Man, he may be treated as born in the registration district and sub-district in which the court sits (r 24(4));

(*ii*) Name and surname of the child (the ones stated in the adoption application, or if not stated there, the child's original name or names and the applicant's surname.

(*iii*) Sex of child;

(*iv*) Name, surname, address and occupation of adopter or adopters;

(*v*) Date of the order and description of the court making it.

The form of order also directs the marking of the relevant entry in the birth or adoption register (see chap 28).

Within 7 days of the making of an adoption order the registrar or clerk must send a copy of it, and of any Welsh translation made, to the Registrar General (AR, r 52(4); MC(A)R, r 31(4)). At the same time he sends the completed ADOPTION PROCEEDINGS UNIT RETURN required under s 58A of the AA 1976.

5 Alteration and amendment of orders

The court may change its mind and recall its order at any time before it is passed and entered. Once the oral judgment has been pronounced, however, it is to be assumed that it is valid and effective save in the most exceptional circumstances (*In re Barrell Enterprises* [1973] 1 WLR 19; *R* v *Cambridge County Court, ex*

parte Ireland (1984) *The Times*, 25 June). In *R* v *Colchester and Clacton County Court* (1979) 9 Fam Law 155 (DC), in the absence of any reason given by a county court judge for a change of mind after having pronounced an adoption order, an order of mandamus went to compel him to perfect his order.

The court has statutory power to amend an adoption order which it has made by correcting errors and, as regards pre-1950 orders, by inserting certain particulars. The possibilities may be summarised as follows:

Provision of AA 1958	Nature of amendment	On application of:	Court must be satisfied that:
1 s 24(1)	Correction of any error in the particulars contained in the order	Adopter or adopted person	No specific requirement, but the power appears to be discretionary (see below)
2 s 24(1)(*a*)	Substitution or addition of new name (see below) in particulars to be entered in Adopted Children Register	Adopter or adopted person	Within one year from date of order a new name has been given to the adopted person (whether in baptism or otherwise), or taken by him either in lieu of or in addition to a name specified in the particulars
3 s 24(1)(*b*); Sched 5, para 6(1)	Revocation of a direction for marking an entry in Registers of Births or Adopted Children Register included in the order under s 21(4) or (5) of the Act (see p 174), or under s 18 of AA 1950	Any person concerned	The direction was wrongly included in the order

4 Sched 5, para 6(2)	Amendment of particulars specified in an order made under previous Adoption Acts to bring the order into the form it would have taken if s 21 of the Adoption Act 1958 (see 'The Registrar General' above) had applied to it	Adopter or adopted person	No specific requirement but the paragraph is permissive. If the application is for amendment of an order not specifying the surname of the adopted person, his surname one year after the order may be added in the particulars instead of the adopter's surname (if different)

These powers are conferred in each case only on the court which made the original order (AA 1958, s 24(1)). In relation, however, to a magistrates' court this includes a court acting for the same petty sessions area (s 24(7)). Under the Rules, the application may be made ex parte in the first instance, but the court may require notice to such persons as it thinks fit. FORM 9 is to be used in the domestic court (see Appendix 1) (AR, r 49(1); MC(A)R, r 28(1), (2)).

Head *1* above is a power in the widest terms to correct any error and is not a mere rule for correcting slips. In *R* v *Chelsea Juvenile Court Justices* (*Re An Infant*) [1955] 1 WLR 52 (DC), mandamus went to order justices to hear and determine an application under s 21(1) of the AA 1950 (then in force) to substitute in the order a new recital of the child's identity and a different date of birth as a result of new evidence.

The amendment or revocation must be notified, by the registrar or clerk, to the Registrar General with sufficient particulars to enable the latter to identify the case (AR, r 49(2); MC(A)R, r 28(3)).

6 Terms and conditions

An adoption order may contain such terms and conditions as the court thinks fit (CA 1975, s 8(7)).

Rees J in *In re J (Adoption Order)* [1973] Fam 106, at 115E,

said that on the face of it the court had unfettered power to impose any term or condition. A term or condition, however, must not be inconsistent with the fundamental concept of adoption itself (see now s 8(1) of the CA 1975), and it would not be a valid exercise of the power given (by s 8(7)) to make a final order of adoption subject to the condition that the child should remain in the care and control of some person other than the adopters. Also, any condition imposed must be for the welfare of the child.

Rees J made an adoption order with the condition that the father should have access to the child. It was an exceptional case where there were very strong grounds to support the view that at the right time and in the right manner contact between the child and his father was likely to be for the child's real and lasting benefit. A detailed agreement about access had been reached by the parties and approved by the Official Solicitor as guardian ad litem who would supervise any access.

In *In re S* [1976] Fam 1, the Court of Appeal, approving *In re J* (supra), held that it is only in a most exceptional case that any conditions concerning access should be imposed. As in *In re J*, the parties were in agreement and a schedule of conditions was put before the court. Confirming the approach of Rees J in the earlier case, Cairns LJ said that, 'no condition should be imposed which could be regarded as detracting from the rights and duties of the adoptive parents . . . it does appear to me that the conditions which are asked to be included in the order here are such as not to affect the rights and responsibilities of the adoptive parents in relation to the matter of access' (at 6D–F). It was agreed that the court welfare officer would act as an intermediary.

In *In re H* (1984) *The Times*, 21 November, the Court of Appeal, indicated that in the absence of agreement between the parties, a condition relating to access would not be attached to an adoption order. See also the view expressed by Roskill LJ in *Re C (Wardship and Adoption)* [1981] FLR 177, at 192, that the court has *jurisdiction* to impose a condition as to access in the absence of agreement. Such conditions as the court thinks fit can be imposed in a 'quite exceptional case'. See also *In re M* (1985) *The Times*, 9 May (CA).

In *In re J* (supra), Rees J considered the question of how a term or condition could be enforced if adopters broke it. One method is to extract from each of the adopters an undertaking to comply with the conditions imposed on the making of the adoption order. The undertaking might then be enforced by committal

proceedings. The conditions as pointed out by Rees J, would need to be drafted with care and precision so that a breach could be strictly proved (see also *In re G (T J) (An Infant)* [1962] 2 QB 73 (CA)).

Another method is to make the child a ward of court, and to seek directions from the court as to compliance with the conditions of the adoption order, or the undertakings given by the adopters. One disadvantage of wardship however, might be that the whole question of the child's welfare could be opened up again, leading to prolonged litigation.

In exceptional circumstances, it is suggested, that a condition as to religious upbringing may be imposed. It would appear then that the present prohibition on a parent's agreement to an adoption order or a freeing order being subject to such a condition, or the duty now placed on agencies to try and secure placements into families of appropriate religious persuasions, will not necessarily have rendered such a condition obsolete.

Chapter 13

Applications Concerning the Removal or Return of a Child

1 Restrictions on removal where adoption agreed or freeing application made (AA 1958, s 34)

(a) Adoption agreed

While an application for an adoption order is pending and the parent or guardian *has agreed* to the making of an adoption order (whether or not he knows the applicant's identity), he must not remove the child from the actual custody of the person with whom the child has his home against that person's will, except with the court's leave (AA 1958, s 34(1), as substituted by CA 1975, s 29). It is not clear at what precise stage the parent or guardian will be taken to have agreed to adoption. It may be after all the formalities have been completed (see chap 6).

If the person with custody consents, the child may be removed by the parent or guardian. This may not always be in the interests of the child, and will, it would appear, occur without the intervention of the court, and without requiring the consent of any relevant adoption agency. An interested party may, however, consider invoking the wardship jurisdiction (see chap 21).

(b) Freeing application made

While an application is pending for an order freeing a child for adoption (see chap 20), and:
  (1) the child is in the care of the adoption agency making the application; and
  (2) the application was not made with the consent of each parent or guardian of the child,
no parent or guardian who did *not* consent to the application is entitled to remove the child, against the will of the person with

whom the child has his home, without the court's leave (AA 1958, s 34(2)).

The same comments in respect of the giving of consent made under (a) above apply in the case of this further restriction. Indeed, under s 34(2), the child will be in the care of the agency, and the person empowered to consent to removal may not be the eventual applicant for an adoption order.

2 Restrictions on removal where applicant has provided home for five years (AA 1958, s 34A)

Section 34A, which mainly protects foster parents who wish to adopt, provides wider restrictions than under s 34 in that, subject to the relevant conditions being met, *no-one* is entitled to remove the child.

By s 34A:

(a) while an adoption application is pending in respect of a child who has had his home with the applicant for five years preceding the application, no-one is entitled, against the will of the applicant, to remove the child from the applicant's actual custody, except with the leave of the court or under authority conferred by any enactment or on the arrest of the child (s 34A(1)).

(b) Subsection (2) provides the same protection at an earlier time. A prospective adopter can give notice to the local authority within whose area he has his home of his intention to apply for an adoption order and, subject to the same conditions as in subs (1), the child cannot be removed before either the application for the adoption order is made, or three months have expired since the local authority received the notice, whichever occurs first (s 34A(2)).

Once, of course, the adoption application is made subs (1) continues the protection. If an adoption application is not made within three months, a fresh notice cannot be served until after twenty-eight days from the expiry of the previous notice (s 34A(5)). During the period of twenty-eight days the child could, therefore, be removed.

Section 34A principally restrains parents or guardians who may, for example, find their recollections of the child being stirred by being asked to agree to an adoption. In contrast to s 34 (see above), it is irrelevant whether or not parents or guardians have agreed to adoption, or are not prepared to do so.

In cases where s 34A(1) or (2) applies, and where the child was in the care of a local authority before he began to have his home with the applicant or, as the case may be, the prospective adopter, and the child remains in the care of that local authority or any other, the local authority must not remove the child from the actual custody of the applicant or prospective adopter except in accordance with ss 35 and 36 of the AA 1958 (see pp 29 and 30), or with the leave of a court (s 34A(3), as amended).

A local authority must, not more than seven days after the receipt of a s 34A notice, inform any other authority or voluntary organisation in whose care the child is known by it to be, that it has received the notice (s 34A(4)).

For the criminal offences and penalties for contravention of ss 34 and 34A, see chap 30.

3 Breaches of restrictions

The person from whose actual custody a child has been removed in breach of ss 34 or 34A of the AA 1958 can apply to an authorised court (see p 52) for an order that the person who has unlawfully removed the child, return him to the applicant (CA 1975, s 30(1)). For the particular court, see under 'jurisdiction' below.

Where the applicant has reasonable grounds for believing that another person is intending to remove the child from his actual custody in breach of either ss 34 or 34A of the 1958 Act, he can apply to the court for an order prohibiting such removal (CA 1975, s 30(2)). Alternatively, wardship proceedings may be more effective or convenient in the circumstances.

If an order to return the child has been made by the High Court or a county court, and the court which made the order (or in the case of a county court order, any county court) is satisfied that the child has not been returned, it may, by way of an additional power of enforcement, make an order authorising one of its officers to search specified premises and return the child, if found, to the applicant (ibid, s 30(3)). If a justice of the peace is satisfied by information on oath that there are reasonable grounds for believing that a child to whom the return order relates (whether made by the High Court, a county court, or a magistrates' court) is in specified premises, he may issue a search warrant to a constable who is to return the child, if found, to the applicant (CA 1975, s 30(4)). The search warrant must be in FORM 10 of the

Magistrates' Courts (Children and Young Persons) Rules 1970, or in a form to the like effect (MC(A)R, r 27(11)).

4 Jurisdiction and procedure

(a) *Jurisdiction*

An application:

— under s 34(1) or (2), or s 34A(1) or (2) of the AA 1958 for leave to remove a child from the actual custody of the person with whom the child has his home; or

— under s 30(1) of the CA 1975 for an order for the return of a child removed in breach of ss 34 or 34A of the 1958 Act; or

— under s 30(2) of the 1975 Act for an order forbidding removal of a child,

must be made:

(1) if there is a pending adoption application, or application for a freeing order, or for revocation of a freeing order, in the court where the application is pending;

(2) if no such application is pending, in the 'appropriate court' which may be the High Court, the county court within whose district the applicant lives, or the magistrates' court in whose area he lives, or in the case of an application under s 34A(2), the county court within whose district or the magistrates' court within whose area the child is, also has jurisdiction (AR, r 47(2), (3); MC(A) R, r 27(2)).

(b) *Procedure: Serial numbers; High Court and county court*

Serial numbers. The confidential serial number procedure (see p 61) applies to the applications described above where a serial number has already been assigned to a person. In addition, where a person proposes to apply for an adoption order but has occasion earlier to seek an order for the child's return or to restrain his removal, he may apply for a serial number for the purposes of the s 30 application with the same consequences as if it had already been assigned to him in adoption proceedings (AR, r 47(6); MC(A)R, r 27(4)).

High Court and county court. If there is a pending adoption application, freeing application, or application to revoke a freeing

order, the application is by process on notice in those proceedings (AR, r 47(2)(*a*)). Otherwise there must be an originating summons or application as appropriate (AR, r 47(2)(*b*)). Any respondent to the originating summons or application who wishes to claim relief must do so by means of an answer made within 7 days of the service of the summons or application on him (r 47(4)). In an 'intended removal' case, for example, the respondent may want to cross-apply for leave to remove the child. The serial number sub-rule (see above), and other provisions noted below, apply in respect of the respondent as if the answer were an originating process and he were the applicant (r 47(11)).

The registrar must serve a copy of the process, and of any answer thereto, and a notice of the hearing date:

(1) where adoption etc proceedings are pending (including a case where they have been commenced after the removal etc application) on all the parties to those proceedings and on the reporting officer and guardian ad litem (if any);

(2) in any other case, on any person against whom an order is sought in the application, and on any local authority to whom the prospective adopter has given notice under s 18 of the CA 1975 (see chap 5); and

(3) in any case, on such other person or body, not being the child, as the court thinks fit (r 47(5)).

A prospective adopter who is served with a r 47 application or answer, and who wishes to oppose it, must file his adoption application within 14 days, or before or at the hearing of the application, whichever is the sooner (r 47(7)). The court may at any time give directions, and if giving directions in respect of r 47(7), must give further directions as to the conduct of the r 47 application or answer, and in particular as to the appointment of a guardian ad litem of the child (r 47(8)).

(*c*) *Procedure: magistrates' court*

The application is by complaint (MC(A)R, r 27(2)). The respondents are the same persons or bodies who would be served with copies of the process etc on a High Court or county court application in pending adoption etc proceedings, except for the reporting officer and guardian ad litem (if any) (r 27(3)). The justices' clerk must serve notice of the hearing and a copy of the complaint on the reporting officer and guardian ad litem (if any), and they may attend the hearing and be heard on the question of whether the application made should be granted (r 27(5)).

A duly authorised member or employee of a party which is a local authority, adoption agency or other body may address the court at the hearing of the application (r 27(8)). The rules concerning directions and about a prospective adopter filing his adoption application if he wishes to oppose the r 27 application, are the same as in the High Court or county court (r 27(6), and (7)).

(d) *After determination*

Where a court grants an application to remove a child from the actual custody of the person with whom he has his home, or refuses to order his return or restrain his intended removal, it may, if an adoption application has been made, treat the hearing of the application as the hearing of the adoption application, and refuse an adoption order accordingly (AR, r 47(9); MC(A)R, r 27(9)).

Notice of the determination of an application under r 47 or r 27, as the case may be, must be served by the registrar or justices' clerk on all parties (sub-rule (10)).

(e) *Enforcement proceedings in the magistrates' court*

Original proceedings under the Adoption Acts, including applications for the removal or return etc of a child, are domestic proceedings. Proceedings for enforcement of an order under these Acts, however, are not domestic proceedings (MCA 1980, s 65(1)(i)), and are therefore normally heard in open court, unless the court directs them to be treated as domestic proceedings (s 65(2)), or they are heard at the same time as ordinary domestic proceedings between the same parties (s 65(3)). A separate bench, sitting in open court, therefore, may have to be constituted for enforcement proceedings regarding, for example, an order for the return of a child.

(f) *Wardship proceedings*

As noted above, wardship proceedings may be more effective or convenient when there is a threatened or apprehended removal of the child. When, however, ss 34 or 34A of the 1958 Act do *not* apply to the removal or threat of it (eg adoption not agreed, or break in the five-year period), wardship will be necessary. See also chap 21 for adoption and wardship generally.

Chapter 14

Supervision or Care after the Refusal of Adoption Order

Where the court refuses to make the adoption order, it may, if it appears that there are exceptional circumstances, order:
(a) that the child shall be under the supervision of a specified local authority or probation officer (CA 1975, s 17(1)(a));
(b) that the child be committed to the care of a specified local authority, (ibid, s 17(1)(b)).

The supplementary provisions in ss 3 and 4 of the Guardianship Act 1973, as amended, are applied to a s 17 order as they apply to an order under s 2 of the 1973 Act (ibid, s 17(3)). These deal, inter alia, with variation and discharge of the order, and the appointment of the particular probation officer.

1 Supervision order

The exceptional circumstances must be such as to make it desirable that the child should be under the supervision of an independent person. A supervision order ceases to have effect when the child attains the age of eighteen (Guardianship Act 1973, s 3(2) as amended).

2 Committal into care

The exceptional circumstances must be such as to make it impracticable or undesirable for the child to be entrusted to either of his parents or to any other individual. In respect of 'exceptional circumstances', see F v F [1959] 1 WLR 863, and G v G (1962) 106 SJ 858.

The order under s 17(1)(b) may require the payment by either parent to the local authority, while it has the care of the child, of

such weekly or other periodical sum as the court thinks reasonable towards the maintenance of the child (CA 1975, s 17(2)).

Where a court proposes to make an order committing the child into care, it must give the local authority in whose area the child is an opportunity of making representations. Where that authority is a party to the adoption application and represented before the court when the adoption order is refused, the court may proceed forthwith to hear its representations as to the making of an order committing the child into care, or as to maintenance payments (AR, r 26(2); MC(A)R, r 26(2)). If the local authority is not a party or is not represented before the court, or if it makes representations about the making of an order for maintenance, the court must adjourn the hearing, and the registrar or the justices' clerk, as the case may be, must, not less than 14 days before the date fixed, send notice of the further hearing in FORM 8 to the authority, to the applicant, to each parent, and to the guardian ad litem (if appointed). Notice to an authority who is not a party to the proceedings must be accompanied by copies of any previous notices of hearing or, if applicable, notice of further proceedings after an interim order, served on the respondents (r 26(3)).

Chapter 15

Interim Orders

1 Nature of the order

The Court may postpone the determination of an application for an adoption order and make an interim order vesting the legal custody of the child in the applicants for a probationary period not exceeding two years, upon such terms for the maintenance of the child and otherwise as the court thinks fit (CA 1975, s 19).

Before an interim order may be made the requirements of the CA 1975, s 12(1) (parental agreement, dispensation, or child free for adoption), and s 18(1) (notice to local authority in non-agency placement) must have been complied with (s 19(1)).

'Probationary' period imports a process of investigation or experiment in relation to all the circumstances relevant to the proposed adoption, and not merely to the suitability of the applicants (per Buckley LJ in *S* v *Huddersfield BC* [1975] Fam 113 (CA), at 124). In the *Huddersfield Case* an interim order was made in favour of foster parents who had applied for an adoption order. The natural parent was granted visiting and staying access, and a supervision order was made in respect of the child, the whole order being designed to test out the desirability of the eventual integration of the child into the natural parent's new family.

The court may extend, by a further order, up to a total period of two years, an order made in the first instance for a lesser period (s 19(2)).

2 Proceedings after an interim order

Where an interim order has been made, the registrar or justices' clerk must list the case for further hearing on a date before the

order expires. Notice of the hearing must be sent in FORM 8 (see Appendix 1) to all the parties and to the guardian ad litem (if appointed) not less than one month before the date fixed (r 25 of the respective rules). FORM 8 will require adapting as described in the notes to it, as it is primarily used for notice of an original hearing.

3 Consequences of the order

An interim order does not rank as an adoption order as regards its effect.

An interim order may be made notwithstanding that it restricts the parental rights and duties of a local authority, vested in it pursuant to s 3 of the CCA 1980 (*S* v *Huddersfield BC* (supra)).

If the child was placed with the applicant by an agency, and an interim order expires without an adoption order being made, the child must be returned to the agency (AA 1958, s 35(4), and see p 30).

Chapter 16

Orders to Facilitate Adoption Abroad

Where an authorised court is satisfied on an application made in relation to a child by a person who is *not* domiciled in England and Wales or in Scotland that the applicant intends to adopt the child under the law of or within the country in which the applicant is domiciled, the court may make an order vesting in him the parental rights and duties relating to the child (CA 1975, s 25). This provision, which came into force on 27 May 1984, replaces the former system of provisional adoption under s 53 of the AA 1958.

1 Jurisdiction

A magistrates' court is not an 'authorised court' for the purposes of s 25, and cannot make an order (CA 1975, s 100(6)).

A s 25 order, which is made in FORM 15 (see Appendix 1), authorises the applicant to remove the child from Great Britain for the purpose of adopting him under the law of or within the country in which the applicant is domiciled. It vests in the applicant the parental rights and duties relating to the child (including the legal custody). (For the general restrictions on sending children abroad for adoption, save under a s 25 order, see p 187).

2 Requirements

All the requirements relating to the adopter's qualifications (apart from domicile), the eligibility of the child, and parental agreement applicable to the making of an ordinary adoption application must be satisfied before a s 25 order may be made (s 25(2)). The trial period (see chap 5) is, however, twenty-six weeks and

not thirteen, and the order must not be made until the child is thirty-two weeks old (ibid).

The provisions about placement, arrangements for adoption, and supervision (including ss 34–48 of the AA 1958 (see chap 4)) apply when the application made or contemplated is one under s 25 in the same way as they do regarding adoptions in this country (s 25(4)).

3 Further provisions

A s 25 order does not have the effect in English law of an adoption order (CA 1975, s 25(2), excluding s 8(1) and (9), and consequently Sched 1 of the 1975 Act).

An interim order under s 19 of the 1975 Act cannot be made on a s 25 application, and ss 14–16, s 23 (relating to freeing for adoption (see chap 20), and s 24 (convention adoption orders) have no application to orders under s 25 (s 25(2)).

4 Procedure and evidence

The proceedings are commenced in:
- (i) *High Court:* by filing an originating summons in FORM 6 (see Appendix 1), issued out of the Principal Registry of the Family Division (AR, r 48(1)(*a*); or
- (ii) *County Court:* by filing in the office of the county court within whose district the child is an originating application in FORM 6 (r 48(1)(*b*)).

The same rules as for an adoption application apply, save that r 15(1) (commencement of proceedings), and r 52(1)(*d*) (form of order) are not applicable (r 48(2)). In addition, an applicant must file with the process expert evidence of the law of adoption in the country in which he is domiciled. An affidavit as to that law sworn by such a person as is mentioned in s 4(1) of the Civil Evidence Act 1972 is admissible without notice (ie a person who is suitably qualified on account of his knowledge or experience to give evidence as to that law) (r 48(3), and see also s 4(2)).

Chapter 17

Costs

On the determination of proceedings to which the AR apply or of an application under the MC(A)R, or in either case on the making of an interim order, the judge or the magistrates' court, as the case may be, may make such order as to the costs as he or it thinks just (AR, r 51(1); MC(A)R, r 30(1)).

In particular, the applicant may be ordered to pay:

(a) the expenses incurred by the reporting officer and the guardian ad litem, if appointed, (r 51(1)(a); r 30(1)(a)); and

(b) the expenses incurred by any respondent in attending the hearing, or such part of those expenses as the court thinks proper (r 51(1)(b); r 30(1)(b)).

The 'determination of an application' includes a refusal of it. In the magistrates' court the expression is expressly said to include a refusal to proceed with the application or its withdrawal (MC(A)R, r 30(2)).

As to the applicant's undertaking to meet the proper costs of the Official Solicitor, see p 67.

Chapter 18

Appeals

1 High Court and County Court

(a) *High Court*

An appeal lies to the Court of Appeal from the decision of the judge in making or refusing to make an adoption order. Leave to appeal appears to be required as the appeal is in respect of a *final* order made by a judge in *chambers* (see RSC, Ord 58, r 6(2), and the full discussion on pp 799 and 800 of vol 1 of *The Supreme Court Practice 1985*), If, however, the adoption application is heard in chambers, but judgment is given and the order made in *open* it would seem that leave to appeal is not then required.

If the case at first instance concerns adoption and wardship proceedings, then leave to appeal may be required in respect of the former but not in respect of the latter. No leave is required regarding the wardship order as a result of s 18(1)(*h*)(i) of the Supreme Court Act 1981, which exempts from the requirement of leave any interlocutory order or judgment made or given by the High Court where the custody, education or welfare of a minor is concerned. Exceptionally, an order *discharging* the wardship may well be a final order, as opposed to an interlocutory order, so that leave will be required if the order was made in chambers.

An application for leave to appeal should be made to the judge at first instance and, if refused, may then be made to a single judge of the Court of Appeal. For the procedure generally in respect of appeals to the Court of Appeal, see RSC, Ord 59, and *Practice Note (Court of Appeal: New Procedure)* [1982] 1 WLR 1312.

The notice of appeal must be served within four weeks from the date on which the judgment or order of the court below was

97

signed, entered or otherwise perfected (Ord 59, r 4(1)). The period for appealing may be extended by the full Court of Appeal, a single Lord Justice, and the Registrar of Civil Appeals (Ord 3, r 5(4)). Applications for an extension are normally made to the Registrar, but if leave to appeal is also required, a composite application should be made to a single Lord Justice. In *In re F(R) (An Infant)* [1970] 1 QB 385 (CA), Salmon LJ said that an extension of time for appealing from an adoption order is not granted lightly. The child's interests have to be taken into account, and particularly what has happened between the date when the order was made and the date of the application.

The Court of Appeal may in a proper case admit fresh evidence of events since the hearing below (see *Re S (an Infant)* [1973] 3 All ER 88, *Re El-G (Minors)* [1983] FLR 589, and *Re R (A Minor) (Wardship)* [1984] FLR 826).

As to the necessity of hearing appeals as soon as possible and the irrelevance of counsel's convenience, see *Practice Note (Minors: Listing of Appeals)* [1984] 1 WLR 1125.

Appeals regarding freeing applications (see chap 20) and ss 34, 34A and 35(2) of the AA 1958 also lie to the Court of Appeal.

For an unsuccessful attempt to circumvent the appeal procedure by the use of wardship, see *Re S (A Minor)* (1978) 122 SJ 759, referred to on p 123.

The guardian ad litem, almost invariably the Official Solicitor, remains in the same capacity for the appeal (*Re S* [1959] 1 WLR 921).

(b) County Court

Appeals lie to the Court of Appeal from an order of the County Court making or refusing to make adoption orders, freeing orders, or orders in respect of ss 34, 34A and 35(2) of the AA 1958. Leave to appeal is *not* required. Appeals now lie on questions of fact as well as on questions of law (County Courts Act 1984, s 77). The procedure is set out in RSC, Ord 59 (note in particular r 19: Appeal from county court). Notice of appeal must be served within four weeks from *the date of the judgment or order of the court below* (words in Ord 59, r 4(1), substituted by r 19(3)(a)).

The guardian ad litem remains in the same capacity for the appeal (*Re S (supra)*), but it would seem that as the child cannot be a respondent to the various proceedings in the County Court (unlike the position in the High Court), the guardian does not have a right of appeal in his own capacity or on behalf of the

child (see r 15(3) AR (adoption), r 4(3) AR (freeing applications). Judicial Review under RSC, Ord 53 will also be available in appropriate circumstances, see, for example, *R* v *Colchester and Clacton County Court* (1979) 9 Fam Law 155 (the judge made an adoption order but later reconsidered the case and thought that the child should be warded; he refused to perfect his order: an order of mandamus went to compel the judge to perfect it as he had not given any reason for his change of mind, had not exercised his discretion judicially and was not justified in varying or altering the original order). See also *R* v *Beverley CC, ex p Brown* (1985) *The Times*, 25 January (grandfather not informed of date of hearing by guardian ad litem despite having made it clear he was an interested party).

(c) The approach of the Court of Appeal

In *In re W (An Infant)* [1971] AC 682, Lord Hailsham LC, in considering the question whether agreement to an adoption order had been unreasonably withheld, said that:

In an adoption case, a . . . judge applying the test of reasonableness must be entitled to come to his own conclusions, on the totality of the facts, and a revising court should only dispute his decision where it feels reasonably confident that he has erred in law or acted without adequate evidence or where it feels that his judgment of the witnesses and their demeanour has played so little part in his reasoning that the revising court is in a position as good as that of the trial judge to form an opinion. (p 700 A–C, and see also Lord Guest at p 724 E–G)

(d) Further appeal

An appeal lies from the Court of Appeal to the House of Lords with the leave of the former or the latter (Administration of Justice (Appeals) Act 1934, s 1).

2 Magistrates' Court

Where a magistrates' court makes or refuses to make an order on an application for an adoption order, a freeing order, or under ss 34, 34A and 35(2) of the AA 1958, an appeal lies to the Divisional Court of the Family Division (s 101(2), CA 1975, as amended by Sched 2, para 27, Hassassa 1983, and RSC, Ord 90, r 9).

Procedure is governed by RSC, Ord 90, r 9, incorporating r 16 with the necessary modifications.

The notice of motion must be served and the appeal entered within six weeks after the date of the order or determination appealed against (RSC, Ord 90, r 16(2) incorporating and substituting the period in Ord 55, r 4(2)). Order 55 applies generally save in so far as it is not inconsistent with the particular rules applicable to appeals in adoption matters from magistrates' courts (Ord 55, r 1(4)).

See also *Practice Note (Adoption: Appeal)* [1973] 1 WLR 44.

A further appeal lies from the Divisional Court of the Family Division to the Court of Appeal, but only with the leave of the former or the latter (s 18(1)(*c*) and (*e*), Supreme Court Act 1981). An appeal to the House of Lords then lies with the leave of the Court of Appeal or the House of Lords.

In *In re G(DM) (An Infant)* [1962] 1 WLR 731 (DC), it was said that the principles upon which the High Court and the Court of Appeal acted in cases relating to the guardianship, custody and care and control of infants appeared to be equally applicable in cases of adoption, and that while the court would interfere if the justices acted on a wrong view of the law or on findings of fact not justified by the evidence, and in certain other exceptional circumstances, it would not interfere with the exercise by them of their discretion, unless it came to the clear conclusion that such exercise was wrong, in the sense of not being the course most beneficial to the child.

Judicial Review under RSC, Ord 53 will be available in appropriate circumstances, see above under 'County Court'. On the other hand, there appears to be no basis now in adoption cases for a case stated under the MCA 1980, since the CA 1975, s 101(2) has been amended by Hassassa 1983 to provide for appeals proper in all adoption proceedings before magistrates.

Chapter 19

Fresh Proceedings in Respect of the Same Child

1 Refusal of previous adoption application

Section 22(4) of the CA 1975 provides that the court must not proceed to hear an application for an adoption order in relation to a child, where a previous application for a British adoption order, made in relation to the child by the same persons, was refused by any court unless:

(*a*) in refusing the previous application the court directed that s 22(4) should not apply, or

(*b*) it appears to the court that because of a change in circumstances or for any other reason it is proper to proceed with the application.

A 'British adoption order' means an adoption order, or any provision for the adoption of a child effected under the law of Northern Ireland, or any British territory outside the United Kingdom (CA 1975, s 107(1)).

If it appears to a registrar or justices' clerk, as the case may be, on receipt of the originating process for an adoption order, that the provisions of s 22(4) may preclude the court from proceeding to hear the application, he must refer the process to the judge or court (r 16 of the respective rules, and see p 61).

New applicants for an adoption order, where there has been a previous refusal of an order to other persons in respect of the same child, are not, of course, caught by the provisions of s 22(4).

2 Re-adoption orders

There is no bar on an adoption order being made, notwithstanding that the child is already an adopted child (CA 1975, s 8(8)). There is no restriction on the number of times a child may

be adopted. An adopted child may be the subject of a subsequent interim order or one leading to adoption abroad.

For an application for a further order a certified copy of the entry of the previous adoption in the Adopted Children Register is required in place of the birth certificate (see FORM 1, Appendix 1). It is the adopter under the last previously made order who is deemed to be the child's parent, so that, for instance, it is his agreement and not that of the natural parent which is required to the making of the new adoption order (see *Re RM* (1941) WN 244).

Chapter 20

Freeing for Adoption

1 Introduction

The new freeing procedure provides for the giving of or dispensing with agreement to the making of an adoption order by a parent or guardian to be dealt with at an early stage in the adoption process. It seeks to avoid some of the disadvantages of the alternative consent procedure already considered in chapter 6. That alternative procedure requires agreement to a specific adoption (as opposed to agreement to adoption generally under freeing), and the question of agreement cannot be resolved finally until the hearing of the adoption application when the child has already been placed with the prospective adopters. This frequently causes unnecessary strain on the natural mother and encourages indecisiveness; can put the welfare of the child at risk whilst his future is in doubt and there is a possibility that he may be moved; and may make the adoption parents anxious and reluctant to give total commitment to a child whom they may not be allowed to keep (see the 'Houghton Report', Cmnd 5107, paras 168 and 169, and the 'Second Report to Parliament on the Children Act 1975', para 42).

Section 12(6) of the CA 1975, states that 'a child is free for adoption if he is the subject of an order under s 14 and the order has not been revoked under s 16.' Sections 14, 15, 16 and 23 of the CA 1975, which relate to freeing, came into force on the 27 May 1984.

Section 14 provides for the application for a freeing order to be made by an adoption agency (an approved adoption society or local authority). A preliminary hearing takes place at which the agreement of the parent or guardian may be given or dispensed with on any of the grounds in s 12(2) of the Act (see p 41). This

will, of course, be before the adoption application is heard and usually before the child has been placed for adoption. If the freeing order is made the parental rights and duties relating to the child vest in the adoption agency until either the order is revoked under s 16 (see below), or an adoption order is made (s 14(6), and see below under 'effect of the order'). Section 15 provides for certain progress reports, and s 23 provides for the transfer of parental rights and duties, vested under s 14(6), between adoption agencies.

2 Making a freeing order (a s 14 order)

Before making an order the court must be satisfied that in the case of each parent or guardian:

(1) he freely, and with full understanding of what is involved, agrees generally and unconditionally to the making of an adoption order, or

(2) his agreement to the making of an adoption order should be dispensed with on a ground specified in s 12(2) (see p 41) (s 14(1)).

An application for a freeing order, however, can only be made if:

(1) it is made with the consent of at least *one* parent or guardian *or*

(2) the child is in the care of the adoption agency and the agency is applying to the court to dispense with the agreement of *each* parent or guardian (s 14(2)).

For the meaning of 'parent or guardian', see pp 37 and 38.

As noted above, the agreement of the parent or guardian must be given *generally* (and therefore not to a specific adoption) and unconditionally to the making of an adoption order (s 14(1)(*a*)). Accordingly, no stipulation about, for example, the religious upbringing of the child can be made as a condition of agreement (see p 39 for the similar position regarding s 12(1)(*b*)(i)). It follows, of course, that in addition specific adopters cannot be stipulated.

The court will not dispense with the agreement of a parent or guardian unless the child is already placed for adoption or the court is satisfied that it is likely that the child will be placed for adoption (s 14(3)). It will be for the applicant to put in evidence on this aspect and to satisfy the court on the balance of probabilities (which is the onus and standard of proof for the other require-

ments of s 14, save perhaps for those in s 14(7) and (8) (see below)).

It should be noted for the purpose of s 14(2)(*b*), that in the situation where a parent or guardian does *not* consent to the making of the freeing application, but where an application may nevertheless be made if the child is in the care of the adoption agency (being an approved adoption society or local authority) and the agency is applying to dispense with the agreement of each parent or guardian, that no minimum period is specified in respect of the child having been in care. This, it may be thought is somewhat surprising and indeed may deter some parents from placing their children in care once the provision becomes widely known. The phrase 'is in the care of' is not defined in the Act and presumably applies to children in care under a court order, pursuant to a parental rights resolution or in 'voluntary care'.

Agreement may be dispensed with on any one of the grounds specified in s 12(2), and on the same basis as already considered in respect of an ordinary adoption application (see pp 41–51). Section 12(2)(*b*) provides the frequently used ground that the parent or guardian 'is withholding his agreement unreasonably'. Bearing in mind that the freeing application will be made at an earlier stage in the adoption process than a full application, it is suggested that the question surrounding access to the parent or guardian is likely to be of major importance, and the court will expect full evidence to be placed before it on this aspect. (For the possible relationship of access applications in the Juvenile Courts under s 12C of the CCA 1980 to freeing applications, see below under 'procedure'). It is also possible to envisage situations where it could be argued with some force that it cannot be unreasonable for a parent to refuse agreement to adoption in general because he or she wants to know something about the prospective adopters and to ensure that they form a good relationship with the child and are of a certain ethnic origin or practise a particular religion. This would be a quite separate matter, of course, from the prohibition against conditional agreement (see above).

(*a*) Father of an illegitimate child

Before making an order under s 14, in the case of an illegitimate child whose father is not its guardian (see s 107(1), CA 1975, and p 37), the court must satisfy itself in relation to anyone claiming to be the father that either he has no intention of applying for

legal custody under s 9 of the GMA 1971, or if he did apply that the application would be likely to be refused (s 14(8)).

If the putative father is a guardian of the child, a s 14 application cannot be granted unless either his agreement is forthcoming or it is dispensed with. Where he is not a guardian and intends to apply for legal custody, and the court is not satisfied that his application would be likely to be refused, the freeing application will presumably be adjourned and the two applications brought on together in the same court. The words in s 14(8), 'in relation to anyone claiming to be the father' envisage a possible preliminary issue regarding paternity.

For the adoption agency's duties in respect of the father of an illegitimate child, see p 245, and for the reporting officer's duties, see below.

(b) Declaration (s 14(7))

In addition, before making a s 14 order, freeing a child for adoption, the court must be satisfied that each parent or guardian who can be found has been given an opportunity of making, if he so wishes, a declaration that he prefers not to be involved in future questions concerning the adoption of the child. The court must record any declaration made (s 14(7)). The reporting officer (see below) must confirm that the parent or guardian has been given the opportunity of making a declaration under s 14(7) (r 5(4)(b) of each set of Rules). Any declaration made will be contained in FORM 2 (Agreement to an Adoption Order (Freeing Cases)) in Sched 1 to the Rules (see Appendix 1). If the declaration is made, therefore, the parent has no further rights regarding the child. Where a declaration is not made the parent may use ss 15 and 16 of the Act (see below).

(c) Progress reports to former parent (s 15)

A parent or guardian (referred to in the section as 'the former parent') who was given an opportunity of making a declaration under s 14(7) but did not do so, is entitled to receive a progress report on the child from the adoption agency within 14 days after the first anniversary of the making of the freeing order under s 14. The report must be made by the agency (unless it has already notified him that an adoption order has been made) and must inform him whether an adoption order has been made and, if not, whether the child has his home with a person with whom he has been placed for adoption (s 15(1) and (2)). Thereafter, he must

be notified of the making of an adoption order, if it has not already been made, or of any placement for adoption, or the cessation of any such placement (s 15(3)). The former parent may at any time make a declaration to the agency that he prefers not to be involved in future questions concerning the adoption of his child. The agency must then ensure that the declaration is recorded by the court which made the s 14 order, and the agency is released from having to make any further progress reports (s 15(4)).

3 Effect of s 14 order

On the making of the order declaring the child free for adoption the parental rights relating to the child vest in the approved adoption society or local authority (s 14(6)). They will continue to do so until either the s 14 order is revoked under s 16 (see below) or an adoption order is made. The s 14 order does not affect the parental rights and duties so far as they relate to any period before the making of the order (see s 8(2), applied by s 14(6)). Any parental right or duty, however, which was vested in a parent or guardian or in any other person by virtue of an order of the court, immediately before the making of the s 14 order, will be extinguished. Also extinguished will be any duty pursuant to an agreement or court order to make maintenance payments for the child for any period after the making of the s 14 order, except a duty arising by virtue of an agreement which constitutes a trust or which expressly provides that the duty is not to be extinguished by the making of a s 14 order (s 8(3) and (4), applied by s 14(6)).

4 Revocation of a freeing order

An application to revoke a freeing order can only be made by 'the former parent' as defined at p 106 above (ie one who did not make a s 14(7) declaration), and only *more than* twelve months after the making of the freeing order (s 16(1)). This requirement provides the adoption agency with a reasonable period within which to place the child for adoption. It may, nevertheless, not be long enough to place some disturbed or handicapped children.

Additionally, s 16(1) provides that an application to revoke can only be made if:

(*i*) an adoption order has not already been made, and

(*ii*) the child does *not* have his home with a person with whom he has been placed for adoption.

The former parent must apply to the court which made the freeing order on the ground that he wishes to resume the parental rights and duties (s 16(1)).

Whilst the application to revoke is pending the adoption agency having the parental rights and duties must not place the child for adoption without the leave of the court (s 16(2)). Unless the application to revoke is obviously hopeless, it is suggested that leave will not be obtained without very compelling reasons. Placement may, for example, unfairly pre-empt the former parent's pending application or could be very damaging to the child if the parent eventually succeeds and the child has then to be moved again.

In deciding the application the court will apply s 3 of the CA 1975 (first consideration being given to the welfare of the child, see p 3). Other matters that will be considered by the court will presumably include the wishes and circumstances of the former parent, the reasons for the application and any delay in making it, the agency's efforts to place the child and their plans, and (where appropriate) the wishes and feelings of the child.

If the application is dismissed on the ground that 'to allow it would contravene the principle embodied in s 3', the applicant will not be able to make a further application without the leave of the court, and the adoption agency is released from the duty of providing him with any more progress reports. Leave to make a further application will only be given if it appears to the court that because of a change of circumstances or for any other reason it is proper to allow the application to be made (s 16(4) and (5)).

Where an order under s 14 is revoked the parental rights and duties relating to the child are vested in the individual or individuals in whom they vested immediately before the order was made (s 16(3)(*a*)). If the parental rights and duties, or any of them, vested in a local authority (eg under a care order or parental rights resolution) or voluntary organisation immediately before the order freeing the child for adoption was made, those rights and duties are vested in the individual or individuals in whom they vested *immediately before* they were vested in the authority or organisation (s 16(3)(*b*)). In view of these provisions the court will have to look most carefully at the effect of revocation particularly, for example, where two parents have separated or where one of the parents made a s 14(7) declaration (see above), or the

child was in care following ill-treatment or lack of care by the parent.

Any duty in respect of payents for the child's maintenance, extinguished on the making of the s 14 order, revives on its revocation (s 16(3)(c)).

Revocation does not affect any right or duty so far as it relates to any period before the date of the revocation (s 16(3)).

5 Transfer of parental rights and duties between adoption agencies

Section 23 of the CA 1975 provides that on the joint application of an approved adoption society or local authority in which the parental rights and duties relating to a child who is in Great Britain are vested under s 14(6), and any other approved society or authority, the court may, if it thinks fit, order the transfer of the parental rights and duties to the latter society or authority.

— For the restrictions on the removal of a child while an application is pending for a s 14 order, see p 84.

— Regarding the possible relationship between freeing and wardship, see chap 21.

6 Procedure

(a) *Application for a freeing order*

(1) *Commencing proceedings.* An adoption agency applying for a s 14 order does so as follows:

   (i) *High Court*: by filing an originating summons in FORM 1 (see Appendix 1) issued out of the Principal Registry of the Family Division;

  (ii) *County Court*: by filing in the office of the appropriate county court an originating application in FORM 1 (see Appendix 1). (The appropriate court is one having authority by virtue of s 100(2) of the CA 1975 (see p 52));

 (iii) *Domestic Court*: by an application in FORM 1 (see Appendix 1) which is deemed to be a complaint within the MCA 1980 and the Magistrates' Courts Rules 1981. The court must be one acting for the area in which either the child or a parent or guardian is at the date of the application (MC(A)R, r 4(1)). The application must be delivered or sent by post to that court together with all the documents referred to in the application.

In view of the likely length and complexity of contested freeing applications, the appropriate venue for them is likely to be the High Court or County Court. See also p 54.

(2) *Process*. FORM 1 and its accompanying notes, which are set out in Appendix 1, correspond mutatis mutandis with FORM 6 (originating process for an adoption order), as described on p 60, as regards the particulars to be given about the child, parental agreement etc. The form must have attached to it the appropriate birth certificate (or adoption certificate if the child was the subject of a previous adoption). If no certificate is available, the place of birth must be entered on the form, including the country if known.

The applicant agency must pay the appropriate fee and supply three copies of FORM 1, with any other documents required to be supplied (see below), and three copies of a report in writing covering all the relevant matters set out in Sched 2 to the Rules (see Appendix 2). The report therefore covers the same matters as those required in connection with the hearing of an adoption application (see p 71), except that the particulars required relating to the prospective adopter will not be applicable at the freeing stage (see para 4 of Sched 2).

The documents required to be attached are:

(*i*) the birth or adoption certificate (see above);

(*ii*) any document signifying agreement to adoption (FORM 2) if executed outside England and Wales before the proceedings (r 8(1)); and

(*iii*) if appropriate, a statement of facts supporting the applicant agency's request for a parent or guardian's agreement to be dispensed with by the court (r 7(1); see p 70).

Where the applicant agency has been informed by a person with whom the child has been placed for adoption that he wishes his identity to remain confidential, the statement of facts under r 7 must be framed in such a way as not to disclose the identity of that person (r 7(2)).

(3) *Parties*. The applicant in a freeing application is the adoption agency, and the respondents are the persons and bodies set out in r 4(2) as follows:

(*i*) each parent or guardian of the child;

(*ii*) any local authority having the powers and duties of a parent or guardian by virtue of s 10 of the CCA 1980;

(*iii*) any local authority in whom the parental rights and duties in respect of the child are vested, whether jointly or not, by virtue of s 3 of the CCA 1980;

(*iv*) any voluntary organisation in whom the parental rights and duties in respect of the child are vested, whether jointly or not, by virtue of s 64 of the CCA 1980;

(*v*) any local authority or voluntary organisation in whose care the child is under s 2 of the CCA 1980 or under or within the meaning of any other enactment;

(*vi*) any person liable by virtue of any order or agreement to contribute to the maintenance of the child; and

(*vii*) in the High Court only, the child.

The court may at any time direct that any other person or body, (except the child in a county court or domestic court) be made a respondent to the process (r 4(3)).

(4) *Reporting officer and guardian ad litem.* As in the case of an application for an adoption order the rules as to appointment operate as follows:

(*i*) *Reporting officer*: appointed by the registrar or clerk as soon as practicable after the originating process has been filed, or at any stage thereafter, if it appears that a parent or guardian of the child is willing to agree to the making of an adoption order and is in England and Wales (r 5(1)); and

(*ii*) *Guardian ad litem*: appointed as soon as practicable after the originating process has been filed or after receipt of the statement of facts supplied under r 7 (see above), if it appears that a parent or guardian of the child is *unwilling* to agree to adoption (r 6(1)); and may be appointed at any time where there are special circumstances and it appears to the court that the welfare of the child requires it (r 6(2)).

The selection and roles of these officers are generally as described in chap 9, the Official Solicitor being usually appointed, if he consents, in the High Court (see rr 5 and 6).

The reporting officer's duties in freeing cases are set out in r 5(4). In addition to those described in chap 9, a reporting officer must confirm that a parent or guardian has been given the opportunity of making a s 14(7) declaration (see above), and where it is proposed to free an illegitimate child for adoption and his father is not his guardian (see above), he must interview any person claiming to be the father in order to be able to advise the court whether that person intends to apply for custody of the child under s 9 of the GMA 1971 and, if so, the likely outcome of the application (see s 14(8) above). If there is more than one reporting

officer the registrar or clerk nominates one of them to interview the person.

The form of agreement for use in freeing cases is FORM 2 (see Appendix 1).

The guardian ad litem performs the same duties on a freeing application as on an adoption application (AR, r 6(6); MC(A)R, r 6(5)) (see chap 9).

On the appointment of a reporting officer or of a guardian ad litem, the registrar or clerk sends to the person appointed a copy of the application and of the documents attached; and if a statement of facts is lodged later in a dispensation case, a copy of it is sent to both the reporting officer and the guardian ad litem (r 5(1); r 6(1) and (2); r 7(4)).

Any report made to the court (under r 5 or r 6) by either the reporting officer or the guardian ad litem is confidential.

(5) *Further procedural matters on a freeing application.* Rules 7 (statement of facts in dispensation cases), 9 (notice of hearing (in FORM 3, see Appendix 1)), 10 (the hearing), and 11 (identity of child etc) correspond with the similarly headed rules (19, 21, 23 and 24) which detail the procedure on adoption applications, and whch are described in chaps 10 and 11. No serial numbers are assigned at the freeing stage, but the obligation to conduct the proceedings at the hearing so as not to reveal a person's identity applies where the court is informed by the applicant agency that the child has been placed with the person (whether alone or jointly with another) for adoption, and that he wishes his identity to remain confidential (r 10(3)).

(6) *Freeing order.* The prescribed form (AR, r 52(1); MC(A)R, r 31(1)) is FORM 12 scheduled to the AR, and FORM 10 scheduled to the MC(A)R (see Appendix 1). As noted above it vests the parental rights and duties relating to the child in the applicant agency, records facts that may be relevant in any future adoption application, and directs that the order shall be sufficient proof of those facts for the purposes of such an application. If a parent or guardian has made a s 14(7) declaration (see above), that fact is also recorded.

(7) *Freeing applications and duplication of proceedings.* Procedural complications and conflicts of jurisdiction may well arise when freeing applications (or adoption applications) are made in respect of children in care. Where a parent or guardian opposes the freeing application, or anticipates it being made, he may

himself apply to the Juvenile Court to try, for example, to revoke the care order in respect of the child, the parental rights resolution, or to obtain access under s 12C of the CCA 1980. As the freeing application is likely to be made in the county court or the High Court possible difficulties in respect of co-ordinating hearings with different parties, different waiting periods, different statutory approaches and appeal provisions, are obvious. In addition a different guardian ad litem may be appointed in each application. As yet no firm practice or principles have emerged but the following cases may provide some guidance. In *Southwark LBC* v *H* (1985) *The Times*, 6 April (DC), the view was expressed obiter that, in a case where there was an access application by the natural mother to the juvenile court and an adoption application by foster parents, the proper approach was to decide first whether the natural mother should have access. That was the approach approved by the Court of Appeal in *In Re M*, 1984, 11 October, unreported.

In *R* v *Slough Justices, ex parte B* (1984) *The Times*, 15 December (DC), a boy aged two was in care under s 1 of the CYPA 1969. The local authority had written to the natural parents stopping access and stating that it was their intention to apply to the High Court for a freeing order under s 14, CA 1975. The parents applied to the Juvenile Court under s 12C of the CCA 1980 for access to their child and, on the same date, the local authority put in their freeing application to the High Court. The justices, on the local authority's application to them for the access summons to be adjourned generally, granted it so that the High Court freeing application could be heard first. The parents sought judicial review of the justices' decision. Wood J held that judicial review was not the appropriate course; the parents should appeal the justices' decision to the Divisional Court of the Family Division, so that both the appeal and the freeing application would be in the control of the High Court.

In *R* v *Tower Hamlets Juvenile Court, ex parte London Borough of Tower Hamlets* [1984] FLR 907 (DC), a child aged eight was in care under s 1 of the CYPA 1969. The child's foster parents began *adoption* proceedings in the High Court. The natural parents then began wardship proceedings, but the court refused to exercise the jurisdiction on the principles laid down in *A* v *Liverpool CC* [1982] AC 363. The natural parents then applied to revoke the care order under s 21 of the 1969 Act in the juvenile court. The local authority's application to adjourn the care

proceedings, pending the outcome of the adoption application in the High Court, was refused by the justices, who decided to proceed with the hearing because if they were to await the outcome of the adoption application, and no adoption order was made, there would be further delay in deciding the child's future.

The local authority were granted an order of certiorari to quash the magistrates' decision. The juvenile court hearing was halted and the adoption application given priority. Bush J said that the powers of the High Court on the adoption application were very wide indeed: either the court would order adoption or it would, in its general jurisdiction, make arrangements for the child's future. The court's duties in adoption proceedings were wholly inconsistent with the purported exercise of jurisdiction in the care proceedings. Even if the justices, for example, discharged the care order, the child could not be returned to the parents because s 34A of the AA 1958 (see p 85) prohibited the removal of the child from the adoption applicants without the leave of the High Court. It was also a factor to be taken into account that the Official Solicitor, as guardian ad litem in the adoption application, had expressed the view that the adoption proceedings should have priority.

See also *Re J (a Minor)* (1984) Adoption and Fostering 56, CA.

For the local authority, wardship may provide the way out of the procedural difficulties.

(b) *Application to revoke a freeing order*

The application is made in FORM 4, scheduled to the respective rules (see Appendix 1). As noted above the application is made to the court which made the freeing order and is made on the ground that the parent or guardian wishes to resume the parental rights or duties (see s 16(1), CA 1975).

Rule 12(2) requires that notice of the proceedings shall be served on:

(*i*) all parties, *except* the authorities and organisations listed at (3)(*ii*) to (*v*), inclusive, on p 110, and

(*ii*) any adoption agency in which the parental rights and duties relating to the child are vested by virtue of s 23 of the CA 1975 (see above).

A guardian ad litem for the child must be appointed by the registrar or clerk as soon as practicable after receipt of the application, and must be sent a copy of the application and any documents attached to it (r 12(3)). He has similar duties to those he has on a freeing application (see r 12(4)).

(c) *Application for transfer of parental rights and duties between adoption agencies*

An application under s 23 of the CA 1975 (see above) is made in FORM 5 (see Appendix 1).

In the High Court or county court the application is to be made in the freeing proceedings (AR, r 13).

In a domestic court, it is made to a court acting for the area within which the child is at the date of the application (MC(A)R, r 13).

Notice of any order made under s 23 must be sent by the court to the court which made the freeing order under s 14 of the CA 1975 (if a different court), and to any former parent (see s 15, and above) of the child (r 13(2)).

Chapter 21

Adoption Orders, Freeing Orders, and Wardship

ADOPTION ORDERS, AND WARDSHIP

Lord MacDermott in *J* v *C* [1970] Act 668, at p 714, said that care and control orders in wardship and adoption proceedings are so different in concept, nature and legal consequences that one cannot validly argue from either of these jurisdictions to the other. Lord Upjohn in the same case, at p 719, said:

> An adoption order, if made, is the antithesis of an order made in wardship proceedings. In the former case the rights and obligations of the true parents in relation to the infant are extinguished and the adopted child stands in relation to the adopter exclusively in the position of a child born to the adopter in wedlock.

Lord Upjohn went on to emphasise that wardship orders could be reviewed at any time and did not sever the infant's ties with his parents.

The fundamental difference between wardship and adoption is important because it is sometimes submitted that in effect an order in wardship for care and control, for example, to foster parents with a direction that the minor should spend his childhood with them, provides as much security as an adoption order. This it is suggested is not so (see, for example, *In re F* [1982] 1 WLR 102, and *In re B(MF)* [1972] 1 WLR 102, at p 104). The fact that the wardship order does not sever the infant's ties with its natural parents, and can be reviewed at any time, is bound to lead to unease in the minds of the foster parents or others looking after the child. If an application is made to review the order, even if it is unlikely to be successful, it means that the foster parents, for example, will have to be involved in further proceedings with the

116

anxiety and uncertainty that goes with them. In addition they may well have the legal expenses to bear.

Adoption and wardship may of course interact favourably. Adoption may well be the appropriate long-term plan for a ward. Increasingly local authorities are putting forward adoption as their plan for a ward who has been with foster parents who wish to continue caring for the child. Alternatively, the local authority may ask the court for leave to place the child for adoption so that they can find adoptive parents.

Wardship has a further role to play in respect of adoption in that it can be used within certain limits to deal with the situation where an adoption application fails, or after an adoption order has been made and either something appears to have gone wrong with the placement or its security is otherwise threatened. For the interaction of freeing for adoption and wardship, see p 126.

1 Adopting a ward

In *Re CB (Wardship: Local Authority)* [1981] 1 WLR 379, at p 387 (CA), Ormrod LJ re-affirmed that it is for the court to decide all the serious issues relating to the ward. Any question of, for example, placing the ward for adoption or commencing adoption proceedings is within this principle. Once a child is a ward of court no important step in the child's life may be taken without the court's approval (see *Re S (Infants)* [1967] 1 WLR 396).

In *Re F (Wardship: Adoption)* [1984] FLR 60 (CA), it was stated that before placing a ward with long-term foster parents with a view to adoption, the local authority must obtain the leave of the wardship judge so to prepare and place the child. The Court of Appeal approved the decision of Hollings J in *Re G (Wardship: Adoption)* [1981] 2 FLR 382, and disapproved the case of *Re K (Application in Wardship)* [1981] 2 FLR 381. In *Re G*, Hollings J dealt with the effect of an application to place a ward for adoption. He considered that, in the wardship jurisdiction, the court was not making any decision in possible future adoption proceedings if the court took the view that it was in the ward's interests to be in the care of a local authority and to direct that the local authority could prepare the ward for adoption, and that the ward could be placed with prospective adopters. By such a direction the court was assisting the adoptive process and was not prejudging the adoption matter. It would be for the trial judge in

any future adoption proceedings to decide whether a particular child should be adopted.

In *Re W (Wardship: Adoption)* [1982] 3 FLR 356, the Court of Appeal emphasised that where, during wardship proceedings, local authorities are seeking orders for leave to place a ward with a view to adoption, with or without the further order that there should be no access, then notice should be given in good time to the natural parents or their solicitors so that the case may be prepared accordingly by them.

In *F v S (Adoption: Ward)* [1973] Fam 203 (CA), it was decided that the leave of the court was required to commence proceedings for the adoption of a ward of court. The test to be applied by the court in deciding whether to give leave was whether an application for adoption might reasonably succeed: it was not whether adoption was in the best interests of the child, because that was the very issue to be decided in the proceedings (per Orr LJ at p 208). This decision may be queried in the future as a result of s 3 of the CA 1975 which provides that, 'in reaching any decision relating to the adoption of a child, a court . . . shall have regard to all the circumstances, first consideration being given to the need to safeguard and promote the welfare of the child throughout his childhood'. The application of the section, however, is as yet uncertain, particularly in respect of which matters are 'decisions relating to adoption' (see *Re P* [1977] Fam 25, and Lord Simon in *Re D* [1977] AC 602, at 641). *F v S* was referred to and re-affirmed without comment in the Court of Appeal in *Re F (Wardship: Adoption)* [1984] FLR 60. The requirement to seek leave is procedural, does not go to jurisdiction and can be dispensed with (see *Re H* (1981) Fam Law 146, and also RSC, Ord 90, r 4A which allows for an application to be made ex parte to a registrar).

The question of the confidentiality of wardship proceedings must be carefully considered if the court gives leave to commence adoption proceedings. Butler-Sloss J in *In re C (Minors)* (1984) *The Times*, 19 June, held that it was a serious breach of the confidentiality of wardship proceedings to show documents relating to those proceedings to a person who was not a party to the suit, without the leave of the court. A local authority, for example, must therefore obtain leave before showing or passing on any of the wardship documents relating to the proceedings to other agencies or to the prospective adopters or their solicitors if they were not parties to the wardship. The principle also applies

to the oral publication of information relating to the wardship proceedings (see s 12 of the Administration of Justice Act 1960, and *Re F (orse A) (A Minor) (Publication of Information)* [1977] Fam 58 (CA)). The question of confidentiality is a matter of great importance in respect of both wardship and adoption and it is suggested that practitioners should be most alert to its application and implications (see chap 1).

If leave is given to commence adoption proceedings in respect of a ward where the child is already with the prospective adopters who, for example, have been the foster parents for some time, then the wardship and the adoption proceedings should be heard together in the High Court and brought on as quickly as possible. At the hearing the judge will then consider whether or not the adoption order should be made. If the adoption application fails, he will go on to consider what order to make in the wardship case. The burden of proof is on the applicant for the adoption order, and he will open the proceedings and call his evidence in the normal way.

When an adoption order is made the child will usually be dewarded. The court, however, sometimes continues the wardship. This may occur, for example, if the natural parents are aware of the identities of the adoptive parents and know their address, or can easily discover it, and there is a real likelihood that difficulties may arise in the future because of this knowledge. The judge will usually give a direction that the adoptive parents need not come back to court for the normal reasons, such as when an important step in the ward's life is about to be taken, but only if they require the assistance of the court, for example by way of injunctive relief, in the future. It will be a wardship for the sole purpose of protecting the ward and the adoptive parents from the possible future actions of the natural parents. The continuation of the wardship proceedings in theory allows the natural parents to make applications to the court. It would be wise for the adoptive parents to seek an order that the natural parents or either of them make no application in the wardship proceedings *without the leave of the court*, and that the adoptive parents should not be required to file evidence or take any part in such application unless so directed by the judge or unless they so desire. There is no jurisdiction in the court, save under the procedure for dealing with vexatious litigants, to make an order that no application be made nor any step taken in the proceedings (see *Re P (Wardship: Prohibition on Applications)* [1982] 3 FLR 420 (CA)).

In *Re W (A Minor)* (1984) 4 Adoption and Fostering 56 (CA) 9 July, it was said that the court had to be careful not to permit the wardship process to be used as the early or masked start of adoption proceedings. It would be an abuse of the wardship process if orders were obtained by local authorities or other agencies denying all access to the natural parent so as to distort the position when the question of unreasonbly withholding agreement came to be considered in adoption. If there was a delay in, for example foster parents, bringing adoption proceedings so that the natural parent's position might be prejudiced, the natural parent should apply for access to the wardship judge.

In *Re E (A Minor) (Wardship: Court's Duty)* [1984] FLR 457, the House of Lords said that the court must consider a course of action even if it had not been advocated by the parties. The choice in the case was not only adoption or care and control to the father: access should be tried.

2 Warding an adopted child

The making of an adoption order does not preclude the child being warded subsequently.

In *Re O (A Minor)* [1978] Fam 196, CA, the natural mother of a boy aged twelve warded him two years after the making of an adoption order in respect of him. The adoption order in favour of the adoptive father was made with the agreement of both natural parents. The natural mother lived with the boy and the adoptive father, after obtaining a legal separation from the natural father, both before and after the adoption. The natural father died in 1974, the same year that the adoption order was made. The mother went abroad in 1976 for medical treatment. When she returned the adoptive father would not let her contact the child. The mother sought care and control in the wardship proceedings.

The Court of Appeal held that, in an application by a natural parent against an adoptive parent, the test should be whether or not it is in the best interests of the child that the wardship should be carried through to its conclusion after a full investigation or whether, on the facts as they are put before the court on both sides and by the guardian ad litem, the court can see that it is not in the interests of the child to pursue the wardship proceedings further. In a normal adoption situation where the natural parents have parted with the child and have not seen the child at all and

the adoptive parents have assumed the parental role, a natural parent would have to make out an extremely strong prima facie case to justify the wardship proceeding further (per Ormrod LJ at p 208). The Court of Appeal decided that the case before them was unprecedented and that as the intention of the adoptive father and the mother was that the mother should continue to care for the child after the adoption, there was an overwhelming case for investigating the mother's allegations in full and therefore continuing the wardship.

At first instance Latey J gave examples of situations where the intervention of the court might be justified:

(a) where there is a strong prima facie case of ill-treatment or serious neglect of a child by an adoptive parent; or

(b) where the adoptive parent:

(i) has been sentenced to a long term of imprisonment; or

(ii) is incapacitated by chronic illness from caring for the child; or

(iii) has died.

Apart from the case where the natural parent or parents ward the child, the fact of a child being an adopted child will not be of any particular significance one way or the other in respect of the wardship.

In *Re J (Adoption Order: Conditions)* [1973] Fam 106, at p 116, Rees J, when considering how any terms and conditions attached to an adoption order (now pursuant to s 8(7) of the CA 1975) could be enforced, or any undertakings given by the adopters, suggested that the child could be warded and directions sought from the court as to compliance with the relevant terms, conditions or undertakings. An alternative method was to seek an undertaking from the adopter upon the making of the adoption order to comply with the condition imposed. The undertaking, if drafted with care and precision, might be enforced by appropriate committal proceedings. Rees J appeared to incline towards the use of wardship as being the more advantageous method of enforcement. See also *Re G (TJ) (An Infant)* [1963] 2 QB 73.

At some point in time after the adoption order has been made the adoptive parents may wish to invoke the protective jurisdiction of the wardship court if their whereabouts are, for example, discovered by the natural parents and they wish to apply for injunctive or other relief from the court. *Re P (Wardship: Prohibition on Applications)* [1982] 3 FLR 420 (CA) on p 119 should be noted, as the same considerations apply in principle whether or

not the wardship is continued on the making of the adoption order or brought into existence later. It may indeed be a second wardship as the first wardship may have been discharged on the making of the adoption order.

3 Warding a child after the failure of an adoption application

An adoption application may well fail because adoption is not in the best interests of the child. Alternatively, this first test may be successfully passed but the application may fail because the court is not prepared to dispense with the agreement of the parent or guardian under s 12 of the CA 1975 (for example under s 12(2)(*b*), if the agreement is not being withheld unreasonably). The applicants may then face the prospect of having to hand the child over either immediately or within a few weeks of the hearing, depending upon who actually arranged the adoption (see s 35, AA 1958, and see chap 4). The argument may well be open to them on the facts that it is in the child's best interests for them to retain care. This will not assist them on appeal if the application failed through the absence of the parent or guardian's agreement. It may, however, avail the applicants if they make the child a ward of court. The precise situations in which the court will exercise the wardship jurisdiction are not clear and the limits have yet to be worked out.

In *Re E (An Infant)* [1964] 1 WLR 51, a decision at first instance, provides an example of the successful use of wardship by a couple whose adoption application had failed. The mother of a two-month-old illegitimate baby handed him over for adoption. The mother, who was a Roman Catholic, changed her mind about adoption when she discovered that the proposed adoptive parents were not Roman Catholics. Subsequently the adoption application failed because the judge decided that the mother's agreement was not being withheld unreasonably. The Court of Appeal refused the prospective adoptive parents leave to appeal and they warded the child and asked that they be granted care and control. The mother, who did not want the child herself, proposed that he should be placed in a Roman Catholic institution and then with a Roman Catholic family for adoption. It was argued on her behalf that the use of the wardship jurisdiction was an abuse of the process of the court, and that the wardship summons should be dismissed because practically the same result as in the adoption proceedings was being sought. Wilberforce J

rejected the mother's argument and agreed to continue the wardship in the interests of the child and to give care and control to the proposed adoptive parents on their undertaking to ensure that the child was brought up in the Roman Catholic faith. In wardship the child's welfare was the first and paramount consideration.

The importance of the prospective adoptive parents pursuing the relevant appeal procedures is shown by the case of *Re S (A Minor)* (1978) 122 SJ 759. After the refusal of her adoption application on the ground that the natural mother was not withholding her agreement unreasonably, a foster mother warded the child, a girl aged twenty-two months. Dunn J said that both parties accepted that the court had jurisdiction. The issue was whether the court should exercise the jurisdiction and hear the merits. Dunn J held that it was an attempt to appeal the decision of the lower court. The foster mother had not appealed the circuit judge's decision dismissing her adoption application, and the High Court should not accept jurisdiction unless there were special or convincing reasons for doing so.

The further case of *Re C (MA) (An Infant)* [1966] 1 WLR 646 should be noted. After the failure of an adoption application, a High Court Judge directed that the child be warded so that the unsuccessful adoption applicants would not have to hand over the child pending an appeal.

One side effect of the warding of a child by unsuccessful adoption applicants is that they will probably retain possession of the child by means of an interim care and control order until the full wardship hearing and will therefore have a stronger argument for the child not to be moved.

Overall it would seem that the court will not allow the wardship jurisdiction to be used unless there is something special or unusual about the case. Wardship cannot be invoked simply to re-litigate a failed adoption application. It may well be prudent to exhaust the appeal procedures arising out of the adoption application before attempting to use wardship. In this connection, however, wardship, if it is needed, would appear in a limited way to be available earlier, simply to preserve the status quo in respect of the child pending the appeal. Whether or not the court would be prepared to continue the wardship and hear the merits of the case after the appeal has failed, would perhaps depend upon whether special or unusual reasons were then forthcoming.

4 Using wardship to oppose an adoption application

Wardship is of particular value to those who are not the parents or guardians of a child. Grandparents and aunts and uncles, for example, may be heard in an adoption application if the court so directs, but they will have no means in the proceedings of putting forward a positive case on their own behalf. Commencing wardship proceedings will allow them not only to take part in opposing the adoption application but also the means to attempt to obtain the care and control of the child.

Wardship may also be used as a tactical measure in circumstances where, for instance, a relation of the child hears of a forthcoming adoption application and wards the child. The prospective adopters, unless the wardship is immediately discharged, will have to obtain the leave of the court to commence adoption proceedings (see *F* v *S* [1973] Fam 203 (CA) considered above). It appears now that the use of wardship in order purely to stifle or delay an adoption application (see eg *Re F* [1970] 1 WLR 192 (CA)) will not be as effective as formerly. The courts are now more accustomed to hearing joint wardship and adoption proceedings and the introduction of wardship may well not significantly delay the hearing, whilst providing a wide range of orders which could well work against those opposing the adoption eventually, for example, by providing the means for the unsuccessful adoption applicant to retain care and control of the child. If the adoption application was made initially in a magistrates' court or county court it is most likely that arrangements will be made for it to proceed in the High Court and be joined with the wardship proceedings.

5 Private placements for adoption

Section 29(1) of the AA 1958, as amended, prohibits a person other than an approved adoption society or local authority from making arrangements for the adoption of a child or placing a child for adoption unless:

(*a*) the proposed adopter is a relative (see s 57(1) of the Act) or

(*b*) he is acting in pursuance of a High Court order (see p 25).

Section 29(3)(*b*) makes a contravention of s 29(1) a summary offence. In addition, a person who receives a child placed with

him in contravention of (s 29(1) is guilty of a summary offence (s 29(3)(*c*)).

In *Re S (A Minor)* (1984) *The Times*, 2 November (CA), it was held that where there had been a breach of s 29 of the AA 1958 a county court had no jurisdiction to hear an application for an adoption order, and such applications *must* be heard by the Family Division of the High Court. The applicant may then presumably receive dispensation from the effects of s 29, by way of a High Court order.

In the earlier case of *Re K (A Minor) (Adoption and Wardship)* (1983) 13 Fam Law 146, an application for adoption had already been made to a county court. The judge then took the view that the applicants were in breach of s 29 and adjourned their application generally as he considered that the placement was unlawful and a High Court order should be sought. The child was warded and in the High Court the applicants were granted care and control, their arrangements were authorised for the purposes of s 29, and they were granted leave to commence adoption proceedings in the High Court. Subsequently an adoption order was made.

It may well be that one solution to the procedural aspect, if a breach of s 29 comes to light during the course of an application to the county court, is for the case to be entirely transferred to the High Court (particularly when s 39 of the Matrimonial and Family Proceedings Act 1984 comes into force, see p 55). Wardship proceedings may provide an alternative method and one that may be quicker and more flexible. If the breach comes to light in the domestic court there is as yet no means of transferring the application to the High Court. Either wardship would have to be used or the adoption application begun again in the High Court.

6 Removal from the jurisdiction for adoption

In *Re M (An Infant) (Adoption: Child's Removal from Jurisdiction)* [1973] Fam 66, an illegitimate girl aged two, a British subject, lived with foster parents in Birmingham and was in the care of the local authority. A married couple, resident and domiciled in Denmark, wanted to adopt her. They wished to take her to Denmark for six months in order to satisfy one of the adoption requirements in respect of continuous care and possession. They then intended to return with the child to England and apply for a provisional adoption order (see now s 25, CA 1975). Section 52

of the AA 1958 imposed an absolute prohibition upon the removal of a child who is a British subject out of Great Britain by a person who is not a parent, guardian or relative with a view to adoption, except under the (then available) authority of a provisional adoption order. The couple warded the child and sought an order allowing them to remove her out of the jurisdiction. Brandon J held that the court did not have jurisdiction to make the order. The expression in s 52 'with a view to adoption' covered the case where, although immediate adoption was not the purpose of the removal, it would be a step in a larger process of which adoption was the ultimate purpose. It was immaterial that the child was a ward of court, what was planned was caught by the absolute prohibition imposed by the statute.

7 Access conditions

For the use of wardship in enforcing terms or conditions, see p 83.

8 Duplication of proceedings

See the discussion on p 112 concerning *freeing applications* and children in care which is equally relevant to the situation where an adoption application is made. Wardship proceedings may provide for the local authority a means of avoiding the procedural complexities.

9 Unlawful removal of child

See p 89, and chap 13 generally.

FREEING FOR ADOPTION AND WARDSHIP

The new freeing procedure (see chap 20) will clearly interact on occasions with wardship. In the absence of any established practice or authority, the following is necessarily somewhat speculative.

1 Freeing a ward for adoption

It is suggested that the leave of the court will be required before commencing an application for a freeing order under s 14 of the

CA 1975 (see *In re CB* [1981] 1 WLR 379 (see p 117), and by analogy *F v S* (*Adoption: Ward*) [1973] Fam 203 (see p 118)). The test to be applied by the court in deciding whether to grant leave will presumably be the same as that evolved in *F v S*: is there a reasonable chance of the application succeeding? It is not whether a freeing order is in the best interests of the ward. See further the matters referred to on p 118.

2 Warding a child free for adoption but unadopted

On the making of an order freeing the child for adoption the parental rights and duties will vest in the adoption agency (s 14(6), CA 1975). It is suggested that prima facie the principle in the House of Lords decision of *A v Liverpool CC* [1982] AC 363 will apply: that the wardship jurisdiction must not be exercised in order to review the day-to-day administration by local authorities regarding the welfare of children in their care.

A person (eg a natural parent) may nevertheless be able to persuade the court to exercise the wardship jurisdiction by bringing his case within the principles set out in the judgment of Lord Greene MR in *Associated Provincial Picture Houses v Wednesbury Corp* [1948] 1 KB 223, at 228 and 229 (ie where the agency has reached a decision by taking into account matters that ought not to have been taken into account, or where it has disregarded matters that should have been taken into account, or where it has reached a decision which no reasonable agency could reach). In addition, the jurisdiction will be exercised if impropriety or breach of statutory duty is shown, or there is something exceptional or something really unusual about the case which necessitates the intervention of the High Court (see *M v Humberside CC* [1979] Fam 114), or if the local authority lacks the power to achieve a certain result which is in the interests of the child.

If, in particular, a natural parent or guardian has signed a s 14(7) declaration that he prefers not to be involved in future questions concerning the adoption of the child (see p 106), he will not be entitled to progress reports under s 15 or to apply to revoke the freeing order under s 16 (see p 107). His only means of being heard if, for example, an exceptional or really unusual situation arises relevant to the child's interests, would seem to be by way of wardship proceedings. Similarly, a parent who has not signed a s 14(7) declaration may have to resort to wardship proceedings if he wishes to be heard by the court at a time prior to the

conditions being fulfilled for him to apply to revoke the order (see p 107, and s 16(1), CA 1975). If any degree of urgency is involved, wardship would in any event appear to be the appropriate remedy.

Wardship proceedings provide a possible means of intervention for a relative (eg a grandparent) who wants to take over the care of the child.

3 Further uses of wardship

(a) Wardship after the failure of a freeing application

Unless there is something exceptional or really unusual about the case, it is submitted, that the court will not allow the jurisdiction to be used to re-litigate a failed freeing application. The appeal procedure, in particular, should first be exhausted (see *Re S (A Minor)* (1978) 122 SJ 759). If a situation arose where it was necessary to preserve the status quo pending appeal, then it would appear that a stay could be granted by the court, as opposed to the position after the failure of an adoption application which has been considered above. There is no equivalent provision to s 35 of the AA 1958 (return of children) in respect of freeing applications. There may be cases, however, in the High Court where the court itself considers it should continue to be involved with the child's future and uses wardship as a means of remaining so.

(b) Wardship after the success of a revocation application

The agency may on general principles be able to rely upon wardship if an exceptional or really unusual situation arose. The appeal procedure, it is suggested, should be used initially. There seems to be no reason why the status quo pending an appeal should not be preserved by a stay granted by the court. It could be argued by the adoption agency, after the 'former parent' has successfully revoked the freeing order, that the test which has been applied by the court only gave 'first consideration' to the welfare of the child (s 3, CA 1975), whereas in wardship the welfare of the child is the 'first and paramount' consideration (s 1, GMA 1971), and so the wardship jurisdiction should be exercised in order to safeguard the child fully (see *Herts CC v A* (1981) *The Times*, 15 December).

(c) Using wardship to oppose a freeing application

Wardship, in exceptional circumstances, may provide the means by which, for example a grandparent, or an aunt or uncle, could

put forward a positive case and seek care and control of the child. If the freeing application was anticipated and the child warded *before* the freeing application was actually made, so long as the wardship was continued the agency would need to obtain the leave of the court before proceeding with their application (see above).

(d) Using wardship to avoid a duplication of proceedings

See p 112, for the circumstances in which a local authority may wish to avoid the procedural complexities by having all the issues ventilated in the High Court, regarding freeing, access and care orders.

(e) Wardship and the unlawful removal of the child

Wardship proceedings may be appropriate in circumstances in which s 34(2) of the AA 1958 does not restrict the removal of the child from the person with whom the child has his home whilst a freeing application is pending (see chap 13).

For wardship generally, see Allan Levy, *Wardship Proceedings*, 1st ed (Oyez Longman 1982).

Chapter 22

Adoption and Custodianship

The provisions regarding custodianship, contained in Part II of the CA 1975 (ss 33–46) will come into force on 1 December 1985. They will meet the difficulty that a non-parent of a child has in initiating proceedings for legal status, other than wardship or adoption applications. The custodianship order, which vests legal custody (see below) of the child in the custodian, is meant primarily for step-parents, relatives, and long-term foster parents. The mother or father of a child is not qualified to make an application (CA 1975, s 33(4)). A custodianship order, unlike an adoption order, will *not* destroy the legal ties between the natural parents and the child. The court (the High Court, a county court or a magistrates' court) may subsequently revoke or vary a custodianship order. In particular circumstances (see under 2 below) an adoption application may result in an order, not for adoption, but for custodianship.

Practitioners will, of course, have to consider carefully, particularly when acting for stepparents, relatives (defined below), and long-term foster parents, whether (if they are qualified to apply) a custodianship application is, in the circumstances, more appropriate than an adoption application. In *Re M (A Child)* (1984), 11 October (unreported) (CA) Ormrod LJ said, 'that a custodianship application should be used in preference to an adoption application in long-term fostering cases, unless the case for dispensing with parental agreement in adoption proceedings is strong, which means cases where the future of the child lies, so far as can be sensibly foreseen, with the foster parents and access is no more than a remote possibility'.

The custodianship provisions are referred to as amended by the DPMCA 1978 and Hassassa 1983.

1 Custodianship provisions: a summary

(a) *Persons qualified to apply*

Section 33(3) of the CA 1975 provides that the following persons are qualified to apply for an order:

(a) a relative or stepparent of the child:
  - (i) who applies with the consent of a person having legal custody of the child, and
  - (ii) with whom the child has had his home for the three months preceding the making of the application;
(b) any person:
  - (i) who applies with the consent of a person having legal custody of the child, and
  - (ii) with whom the child has had his home for a period or periods before the making of the application which amount to at least twelve months and include the three months preceding the making of the application;
(c) any person with whom the child has had his home for a period or periods before the making of the application which amount to at least three years and include the three months preceding the making of the application.

If no person has legal custody or the applicant himself has legal custody, or the person with legal custody cannot be found, then paras (a) and (b) of subs (3) apply with the omission of subpara (i) (CA 1975, s 33(6)).

A stepparent of the child is not qualified if the child was named in an order under para (b) or (c) of s 41(1) of the Matrimonial Causes Act 1973 (arrangements for welfare of children of the family in divorce or nullity proceedings) (ibid, s 33(5)).

Section 33(5), however, will not apply:

(i) if the parent other than the one the stepparent married is dead or cannot be found, or
(ii) if the order referred to in s 33(5) was made under s 41(1)(c) of the 1973 Act and it has since been determined that the child was not a child of the family to whom that section applied (s 33(8)).

A 'relative', in relation to a child, means a grandparent, brother, sister, uncle or aunt, whether of the full blood or half blood or by affinity and includes, where the child is illegitimate, the father of the child and any person who would be a relative to the child within the meaning of this definition if the child were the legitimate child of his mother and father (CA 1975, s 107(1), incorporating s 57(1) of the AA 1958). It is not clear, however, whether

a putative father can apply for an order or whether he is prohibited as 'the father' by s 33(4) (see above).

'Legal custody' means, as respects a child, so much of the parental rights and duties as relate to the *person* of the child (including the place and manner in which his time is spent; but a person shall not by virtue of having legal custody of a child be entitled to effect or arrange for his emigration from the UK unless he is a parent or guardian of the child) (CA 1975, s 86).

Accordingly, since the parental rights and duties are expressed as relating to the person of the child the custodian will have no right:

(*i*) to the administration of the child's property;
(*ii*) to change the child's name;
(*iii*) to change the child's religion;
(*iv*) to agree or withhold agreement to adoption.

In determining whether the child has had his home with the applicant for the specified period, absence of the child at a hospital or boarding school and any other temporary absence is disregarded. The applicant must have had actual custody of the child (CA 1975, s 87(3)). Actual custody means 'actual possession' of the child, whether or not that possession is shared with one or more other persons (s 87(1)).

More than one person may have legal custody of the child; only one of the persons needs to consent for the purposes of s 33(3)(*a*) and (*b*) referred to above.

(*b*) *Procedure*

Applications, as already noted, may be made to a magistrates' court, a county court or the High Court (CA 1975, ss 33(1), 100, and 107(1)). Within 7 days following the application, the applicant must give notice to the local authority in whose area the child resides (s 40(1)). The local authority must then arrange for one of its officers to make a report to the court (s 40(2)). A court dealing with an application can also request a report from a local authority or a probation officer (s 39(1)).

(*c*) *Powers*

The court may:

(1) Make orders regarding access and maintenance (see ss 34, 34A, and 34B);
(2) Commit the child to the care of a local authority, or make a supervision order (ss 34(5), and 36);

(3) Rule on disputes between joint custodians as to a parental right or duty (s 38);

(4) Restrict, while an application is pending, the removal of a child where the applicant has provided his home for three years (s 41);

(5) Order a person to return a child removed in breach of s 41 (s 42);

(6) Restrict the removal of a child from England and Wales (s 43A);

(7) Treat the following applications, in certain circumstances, as if the application were made for a custodianship order:

  (*i*) an application for an *adoption order* (see below) (see s 37(1), and (2));

  (*ii*) an application under s 9 of the GMA 1971 by a father or mother (see s 37(3));

  (*iii*) an application by a party to the marriage under ss 2, 6 or 7 of the DPMCA 1978 (see s 8(3) of the 1978 Act).

(*d*) *Welfare principle*

In deciding applications for custodianship orders, the court must regard the welfare of the child as the first and paramount consideration (GMA 1971, s 1, declared to apply 'for the avoidance of doubt' by s 33(9) of the CA 1975).

2 Custodianship order on application for adoption

(*a*) *CA 1975, s 37(1): relatives and stepparents*

Where on an application for an adoption order by a *relative* of the child or by *the husband or wife of the mother or father of the child (the stepparent)*, whether alone or jointly with his or her spouse, the requirements of s 12 of the CA 1975 are satisfied (child free for adoption, or there is agreement by the parent or guardian, or it has been dispensed with), see chap 6; but, nevertheless, the court is satisfied that:

  (*i*) the child's welfare would not be better safeguarded and promoted by the making of an adoption order in favour of the applicant, than it would by the making of a custodianship order in his favour, and

  (*ii*) that it would be appropriate to make a custodianship order in the applicant's favour,

the court must direct the application to be treated as a custodian-

ship application under s 33 (CA 1975, s 37(1)). An applicant for adoption is to be treated in these circumstances as if qualified to apply for a custodianship order even if he would not be qualified under the terms of s 33(3) (s 37(4)).

If, however, the application was made jointly by the father or mother of the child and his or her spouse, the court must direct the application to be treated as if made by the father's wife or the mother's husband alone (s 37(1)).

Section 37(1), however, does not apply to an application made by a stepparent, whether alone or jointly with another person, in any case where the stepparent is *not* qualified to apply for a custodianship order, as noted above, because in proceedings for divorce or nullity of marriage the child was named in an order made under paragraph (*b*) or (*c*) of s 41(1) of the Matrimonial Causes Act 1973 (arrangements for welfare of children) (ss 37(5), and 33(5) . The stepparent, however, will be qualified if:

(*i*) the child's parent, other than the one the stepparent married, is dead or cannot be found; or

(*ii*) the order was under para (*c*) of s 41(1) of the 1973 Act and it was subsequently determined that the child was not a child of the family to whom s 41 applied (CA 1975, s 33(8)).

In the situation where the stepfather is *not* qualified, the adoption application will be dismissed if a custody order is better than an adoption order (see p 16, and ss 10(3), and 11(4) of the CA 1975) and, of course, a custodianship order cannot be made.

Section 37(1) does not apply to an adoption application made by the child's mother or father alone (see p 15, and s 37(6)).

As noted above, s 37(1) employs different wording from that in ss 10(3), and 11(4). The latter sections require a custody order to be better than an adoption order before the adoption application must be refused. Section 37(1), however, appears to direct the matter to be dealt with by way of custodianship if it could be as well dealt with in that way as by making an adoption order.

(*b*) *CA 1975, s 37(2): person other than relative or stepparent*

Where on an application for an adoption order made:

(i) by a person who is *neither* a relative of the child nor the husband or wife of the mother or father of the child; or

(*ii*) by a married couple *neither* of whom is a relative of the child or the husband or wife of the mother or father of the child,

the requirements of s 12 of the CA 1975 (see above) are satisfied,

but the court is of the opinion that it would be *more appropriate* to make a custodianship order in favour of the applicant, it may direct the application to be treated as if it had been made by the applicant under s 33 (s 37(2)).

It will be noted that the test is different from that in s 37(1).

An applicant for adoption, where necessary, will be treated as if qualified to apply for a custodianship order even if he would not be qualified under the terms of s 33(3) (s 37(4)).

Section 37(2) does not apply to an application for an adoption order made by the child's mother or father alone (s 37(6)).

Chapter 23

Adoption and the European Convention on Human Rights

The UK, one of the original signatories of the European Convention on Human Rights, was the first party to ratify it on 8 March 1951. Subsequently twenty other states have ratified it. It came into operation in September 1953. It was not until 1966, however, that the UK recognised the right of individual petition under Art 25 to the European Commission of Human Rights in Strasbourg. The Convention itself establishes an international protection machinery to examine specific applications alleging violations of the rights which it protects. The main rights protected include the right to life, the right to liberty and security of person, the right to fair administration of justice, and respect for private and family life, home and correspondence. Article 8, dealing with family life, has been central to the applications which have been made to Strasbourg in respect of children's cases. (For a succinct explanation by a member of the European Commission's Secretariat of the protection machinery, its procedure, and the powers of the bodies administering and adjudicating on the Convention, see p 2360 of the *Law Society's Gazette* of 28 September 1983).

Article 8 provides that:

(1) Everyone has the right to respect for his private and family life, his home and his correspondence.

(2) There shall be no interference by a public authority with the exercise of this right except such as is in accordance with the law and is necessary in a democratic society in the interests of national security, public safety or the economic well-being of the country, for the prevention of disorder or crime, for the protection of health or morals, or for the protection of the rights and freedoms of others.

It is important to note that whilst the Convention provides for compensation and costs to be awarded where appropriate (see

Art 50), the Commission, the Council of Ministers, or the Court cannot, for instance, order the return of a child to his natural parents. It has been said that Art 8 gives protection against unjustified interference with family life by public authorities, but does *not* oblige the state to take positive action to restore family life when it has been damaged through the actions of the persons concerned (see *Application no 5416/72* v *Austria* 46 Coll 88, and *Application no 6577/74* v *Federal Republic of Germany* 1 D, and R 91).

Applications to Strasbourg or the threat of them appear, however, to have had in some cases an influence on legislation in the child care field in the UK, eg regarding the Secure Accommodation Regulations 1983, and the insertion of ss 12A–G in the CCA 1980, allowing applications for access to children in care.

Examples of two English adoption cases which became the subject of applications to Strasbourg are set out below in order to demonstrate the approach of the European Commission.

(a) *Application no 7626/76* v *the UK, 11 D, and R 160*

In this application the Commission considered an adoption order made by the High Court in England, the agreement of the mother having been dispensed with on the ground that she was unreasonably withholding it (s 12(2)(*b*), CA 1975, see chap 6). The applicant, the natural mother, maintained that the adoption of her child ordered by the court, against her will, constituted a violation of the right to respect for family life guaranteed by Art 8 (see above).

The applicant was a French national, resident in France, who become pregnant when she was eighteen. The putative father died in an accident during her pregnancy and without knowing of it, their relationship having ended. She came to London to have an abortion. The pregnancy, however, was too advanced and she decided on adoption in England.

Immediately after the birth in England the child was placed with a view to adoption with a married couple, both of whom were doctors. The wife gave up work to care for the child. The applicant returned to France immediately after the birth and did not see the child again. As a result of medical complications she was unable to have any more children and she refused to agree to the adoption of her child. She had the opportunity to put her case at the High Court hearing. Her agreement was dispensed with and the adoption order made. The child was then aged two.

The European Commission confirmed in its decision that the relations between a child born out of wedlock and its natural parents are covered by the concept of 'family life' within the meaning of Art 8. The Commission said that, 'to ascertain whether in a specific case it is dealing with family life it considers not only whether a relationship exists but also whether there is in fact a link that can be considered to establish family life within the meaning of Art 8'. The applicant had from its birth handed the child over for adoption by third parties, and had not seen it since. By reason of her own decision there was no family life between herself and her son during the first months. When, however, she did show a desire to take her child back, or to reserve the right to do so, she was deprived for the future of all possibility of establishing family relations with him by a court decision. In effect the modern law of adoption separates for good the adopted child from its original or natural family.

The Commission held that the adoption, ordered without the mother's agreement, was 'a specific act of interference of a particularly serious nature.' As there had been an interference with respect for family life, the Commission had to consider whether one of the exceptions in para 2 of Art 8 applied.

The Commission noted that it had at its disposal all the evidence carefully collected by the English court. The court went into all the moral, material, sentimental and educational considerations which might tell either in favour of the adoption or of restoring the child to the mother. The court mentioned the views of the psychiatrists called on both sides who agreed on the dangers to the child of a return to his mother. The Commission noted that English law provided that 'the child's interest is the first but not the only consideration'.

It was concluded by the Commission that it was clear that the adoption ordered by the English court,' was in the circumstances of the case a necessary measure to protect the health and overriding interests of the child and justified from the point of view of Art 8, para 2, of the Convention'. The application was therefore 'manifestly ill-founded'.

(b) *Application no 9966/82 v UK [1983] 5 EHRR 299*

The Commission considered an adoption order made in England in favour of foster parents against the wishes of the natural father, who then made the application to Strasbourg. The child was a ward of court.

The father attempted to make the application to the European Commission on his own behalf and on behalf of his legitimate daughter. The Commission, however, rejected his standing to bring the application on behalf of the child, stating that 'although a parent may under normal circumstances bring an application under Art 25 on his or her child's behalf, in the present case the applicant's legal and parental responsibilities towards [his daughter] were terminated [by the adoption order]'. The application was treated as being brought on behalf of the father only. He complained, inter alia, of a breach of Art 8. The Commission noted that the father's agreement had been dispensed with on the ground that it had been unreasonably withheld, and that an adoption order had been made.

The Commission recalled its decision involving the French girl (see (a) above), and followed the same reasoning as in that case. The precise point that was formulated was: whether the interference with the father's right to respect for family life, caused by the adoption order in the face of his opposition, 'was justified within the terms of Art 8, para 2 in the context of the question whether it was in [the child's] best interests to continue to live with the foster [parents] with whom she had been integrated for the previous two years, notwithstanding the final break of her links with her father which the adoption would make irrevocable.' The Commission ruled that the adoption order was 'a necessary measure to protect the health and overriding interests of the child'. The father's application was, therefore, unsuccessful.

Convention and 1968 Act Cases in England and Wales

Chapter 24

The Convention in English Law

A Convention on 'Jurisdiction, Applicable Law and Recognition of Decrees relating to Adoptions' was concluded at the Hague on the 15 November 1965, and signed on behalf of the UK on that date (Cmnd 2613, and set out in (1965) 14 ICLQ 559). It has so far only been ratified by the UK, Austria and Switzerland.

In the UK the Convention was first implemented by the AA 1968 which authorised the recognition of certain overseas adoptions (see p 146), and also paved the way for the conferment on the superior courts in Great Britain of jurisdiction to authorise adoptions in cases in which the ordinary conditions as to domicile, and, in certain circumstances, parental agreement, are not satisfied, though certain alternative qualifications must be. Such adoptions are effected by Convention adoption orders pursuant to s 24 of the CA 1975 which came into force on the 23 October 1978, replacing s 1 of the AA 1968.

The aim of the Convention is to resolve some of the difficulties and legal conflicts which can arise in inter-country adoptions, because the adopters and the child are subject to different personal laws. The Convention uses the concepts of habitual residence and nationality because domicile can mean different things in different legal systems.

Convention applications in England and Wales must be made in the High Court. An adoption order under the Convention, whether made in the UK or in another Convention country, will be recognised in all the countries where the Convention is in force. The resulting adoption order confers the same status on the child as any other adopted child within the scope of Sched 1 of the CA 1975 (see chap 27), and has the same effect as an ordinary adoption order. The mode of application for an order

differs in significant respects from an ordinary application. Only one order has been made in England since 1978.

1 Convention adoption orders

The same conditions as for an ordinary adoption order, save for domicile and, in certain cases, parental agreement, must be fulfilled before a Convention adoption order can be made. In addition the following conditions, imposed by s 24 of the CA 1975, must be satisfied both at the time of the application and when the order is made (for the definitions of UK national, British territory, and Convention country, see (*d*) below):

(*a*) *Child:*

    (*i*) must be a UK national or a national of a Convention country, and

    (*ii*) must habitually reside in British territory or a Convention country, and

    (*iii*) must not be, or have been, married (s 24(2)).

The applicant or applicants and the child must not all be UK nationals living in British territory (s 24(3)).

If the child is not a UK national, there are special requirements regarding 'consents and consultations' (see (*c*) below).

(*b*) *Adopters:*

If the application is made by a married couple, either:

    (*i*) each must be a UK national or a national of a Convention country, and both must habitually reside in Great Britain, or

    (*ii*) both must be UK nationals, and each must habitually reside in British territory or a Convention country (s 24(4)).

If the application is by one person, either:

    (*i*) he must be a UK national or a national of a Convention country, and must habitually reside in Great Britain, or

    (*ii*) he must be a UK national, and must habitually reside in British territory or a Convention country (s 24(5)).

Note also s 24(3), referred to under (*a*) above.

If the applicant is a national of a Convention country, or if a married couple are applicants and both are nationals of the same Convention country, the adoption must not be prohibited by a specified provision of the internal law of that country (s 24(4), and (5)). A 'specified provision' means a provision specified in an

order of the Secretary of State as one notified to the Government of the UK, pursuant to the provisions of the Convention, which relate to prohibitions on an adoption contained in the national law of the Convention country in question (s 24(8)). The Convention provided for such provisions to be notified by each signatory country to the other signatories. Provisions have been notified and specified for Austria and Switzerland (see the Convention Adoption (Austria and Switzerland) Order 1978, SI 1978 No 1431).

(c) *Consents and consultations:*

Where the child is *not* a UK national, the ordinary provisions as to parental agreement contained in s 12(1) of the CA 1975 (see chap 6) do not apply when the application is for a convention adoption order (CA 1975, s 12 (3)). The order must not be made:

(*i*) except in accordance with the provisions, if any, relating to consents and consultations of the internal law relating to adoption of the Convention country of which the child is a national, and

(*ii*) unless the court is satisfied that each person who consents to the order in accordance with that internal law does so with full understanding of what is involved (s 24(6)).

'Consents and consultations' does not include any consent by, or consultation with the applicant and members of his family, including his or her spouse (s 24(7)).

The High Court is to be treated as the authority by whom, under the internal law of the Convention country of which the child is a national, consents may be dispensed with, and the adoption in question may be effected (ibid). A High Court judge may, therefore, have to apply, for example, Austrian law as to dispensing with consent. If the foreign law requires the attendance before that authority of any person who does not reside in Great Britain, that requirement will be treated as satisfied if he has been given a reasonable opportunity of communicating his opinion on the adoption in question to the proper officer of the High Court, or to an appropriate authority of the country in question, for transmission to the court and, in that case, if his opinion has been so transmitted (s 24(7)).

See also 'Procedure' (chap 25).

'Internal law', in relation to any country, means the law applicable in a case where no question arises as to the law in force in any other country (AA 1968, s 11(1)). If there are in force, in a

country whose internal law falls to be ascertained, two or more systems of internal law, the relevant system must be ascertained in accordance with any rule in force throughout that country indicating which of the systems is relevant in the case in question or, if there is no such rule, the system is to be that appearing to the High Court to be most closely connected with the case (AA 1968, s 10(1), applied by CA 1975, s 24(9)). Detailed provisions are contained in s 9(2)–(4) of the AA 1968 as to the treatment of persons appearing to have two nationalities or to have no nationality.

(*d*) *Definitions (CA 1975, s 107(1)):*
    (*i*) *UK National*: a British citizen who has the right of abode in the UK by virtue of s 2 of the Immigration Act 1971, as amended (see British Nationality Act 1981, ss 39, and 51(3)(*a*); SI 1978 No 1432).
    (*ii*) *British territory*: the UK.
    (*iii*) Convention country: any country outside British territory, being a country for the time being designated by the Secretary of State as a country in which, in his opinion, the Hague Convention is in force (Austria and Switzerland were so designated by SI 1978 No 1431).

(*e*) *Custodianship:*
For the circumstances in which a custodianship order may be made, see CA 1975, s 37.

2 High Court's jurisdiction to neutralise overseas adoptions

The AA 1968, pursuant to the Hague Convention, contains provisions with regard to adoptions effected in countries outside Great Britain.

(*a*) *Overseas adoptions*
'Overseas adoptions' are adoptions of such a description as the Secretary of State may by order specify, being a description of adoptions of infants appearing to him to be effected under the law of any country outside Great Britain (AA 1968, s 4(3)).

The only order made so far is the Adoption (Designation of Overseas Adoptions) Order 1973 (SI 1973 No 19). Its schedule lists many Commonwealth countries and British Dependent Territories, and also a number of other countries and territories.

Within the general category of overseas adoptions are 'Convention adoptions' which are overseas adoptions regulated by the Convention (AA 1968, s 5(2), and SI 1978 No 1432, art 3).

Evidence of an overseas adoption may be given by production of a document purporting to be a certified copy of an entry in a public register of adoptions, made according to the law of the country or territory concerned, or a certificate of adoption purporting to be signed as authorised by the appropriate law, or a certified copy of such a certificate (the 1973 Order above, art 4). In the case of Convention adoptions, 'the document' or 'certificate' must show that the adoption is regulated by the Convention. Proof of an overseas adoption by other means is not precluded.

(b) Annulment, revocation and invalidation in England of overseas adoptions

Annulment and revocation of convention adoptions are possible only in the case of those adoptions where immediately before the application is made to the English court the person adopted or the adopter resides in Great Britain or, as the case may be, both adopters reside here (AA 1968, s 7(2)).

The High Court may annul under s 6(1) of the AA 1968 (see below) a Convention adoption order which it has *itself* made (CA 1975, s 24(8A)). There is no power, however, under s 6 to revoke or invalidate such an order.

The annulment or revocation of a Convention adoption will be recognised in the countries in which the Convention is in force.

Annulment. The grounds on which the court may annul a Convention adoption are:

(*i*) That at the time the adoption took effect it was prohibited by a notified provision (see p 144), if under the internal law then in force in the country of which the adopter was then a national or the adopters were then nationals, the adoption could have been impugned on that ground (AA 1968, s 6(1)(*a*));

(*ii*) That at the time the adoption took effect it contravened provisions relating to consents of the internal law relating to adoption of the country of which the adopted person was then a national, if under that law the adoption could then have been impugned on that ground (ibid, s 6(1)(*b*)).

(*iii*) That on any other ground the adoption can be impugned

under the law in force for the time being in the country in which it was effected (ibid, s 6(1)(*c*)).

An application under s 6(1) of the 1968 Act cannot, except with the leave of the court, be made later than two years after the date of the adoption to which it relates (AR, r 37(2)).

Revocation. The High Court may revoke a Convention adoption upon an application by the parties concerned, where a person adopted by his father or mother alone has subsequently become a legitimated person on the marriage of his father and mother (AA 1968, s 6(2)). This complements the power of revoking UK orders, whether made under the Convention or otherwise, on the same ground, as noted on p 153.

Invalidation in Great Britain. The High Court may order that an overseas adoption shall cease to be valid in Great Britain on the ground that:

(*i*) the adoption is contrary to public policy; or

(*ii*) that the authority which purported to authorise the adoption was not competent to entertain the case (AA 1968, s 6(3)).

The High Court has the same power on the same grounds, regarding a determination, made by an authority of a Convention country or a specified country, pursuant to its power under the law of that country, to authorise or review the authorisation of a Convention adoption or a specified order, or to give or review a decision revoking or annulling a convention adoption, a specified order, or an overseas adoption (AA 1968, ss 6(3), 7(4), and 5(1)). Northern Ireland has been specified by SI 1978 No 1432, art 6.

The High Court may also decide the extent, if any, to which a determination has been effected by a subsequent determination (s 6(3)(*b*)).

In deciding whether the authority of a Convention country or a specified country was for the purposes of s 6(3) competent to entertain a particular case, the High Court shall be bound by any finding of fact made by the authority, and stated by the authority to be so made for the purpose of determining whether the authority was competent to entertain the case (AA 1968, s 7(3)).

In addition to the powers given to the High Court by s 6(1)–(3) of the 1968 Act, *any* court in Great Britain may, in any proceedings in that court, decide that, for the purposes of those proceedings, an overseas adoption or a determination shall be treated as invalid on either of the grounds set out in s 6(3) (see above) (AA 1968, s 6(4)).

Chapter 25

Procedure

The Adoption Rules 1984 apply to both applications for Convention adoption orders, and proceedings under s 6 of the AA 1968. In particular, Part IV of the Rules applies specifically to Convention Proceedings, and rr 37–41 within it solely to s 6 proceedings.

Such applications and proceedings must be brought in the High Court (CA 1976, s 100(2), and (5), AR, rr 37(1), and 38). All may be disposed of in chambers (CA 1975, s 21(1), and (2A)).

In view of the rarity of Convention cases only a brief outline of the procedure is set out below.

1 Section 24 applications

The originating summons, which is a modified version of FORM 6 (see Appendix 1), must state that the application is for a Convention adoption order (AR, r 28(1)). Paragraphs 2, 24 or 25 of FORM 6 need not be included (r 28(2)(*a*)). The additional information required by Sched 4 to the Rules must be included to meet the requirements of s 24(2)–(5) of the CA 1975 (see chap 24) (r 28(2)(*b*)); see also r 30.

If proof of the applicant's or the child's nationality depends on a document, the document or a copy of it must be attached to the originating process (r 29(1)). Where the child is not a UK national, the applicant must file with his originating process expert evidence as to the provisions relating to consents and consultations of the internal adoption law of the Convention country of which the child is a national (r 33). See also rr 32, and 34. If the child is a UK national the ordinary rules as to agreement apply.

Notice of hearing is given as for an ordinary High Court adoption application, except that where the child is not a UK national, the registrar must also serve the notice on any person, not being

an applicant, whose consent to the making of the order is required, and on anyone who has to be consulted under the Convention country's internal law (r 35).

For the court's power to make an interim order, see r 43.

2 1968 Act applications

Applications for orders under s 6(1), or (2), to annul or revoke a Convention adoption, must be made in FORM 9 (see Appendix 1) (AR, r 37(1)). An application for an order, or a decision under s 6(3) must be made in FORM 10 (see Appendix 1) (r 38). Evidence in support of applications under s 6 must be given by means of an affidavit in FORM 11 which must be filed within 14 days after the issue of the originating process (r 39(1)). The person whose adoption is in question, and any adopter other than the applicant are to be respondents (rr 37(1), and 38).

Applications under s 6(1) cannot, except with the leave of the court, be made later than two years after the date of the adoption to which it relates (r 37(2)).

Where the application is under s 6(1), or (3) a statement of facts must be exhibited to the affidavit, and expert evidence filed with it (r 39(2)). The court may order any deponent to give oral evidence (r 39(3)).

3 General

A guardian ad litem is required in Convention adoption applications, and a reporting officer (unless the child is not a UK national) in the same circumstances as for non-Convention cases (see chap 9). By r 40 a guardian ad litem (though not a reporting officer) may in special circumstances be appointed by the court, if the adopted person is under eighteen at the date of the application. Appointment is in accordance with r 18 (see p 66).

Other rules deal with expert evidence about specified or notified provisions (r 42), service and translations (rr 45, and 46).

As to notification of orders to the Registrar General, see rr 31, and 41.

Post-Adoption

Chapter 26

Finality or Otherwise of Adoption

1 Adoption Orders in non-Convention cases

(a) Amendment

For the court's powers under s 24 of the AA 1958, see p 79.

(b) Revocation of adoption order after legitimation

Jurisdiction. Although Sched 1, para 3 of the CA 1975 prevents an adopted child from being illegitimate (para 3(3)), and treats him or her in law as if born in wedlock to the adopter or adopters (para 3(1)), it does not stop an adopted child from being legitimated if either natural parent is the sole adoptive parent, and they subsequently marry each other (Legitimacy Act 1975, s 4(1)). This is, of course, subject to the conditions of ss 2, and 3 of the Legitimacy Act being fulfilled.

Accordingly the court retains a power under s 26 of the AA 1958 to revoke an adoption order made solely in favour of one of the natural parents of the child, if the child subsequently becomes legitimated on the marriage of its natural parents. The adoption may have been effected at any time before the legitimation. The event, however, which legitimated the child must have been the parents' marriage. Section 1 of the AA 1960 operates as an extension of s 26 of the AA 1958 in order to meet the case of persons, adopted before 29 October 1959, whose legitimation resulted, not from the marriage itself (that marriage having taken place before the date mentioned), but from the reform in the law effected by s 1 of the Legitimacy Act 1959. This was the section which rendered it immaterial to the legitimising effect of a marriage that a parent had been married to a third party at the child's birth. If such an adoption was in favour of *both* the child's father and his mother,

the adoption can still be revoked. This obsolescent instance is the only joint case in which revocation is possible.

Relevance. An application to revoke an adoption order under s 26 of the AA 1958, or s 1 of the AA 1960, is usually prompted by a desire to have the adoption record expunged from the public registers. The justification for revocation is less compelling from the angle of property law than formerly. Revocation does not affect the proprietary rights provisions of Sched 1 to the CA 1975 (see chap 27), and a child's relationship to its natural father despite adoption by its mother (and vice versa) is preserved by s 4(2)(*a*) of the Legitimacy Act 1976.

Where in exceptional circumstances *after* the marriage of the parents of an illegitimate child, the court had made an adoption order unwittingly in their favour, s 26 of the AA 1958 did not apply, but a declaration of legitimacy was made in order to accord with the fact of the marriage, rather than what Ewbank J treated as the 'fiction' of legitimacy conferred by the adoption (*Veasey* v *A–G*, (1981) *The Times*, 9 October).

Procedure. The application to revoke the adoption order may be made by any of the parties concerned to the court by which the order was made (AA 1958, s 26(1)). In the case of an order made by a magistrates' court, the application may be made to any court for the same petty sessions area (s 26(3)). It may be made ex parte in the first instance, but the court may require notice of the application to be served on such persons as it thinks fit (AR, r 49(1); MC(A)R, r 28(1), and (2)). The application is made in FORM 9 (see Appendix 1).

(c) Setting aside adoption orders

Subject to the court's powers of amendment and revocation in special circumstances (see above), an adoption order has to be acted on unless and until a competent court sets it aside. In *Skinner* v *Carter* [1948] Ch 387, the Court of Appeal considered a case where, following a bigamous marriage, the natural mother and her 'husband', who was not the father, adopted her daughter. Subsequently the 'husband' was convicted of bigamy. He left the mother, and she applied to a magistrates' court for a maintenance order and was successful. Vaisey J, however, allowed the husband's appeal on the ground that the mother, having admitted the marriage was bigamous, could not rely upon the adoption order. The Court of Appeal restored the magistrates' court order, holding that the adoption order had not been set aside, and the

magistrates had no jurisdiction to disregard it or to treat it as a nullity. Lord Greene MR, whilst not expressing an opinion on the point, pointed out that it was by no means certain that non-compliance with the statutory requirements as to an adopter's qualifications would have the effect of making the adoption order void or voidable. It might very well be thought by the legislature that in dealing with questions of status, an order should remain a valid order when made after proper investigations, notwithstanding that later it was found that there was no jurisdiction to make it (per Lord Greene at p 395).

In *Re RA (Minors)* (1974) Fam Law 182, the Divisional Court set aside adoption orders which had been obtained by false representations to magistrates, including statements that the applicants were married to each other, and that the female applicant was the children's aunt, when in fact she was their mother. The adoption orders were considered to be void.

In *In re F (Infants) (Adoption Order: Validity)* [1977] Fam 165 (CA), joint adopters had discovered that the prior marriage of one of them had not been dissolved, as they and the court had believed at the time the adoption orders were made. They went through a second and valid ceremony of marriage. They applied for directions as to the status and effect of the adoption orders.

The Court of Appeal held that the adoption orders were good on their face and valid until set aside by a competent court. The orders were not void but voidable and, therefore, the court was not obliged to set them aside, but had a discretion whether or not to do so. Since there was no party aggrieved by the orders for adoption, it had not been established that the interests of justice would be served by setting the orders aside. The application for leave to appeal out of time against the adoption orders made in the county court, was refused.

2 Convention etc orders

In contrast with the position in non-Convention cases, the AA 1968 contemplates that a Convention adoption, whether made in England or elsewhere, an overseas adoption, or a 'specified' order, may be subject to review and may be annulled, revoked or invalidated.

The English High Court's jurisdiction in this respect under s 6 of the 1968 Act is set out in chap 24, and the procedure in chap 25. Chapter 24 also deals with the limited power of other courts

in Great Britain to treat as invalid certain adoptions and determinations made abroad (AA 1968, s 6(4)). Except as provided by s 6, however, the validity of an overseas adoption, or of a determination in exercise of proper powers of review of Convention orders etc, is not to be impugned in any court in Great Britain (s 6(5)).

Section 5 of the AA 1968 should also be noted. It refers, not to all overseas adoptions and orders, but only those which are Convention or 'regulated' adoptions (see p 147) or, as the case may be, orders made under the Hague Convention in specified countries (Northern Ireland being the only country so far specified: SI 1978 No 1432). The section gives effect in English law to determinations made by competent authorities of Convention countries, or of specified countries, in the exercise of a power to authorise or review the authorisation of a Convention adoption, or an order made either in a specified country or in Great Britain in pursuance of the Hague Convention.

Orders made outside England or Wales, but effective in English law on the principles stated in chap 27, if not affected by the provisions of the AA 1968 (see above), are clearly final or otherwise according to the provisions of the law under which they were made.

For revocation of a Convention adoption after legitimation, under s 6(2) of the AA 1968, see p 148.

Chapter 27

Effects of Adoption

1 General

(a) Modern principle: events after 1975

Adoption by formal process of law has always entailed certain effects on the rights and obligations of the adopter, the adopted person, and the natural parents.

(1) As a result of the CA 1975, Sched 1, para 3(1), an adopted person is, from 1 January 1976, or from the date of the adoption if later, treated in the law of England and Wales as if:

(*i*) he had been born to the adopter in wedlock; and

(*ii*) he were not the child of any other person.

The effect is therefore carried back to the adopted person's birth. Where the adopters are a married couple, the adopted person is treated as having been born of their marriage, whether or not he was in fact born after that marriage had been solemnised. In the case of a sole adopter, however, the hypothetical birth to the adopter 'in wedlock' does not look to a particular marriage (if any) of his.

(2) This principle has effect only as regards things done or events occurring after 31 December 1975, or the date of the adoption if later (para 3(6)). Subject to that (and to any contrary indication) it applies to the construction of enactments or instruments whenever passed or made (para 3(5)).

(3) It applies, subject to (2) above, to an adoption whenever made (para 1(4)), and whether the adoption is, or was—

(*i*) made by order:

—(in England or Wales) under the Adoption of Children Act 1926; or

—(in Scotland) under the Adoption of Children (Scotland) Act 1930; or

—(in England, Wales or Scotland) under the AA 1950, or the AA 1958; or

—(in England, Wales or Scotland) under s 8 of CA 1975, which includes a UK Convention adoption; or

—in Northern Ireland, the Isle of Man or any of the Channel Islands (para 1(2)(*a*), (*b*) and (*c*)); or

(*ii*) an overseas adoption (defined on p 146), or one recognised by English law though effected abroad (para 1(2)(*d*), and (*e*)). English law recognises an adoption made in a jurisdiction in which the adopter was at the time domiciled, (*Re Valentine's Settlement* [1965] Ch 831), at all events if the adopted person was then resident in that jurisdiction (*per* Lord Denning MR, at 843).

(4) As regards some areas of law the application of the modern principle is excluded, modified or explained in Sched 1, or in some other provision of the CA 1975. These instances will be noted in the following pages.

(*b*) *Events before 1976*

Relevance of dates and of enabling Authority:

The general principle stated in Sched 1 to the CA 1975 replaced previous provisions which had dealt piecemeal with the law, and had varied according to the date and the place of the adoption. The stages in the development of those former provisions are mentioned below only where they are necessary to the appreciation of the effects of former adoption orders.

Adoptions outside England and Wales:

(1) *In the British Isles*

The Adoption of Children Act 1926 facilitated adoption only in England and Wales. There followed similar Acts applying to Northern Ireland (1929), and Scotland (1930), and no one has ever doubted that orders made under those Acts, even before they figured by express mention in English statutes, would have effects similar to those of an English adoption. The statute book made this explicit in the AA 1950 by incorporating the Scottish legislation into the consolidation effected by that Act and by numerous cross-references to the separate statute which still regulated the procedure in Northern Ireland.

Next, the AA 1964 gave effect in English law, to a specified extent, to adoption orders made in the Isle of Man, or in any of

the Channel Islands, and extended the effect of Northern Irish orders.

(2) *Elsewhere*

Effect given by statute. Section 4(1) of the AA 1968 extended to an overseas adoption, as defined in the Act (see chap 24), certain provisions of English law. The extension applied as respects anything done or any event occurring *on or after* 1 February 1973. The provisions in question were those in any enactment passed *before* the date mentioned under which a person adopted pursuant to a 1958 Act order was for any purpose treated as the child of the adopter, or any other relationship deduced (see 4 below). In addition, some particular provisions of the 1958 Act were specifically applied to overseas adoptions by s 4(2) of the Act of 1968.

Southern Rhodesian adoptions were recognised as overseas adoptions despite our law's non-recognition of that country's independence (see SI 1972 No 1718). This order was effective from 11 November 1965 until the coming into force of the Zimbabwe Act 1979, on 18 April 1980.

Effect given by common law. Foreign adoption orders which are not within the statutory provisions discussed above (eg because they are not made in the UK or the British Islands, or are not overseas adoptions as defined, or because the adoption or some relevant event antedates the effective commencement of a provision which might otherwise be applicable), may nevertheless always have had some force in the English conflict of laws (see *Re Valentine's Settlement*, referred to at p 161). The *Valentine* case, however, seems to establish that English law's recognition of a foreign adoption did not, even before 1976, confer on the parties to it such rights and obligations as the foreign law might have given, but only the same effects as under a contemporary English adoption.

2 Parental rights and duties

An adoption order now vests in the adopter or the adopters the parental rights and duties relating to the child (CA 1975, s 8(1)). A provisional adoption order under s 53 of the AA 1958 (now repealed), had the same effect (s 53(4), as adapted by SI 1976 No 1744, Sched 3, para 10). So, now, does an order under s 25 of the CA 1975, made with a view to adoption abroad (s 25(1)) (see chap 16).

No adoption order affects the parental rights and duties so far as

they relate to any period before the making of the order (s 8(2)). Thereafter the order operates to extinguish:

(a) any parental right or duty relating to the child which:
    (i) is vested in a person (not being one of the adopters) who was the parent or guardian of the child immediately before the making of the order, or
    (ii) is vested in any other person by virtue of the order of any court; and
(b) any duty arising by virtue of an agreement, or the order of a court to make payments, so far as the payments are in respect of the child's maintenance for any period after the making of the order or any other matter comprised in the parental duties and relating to such a period (s 8(3)).

But (b) does not apply to a duty arising by virtue of an agreement which constitutes a trust, or which expressly provides that the duty is not to be extinguished by the making of an adoption order (s 8(4)).

These specific provisions, supplementing the general principle discussed in 1 (a) above, operate technically from 26 November 1976, when SI 1976 No 1744 brought them into force. The previous corresponding provisions (ss 13(1), and 15(1) of AA 1958) were, however, repealed as from the preceding 1 January, so far as concerned things done after 31 December 1975. It is thought that the general principle was strong enough to tide over the intervening period, and to produce broadly the result now detailed in s 8 of the CA 1975. Sections 13 and 15 are only relevant to a particular thing or event done or occurring before 1976. As to s 15, see also p 170. Section 13(1) and (2) corresponded, with s 8(1), (2) and (3)(a) of CA 1975 as set out above.

It always appears to have been the case that an adopter may appoint a testamentary guardian of the child to act after the adopter's death under the GMA 1971, and that the survivor of a husband and wife who have jointly adopted a child becomes its statutory guardian under s 3 of the same Act. An order for the maintenance of an adopted child may be made under the 1971 Act against its adopter (see, for example, *Skinner* v *Carter* [1948] Ch 387).

Section 13(1), and (2) of the 1958 Act covered only English and Scottish adoption orders. Since s 13 was a provision under which an adopted person is 'for any purpose treated as the child of the adopter, or any other relationship is deduced' by reference to an adoption order, s 1(1)(b) of the 1964 Act (now repealed)

extended it to Northern Ireland, Isle of Man and Channel Islands adoptions, regarding anything done or any event occurring between 16 July 1964, and 1 January 1976.

Section 4(1) of the 1968 Act extended it to overseas adoptions as defined (see chap 24) in respect of anything done or any event occurring after 31 January 1973.

3 Status of adopted person

Adoption is capable of affecting the legal status of the child who is the subject of it. Whether in a particular case it gives the child a status different from that which it had previously must depend on the facts. Schedule 1, para 3 of the CA 1975, which is headed 'Status conferred by adoption', appears to be concerned less with legitimacy, domicile and nationality, than with conferring a notional lineage on the child in place of the natural one. This may or may not affect one or more of the incidents which are usually comprehended within 'status' as that word is used by most lawyers.

(a) Legitimacy

Paragraph 3 of Sched 1 of the CA 1975 prevents an adopted child from being illegitimate (see para 3(3)), for he is treated in law as if born in wedlock to the adopter or adopters. Nevertheless an adopted person can become legitimated (see further chap 26).

(b) Domicile

The situation before 1 January 1974 was that an adopted child's domicile became that of the adoptive parent, and changed during minority with any change of that parent's domicile (see the observations of Lord Denning MR in *Re Valentine's Settlement* [1965] Ch 831 at 842; *Re B (S) (An Infant)* [1968] Ch 204). The Domicile and Matrimonial Proceedings Act 1973 shortened the period of dependent domicile by declaring that the time at which a person first becomes capable of having an independent domicile should be the attainment of the age of sixteen, marriage under that age, or 1 January 1974 in the case of a dependent person who was then already sixteen or had been married (s 3). Section 4 specifically included an adopted child, and stated that if his adoptive parents were alive but lived apart, his domicile was dependent on that of the female adopter in certain circumstances.

The general principle of Sched 1 (see 1(a) above) for the future

covers domicile as well as other matters, and the reference to an adopted child in s 4 of the 1973 Act has been repealed without changing the effect of the section.

(c) Nationality

This topic was formerly partly covered by s 19(1) of the AA 1958, which declared that, where an adoption order was made in respect of a child who was not a citizen of the UK and Colonies, then, if the adopter or, in the case of a joint adoption, the *male* adopter was such a citizen, the child became such a citizen too, as from the date of the order. Orders made in England, Scotland or Northern Ireland (see s 19(2)) had this effect from 1 January 1950. Section 19(1), however, never applied to an overseas adoption as defined in chap 24. As to Isle of Man or Channel Islands adoption orders made between 15 July 1964 and 1 January 1983, see the AA 1964, s 1(3), now repealed.

Section 19 did not apply to provisional adoptions (s 53(4) of the AA 1958), nor did it affect the nationality of persons, whether British subjects or not, adopted by aliens or by British subjects who owed their nationality solely to Dominion citizenship.

Present position:

As part of the overhaul of nationality law effected by the British Nationality Act 1981, s 19 of the 1958 Act was repealed and replaced (and in one significant respect extended) by s 1(5) and (6) of the 1981 Act. With effect from 1 January 1983, a child who is not already a British citizen becomes such a citizen automatically on adoption by an order of a UK Court, provided that the adopter or *either* of two joint adopters is a British citizen. Thus a child adopted by a couple of whom the wife is a British citizen, but the man is not, now takes its adoptive mother's citizenship. Adoptions abroad are not affected by s 1.

By s 1(6) of the 1981 Act, the status conferred by s 1(5) is not affected by the cessation (whether by annulment or otherwise) of the adoption order.

The general principle which treats the child in law as if he had been born to the adopter is expressly stated not to apply to any provision of the British Nationality Acts, the Immigration Act 1971, or any other legal provision determining citizenship of the UK and Colonies or British citizenship, British Dependent Territories citizenship, or British Overseas citizenship (CA 1975, Sched 1, para 7(2), read, according to date, with or without the amendments introduced by the British Nationality Act 1981, Sched 7).

Accordingly a child who has British citizenship will retain it after adoption by an alien.

Section 15(5) of the 1981 Act complements s 1(5) and (6), producing a corresponding transmission of British Dependent Territories citizenship to children adopted in a dependent territory by citizens of such a territory (see Sched 6 of the 1981 Act). No other type of British status is affected by the Nationality or Adoption Acts in England in an adoption context: the effect of adoption (wherever it takes place) on Commonwealth citizenship derived from a country specified in Sched 3 of the Act of 1981 is a matter for the law of that country.

As to the availability of information necessary to establish the parentage of a person adopted under the serial number system, see the suggestion on p 178.

4 Proprietary rights

It was expressly provided by the Adoption of Children Act 1926 that an adoption order did not deprive the child of any right to or interest in property to which, but for the order, he would have been entitled under an intestacy or disposition—whether occurring or made before or after the making of the order—nor confer any such right or interest on him as a child of the adopter. He therefore had no title to a grant of representation to his adopter's estate, nor to share in an intestacy, nor did he take, unless a contrary intention appeared, under a gift expressed to be to a child or issue.

This position was virtually reversed as regards devolution on a death occurring on or after 1 January 1950, and dispositions made after the end of 1949, by the AA 1949. The object was to secure that adopted persons should be treated as children of their adopters for the purposes of any future devolution or disposal of real or personal property.

Only adoption orders made in England, Scotland or Northern Ireland carried the full effect of this statutory reversal. Isle of Man and Channel Islands orders, whenever made, were brought in by s 1(1) of the 1964 Act, as regards anything done or any event occurring on or after 16 July 1964; and overseas adoptions, as defined (see chap 24), as regards events between 31 January 1973 and 1 January 1976, by the AA 1968, s 4(2). As to the effect of other foreign adoptions in this context in the English conflict of laws, see p 159. It would seem that (apart from statute) a foreign

adoption, if it were to qualify for full recognition as affecting the interpretation of words such as 'child' or 'issue' when used by an English testator or settlor, would have to be such that under the relevant law it conferred the same incidents of filial status in relation to the adopter, as would bring the adopted person within the words in question as contemplated by the testator or settlor.

The relevant sections of the AA 1958 are ss 16 and 17. They apply to full adoption orders whenever made, but not to interim or provisional orders (see 1958 Act, ss 8(5), and 53(4)). They do not affect the devolution of any property on the intestacy of a person who died before 1 January 1950, or any disposition made before that date (Sched 5, para 4) and, though they are repealed by the CA 1975, Sched 4, Part I, as from 1 January 1976, as are the provisions mentioned immediately above (see the 1964, and 1968 Acts), that repeal does not affect their application (or the application of references to s 16 or s 17 in any other repealed provision) in relation to an intestacy occurring before 1 January 1976, or to a disposition of property effected by an instrument made before that date (Sched 1, paras 1(5), 5(2), (3). In addition the general principle does not (see 1(a) above) apply in such a case (para 5(1), (3)).

Sections 16 and 17 of the 1958 Act were extensively set out and discussed in editions of this book up to and including the seventh. It is again stressed that these sections are by no means spent, as they affect past devolutions and dispositions which are still of common relevance.

(a) Post-1975 instruments, enactments and intestacies: general rules

The rules of devolution on intestacy are consolidated with those relating to express dispositions by a deeming device. By para 5(3) of Sched 1 of the CA 1975, the provisions of the law of intestate succession are to be treated for this purpose as if contained in an instrument executed by the deceased immediately before his death but while he was of full capacity.

In the case of a will or codicil clearly any deeming provision is not necessary in order to identify it as an instrument; para 1(6) of Sched 1 fixes the date of the testator's death as the date at which it is to be regarded as made.

Subject to what is stated above, and to any contrary indication, the general proposition of Sched 1, as to treating an adopted person in law as having been born to the adopter in wedlock, or

born as a child of the marriage of joint adopters, applies to the construction of enactments or instruments (including the 'instrument' which the Act deems to be constituted by the law of intestacy), passed or made before or after the adoption, but only so far as passed or made after 31 December 1975 (paras 1(5), 3(5)).

(b) *Post-1975 dispositions of property*
(1) *Definitions*
References to dispositions of property include a disposition by the creation of an entailed interest (para 17 of Sched 1 of the CA 1975). A disposition includes the conferring of a power of appointment, and any other disposition of an interest in, or right over property. In its turn, 'power of appointment' includes any discretionary power to transfer a beneficial interest in property without the furnishing of valuable consideration. An oral disposition of property is covered by Sched 1, as if contained in an instrument made when the disposition was made (para 2). An instrument here includes a private Act settling property, but not, in (2), (3), and (4) below, any other enactment (para 6(6)).

(2) *Where date of birth material*
In applying the positive limb of the general principle (see 1(a) above) to a disposition which depends on the date of birth of a child or children of the adoptive parent or parents, the disposition is to be construed as if the adopted child had been born on the date of adoption, and as if two or more children adopted on the same date had been born on that date in the order of their actual births. This does not, however, affect any reference to the child's age (para 6(2)). Parliament has put explanatory examples into the Act. Paragraph 6(3) of Sched 1 thus gives the following instances of phrases in wills on which para 6(2) can operate:

(a) Children [or grandchildren] of A 'living at my death or born afterwards'—with or without the addition of the words 'before any one of such children' [or 'grandchildren'] 'for the time being in existence attains a vested interest, and who attain twenty-one years.' The reference to age twenty-one will not be affected.

(b) A for life (until he has a child', and then to his child or children.

Where a disposition depends on the date of birth of a child who was born illegitimate, and who is adopted by one of his natural parents as sole adopter, the rule of construction in para 6(2) above does not affect entitlement under Part II of the Family Law

Reform Act 1969, which contains provisions about the property rights of illegitimate children (CA 1975, Sched 1, para 14(1), as amended by the Legitimacy Act 1976). Where a disposition depends on the date of birth of an adopted child who is legitimated, or treated as such, Sched 1, para 6(2) of the CA 1975 above continues to apply notwithstanding the new rule of construction generally applicable where the date of birth of the legitimated child is material, ie s 5(4) of the Legitimacy Act 1976 (1976 Act, s 6(2), replacing CA 1975, Sched 1, para 14(2)). The statutory example given in para 14(3) assumes that a testator dies in 1976 bequeathing a legacy to his eldest grandchild living at a specified time, his daughter has an illegitimate child in 1977, and his married son a child in 1978. Subsequently the illegitimate child is adopted by his mother as sole adopter. The daughter's child remains the testator's eldest grandchild *throughout*.

(3) *Interests already vested in possession or expectant thereon*

The negative part of the general principle (see 1(*a*) above), which in normal cases dissociates the child from his former family, does not prejudice any interest vested in possession in the adopted child before the adoption, or any interest expectant—whether immediately or not—upon an interest so vested (para 6(4)). An interest is vested in possession (and not merely in interest), when there exists a right of present enjoyment as distinct from a firm right of future enjoyment (see *Halsbury's Laws of England*, 4th ed (Butterworths 1982), *39*, 487). The case of a pension presently payable to the child (head (*f*) below) is a particular instance of para 6(4).

(4) *Child-bearing age applied to possibility of adopting*

Where it is necessary to determine for the purposes of a disposition of property effected by an instrument whether a woman can have a child, it is to be presumed that once a woman has attained the age of fifty-five she will not adopt a child after the instrument is executed. If she does so adopt, the child is not (despite the general principle) to be treated as her child, or that of any spouse of hers for the purposes of the instrument (para 6(5)).

(5) *Contrary indication*

Rules (2), (3) and (4) above are expressed to be subject to 'any contrary indication' (para 6(1)). These words are perhaps narrower than those used in s 16(2) of the AA 1958: 'unless the contrary intention appears', for it was held in *Re Jones' Will Trusts* [1965] Ch 1124, that this contrary intention need not appear on the face of the instrument. Buckley J admitted evidence that the

testator had discussed his affairs on a certain footing. It is thought that the new context would require a contrary indication to be coupled with the disposition more closely, since the rules themselves are more specific. On the other hand, a contrast with para 16 of Sched 1 (see head (*d*) below), where the words 'expressed in the instrument' are used, provokes some expectation that the *Jones* case would not be entirely irrelevant if the point arose.

(c) Adoption by natural parent

The negative part of the general principle (see 1(*a*) above) has no effect as respects entitlement to property depending on an adopted person's relationship to one of his natural parents, if that parent is also his sole adoptive parent (Sched 1, para 9). It would in those circumstances contradict the positive principle, nor does it apply to the child's natural relationship with the other natural parent, if the child (having a sole adoptive parent) is legitimated (Legitimacy Act 1976, s 4(2)(*a*)).

If the adoption order is revoked under s 26 of the AA 1958, s 1 of the AA 1960, (see chap 26), the revocation does not affect the operation of the whole general principle, as it applies to any instrument made before the date of the child's legitimation leading to the revocation of the order (Legitimacy Act 1976, s 4(2)(*b*)).

(d) Peerages etc and property devolving therewith

By para 10 of Sched 1 of the CA 1975 it is declared that an adoption does not affect the descent of any peerage or dignity or title of honour, nor, by para 16, does it affect the devolution of any property limited (expressly or not) to devolve, as nearly as the law permits, along with any peerage or dignity or title of honour. Para 16 applies, however, only if and so far as a contrary intention is not expressed in the instrument, and has effect subject to the terms of the instrument.

(e) Protection of trustees and personal representatives

Paragraph 15 of the CA 1975, Sched 1, protects trustees and personal representatives who convey or distribute property to or among persons entitled thereto, without enquiring whether any adoption has been effected or revoked, which may affect entitlement. Section 7 of the Legitimacy Act 1976 extends a similar protection against the possibility of a person adopted by one of his natural parents becoming legitimated. Trustees or representatives are not liable to any person if they had no notice at the time

of conveyance or distribution, of such an adoption or possibility. The right of a person to follow the property into the hands of a person other than a purchaser is not prejudiced.

(f) *Child's pension*

A reservation in the second part of the general principle is made by para 8 of Sched 1, which enacts that the negativing in law of the child's relationship to any person other than the adopter or adopters, does not affect entitlement to a pension which is payable to or for the benefit of a child, and is in payment at the time of his adoption.

5 Marriage laws

Section 13(3) of the AA 1958 deemed an adopter and the person whom he was authorised to adopt under an adoption order, whensoever made, and including an order made in Scotland or Northern Ireland (s 13(4), and Sched 5, para 1), to be within the prohibited degrees of consanguinity for the purpose of the law relating *to marriage*. (It was held in Scotland that it was not incest for a man to have intercourse with his adopted daughter: *HM Advocate* v *Mackenzie* [1970] SLT 82.) Adoption orders, whenever made, in the Isle of Man or any of the Channel Islands, had the like effect as respects events occurring on or after 16 July 1964 (1964 Act, s 1(1)(*a*)), as had overseas adoptions, as defined (see chap 24), as respects events on or after 1 February 1973 (AA 1968, s 4(1); SI 1973 No 18).

This statutory relationship continued notwithstanding that the adopted person was subsequently re-adopted by another person. It attached also in the case of provisional adoption (1958 Act, s 53(4)). On the other hand, nothing in s 13(3) invalidated a marriage solemnised before 1 January 1950 (Sched 5, para 1). The subsection did not bring any relatives of the adopter within the fiction of consanguinity with the adopted person.

Though s 13(3) has been repealed as respects things done or events occurring after 31 December 1975 (CA 1975, Sched 4, Part I), the current position in law is exactly as before, because of a contemporaneous amendment of the Marriage Act 1949 (CA 1975, Sched 3, para 8) which inserts the relationships of adoptive or former adoptive mother, daughter, father and son into the catalogue of prohibited degrees; and because para 7(1) of Sched 1 to the 1975 Act negates the application of the general principle

of that Schedule (see 1(*a*) above) to that table of kindred and affinity, or to the incest provisions (ss 10, and 11) of the Sexual Offences Act 1956 (thus apparently giving statutory recognition in England and Wales to the *Mackenzie* decision).

6 Matrimonial proceedings by or against adopter

(*a*) Position of adopted child

The general principle (see 1(*a*) above) applies after 1975. As respects things done or events occurring before 1 January 1976, a child adopted jointly by the parties to a marriage counted in the statutory provisions relating to custody and maintenance, as a child of the family by the effect of s 27(1) of the Matrimonial Proceedings and Property Act 1970, and s 52(1) of the Matrimonial Causes Act 1973, as did a child adopted by only one party who had been treated by *both* spouses as a child of their family; and adoption for this purpose might have been by order under the 1958 Act, an adoption recognised by the 1964 Act, or an overseas adoption as defined (see chap 24).

The main branch of the decision of Davies J in *Crossley* v *Crossley* [1953] P 97 was that, once an adoption order has been made, it supersedes any *previous* custody order, and the child is no longer a child of the marriage of its natural divorced parents. This decision seems entirely sound, and is reinforced by the provisions of the 1975 Act as to the status of an adopted person (p 157 et seq).

(*b*) Adoption as bar to nullity decree

In *W* v *W* [1952] P 152 it was held that, in the particular circumstances, the adoption of a child *jointly* by the parties to a marriage was an act approbating the marriage, and so (with other factors) constituted a bar, as the law then stood, to a decree of nullity on the ground of incapacity to consummate. The bar in question was, however, re-formulated in 1971, and now requires, if the grant of a decree is to be precluded on general grounds, both that the petitioner has so conducted himself *in relation to the respondent* as to lead her reasonably to believe that he would not seek to have the marriage avoided, and also that the grant of a decree would be unjust to the respondent (Matrimonial Causes Act 1973, s 13(1)). In *D* v *D* [1979] 3 WLR 185 it was held that on the facts the respondent was misled by the petitioner's agreeing

(at a time when he knew he had grounds for petitioning for nullity) to the joint adoption of children, but that as the respondent was content to have the marriage annulled, the second limb of the statutory bar was not satisfied.

7 Affiliation orders and agreements; care orders and resolutions

Where an adoption order was made after 31 December 1949, but before 1 January 1976, in respect of an infant who was illegitimate, any affiliation order in force with respect to him, and any agreement whereby his father had undertaken to make payments specifically for his benefit, ceased to have effect (except for recovery of arrears), *unless* the infant was adopted by his mother, being a single woman (s 15(1), and Sched 5, para 3). See also, as to the marriage of a single woman adopter, s 12(2) of the AA 1950 (before April 1959), and s 22(4) of the CA 1958.

Section 15(4) of the AA 1958 provided for the cessation on adoption of certain local authority care orders, and resolutions assuming parental rights, and subs (5) extended s 15 to Northern Irish adoptions.

The general principle now bars affiliation proceedings: s 15(1) is repealed as respects post-1975 events, and as from 26 November 1976 s 15(4) and (5) are replaced as follows:

(a) as regards affiliation orders and agreements by the CA 1975, s 8(3)(b) (see p 160);

(b) as to care orders, by s 21A of CYPA 1969 providing for a care order to cease on the adoption or provisional adoption of the child to whom it relates; and

(c) for resolutions assuming parental rights and duties, by what is now s 5(2) of the CCA 1980, which also provides for cessation of the resolution if the child is adopted.

Like s 15 of the AA 1958, the new enactments applied to provisional as well as to full orders and now apply to orders authorising foreign adoptions under s 25 of CA 1975 (see the provisions cited, CA 1975, s 108(7), and AA 1958, s 53(4) as adapted by SI 1976 No 1744, Sched 3, para 10).

8 Insurance

Certain statutes regulate the business of friendly societies, collecting societies, and industrial assurance companies. In particular, they empower such societies to insure (notwithstanding

that the member or insured person may have no insurable interest) the payment of money on the death of a parent. They also authorise (to a limited extent) insurance for funeral expenses of the child of a member or assured, and in some cases his parent. As regards registered friendly societies, insurance on endowment terms is still, in some circumstances, and was formerly more widely, available in respect of a member's parent.

For the purposes of all these enactments, the adopter under an English or Scottish adoption order (full or provisional), whenever made, is regarded as the parent (AA 1958, s 14(1), and Sched 5, para 2, for events before 1976: see now the general principle (1(a) above). Further, where the insurance is for funeral expenses of a child, and where it was effected by the natural parent before the making of an adoption order, the rights and liabilities under the policy are transferred to the adopter by virtue of the order, he being treated as the person who took out the policy (1975 Act, Sched 1, para 11, re-enacting s 14(2) of the AA 1958).

References in s 11 of the Married Women's Property Act 1882 to a person's children include, and are deemed always to have included, references to children legally adopted by that person. Section 11 of the 1882 Act is the section which creates a trust in favour of the spouse and children of the assured in the case of certain policies effected by a married person. It had previously been held (*Re Clay's Policy* [1973] 2 All ER 548) not to extend to a case where the named beneficiary was an adopted child, but the AA 1958, s 14(3), and Sched 5, para 2, retrospectively reversed this decision. In 1975, the 1958 provisions were repealed as being superfluous in view of the general principle applicable thereafter.

As to the extension of s 14 of the AA 1958, to Northern Irish, Isle of Man, or Channel Island orders, see the AA 1964, s 1(b), and (2). As to overseas adoptions, as regards events occurring between 31 January 1973 and 1 January 1976, see ss 4(1) of the AA 1968, (as to s 14(1), and (3)), and s 4(2) (which specifically covered s 14(2)).

9 Social security

The general principle of Sched 1 of the CA 1975, seems adequate to constitute an adopted person as a member of the beneficiary's family (or, as the case may be, a child for whom the beneficiary is responsible) in both standard and supplementary

benefit cases. The second part of the principle is also true (see *Secretary of State for Social Services* v *Smith* (1983) 127 SJ 663 (CA), in which May LJ applied the negative part of the principle in considering a claim for guardian's allowance). In the *Smith* case the adopter had died, and the natural mother (the adopter's daughter) had resumed care of the child. The court declined to treat her as the child's parent for the purposes of the claim. There are express provisions, however, in certain death grant and industrial death benefit cases (see below).

Before 1976 the inclusion in the statutory schemes of recognition of the adoptive relationship was secured by specific provisions (now repealed) in the relevant Acts. The legislation with regard to supplementary benefits never made express reference to adopted children, but statutory liabilities to maintain children probably fell to be interpreted in the light of s 13 of the AA 1958, so that they fell upon the adoptive parent.

(a) Special provisions of the Children Act

Sched 1, para 7(3), preserves the right of a person to be treated as a 'near relative' of a deceased person for the payment of death grant under s 32 of the Social Security Act 1975, despite the general principle of the schedule (see 1(*a*) above), if apart from that principle he would be so treated. Nor does the principle apply for the purposes of s 70(3)(*b*), or s 73(2) of the Social Security Act, which provide for payment of industrial death benefit to or in respect of an illegitimate child of the deceased, and the child's mother (para 7(4)). Lastly, subject to regulations under s 72 of the Social Security Act, the principle is not to affect the entitlement to an industrial death benefit of a person who would otherwise be treated as a relative of the deceased (para 7(5)).

10 Child's names

From at least 1950 it has been accepted that not only the surname, but also the forenames of the child could be changed on adoption, and the surname almost invariably is so changed.

There is no statutory provision since the repeal of s 21(2) of the AA 1958, but the point is now covered in the prescribed application forms. In all courts these require the child's forename and surname, corresponding with his birth certificate, to be stated, and then go on to propose in a later paragraph that if an adoption

order is made 'the child is to be known by the following names', space being allowed for a surname and 'other names'.

Chapter 28

Adopted Children Register

1 Contents

The Registrar General is required to keep a register, called the Adopted Children Register, at the General Register Office, in which entries of adoptions are recorded as directed by adoption orders (see chap 12). The form of entry to be made in the register is prescribed by the Registrar General, as described on p 78. In the case of Convention adoption orders made under s 24 of the CA 1975, there must be added the words 'Convention order'.

Amendments of the Adopted Children Register will be made after the prescribed officer of the court has sent the adoption order amendments to the Registrar General (AA 1958, s 24(2)(a)).

If the Registrar General is satisfied that an entry in the Register of Births relates to a person adopted under an overseas adoption (see p 146), and that he has sufficient particulars relating to that person to do so, he is to make an entry in the Adopted Children Register (AA 1968, s 8(2)). He may require an English translation of a certificate or certified copy presented as evidence of an overseas adoption or a Convention adoption, as the case may be (SI 1973 No 19, art 4(2); SI 1978 No 1432, art 4(2)).

Entries may be corrected following annulment of the adoption, or on it otherwise ceasing to have effect (AA 1968, s 8(3)).

2 Marking of birth registers

By s 21(4) of the AA 1958, if upon an application for an adoption order, there is proved to the satisfaction of the court in England or Wales the identity of the child with a child to whom any entry in the Register of Births relates, the Registrar General

is directed in the adoption order to cause such entry in the Registers of Births to be marked with the word 'adopted'. A similar procedure is followed with the previous entry in the Adopted Children Register in the case of a re-adoption (AA 1958, s 21(5)).

On a provisional adoption order being made, the marking was 'provisionally adopted', or 'provisionally re-adopted'. For orders under s 25 of the CA 1975 (see chap 16), the registers are to be marked 'proposed foreign adoption' or 'proposed foreign re-adoption' (CA 1975, s 25(3)).

Effect must be given to any directions of a court on the quashing of an adoption order, or the allowing of an appeal against it, by cancelling the markings in the Registers of Births, and the entry in the Adopted Children Register. Both marking and cancellations are in that event to be omitted from all copies of the entries affected (AA 1958, s 24(3) and (6)). A similar procedure occurs where the court, under s 24(1) amends an order, or revokes a direction for marking (s 24(2) and (6)).

There are certain cases in which the Registrar General must or may mark Birth Registers in other circumstances. These are:

(i) AA 1958, s 24(4): Scottish adoption, or cancellation order identifiable with birth registered here, on notification by the Registrar General for Scotland;

(ii) AA 1964, s 3: Northern Ireland, Isle of Man or Channel Islands orders similarly identifiable here, on official notification; and

(iii) AA 1968, s 8(2) and (3): overseas adoptions where Registrar General makes an entry in the Adopted Children Register: see 1 above.

Section 14 of the Births and Deaths Registration Act 1953 provides for the re-registration, on certain conditions, of the births of legitimated persons. If such re-registration takes place *after* the original entry in the Register of Births has been marked 'adopted', the entry made on re-registration is to be similarly marked (AA 1958, s 27; 1964 Act, s 3(4); 1968 Act, s 8(4)). The 1958 provision is stated to be without prejudice to the court's power to revoke an adoption order in consequence of legitimation (s 26: see chap 26). Where that power is exercised, the fact is communicated to the Registrar General (see below), and the entries and markings in the Adopted Children Register, and the Registers of Births must be cancelled. This applies also when the order revoked is a Convention adoption order.

As to local registers, it is provided by reg 37 of the Registration

of Births, Deaths and Marriages Regulations 1968 (SI 1968 No 2049) that a superintendent registrar, or registrar must, on being directed by the Registrar General, mark any entry specified in the direction with the word 'adopted', adding his signature and official description, and send to the Registrar General a certified copy of the entry showing the marking. By reg 38, any certified copy of such entry given under the provisions of the Registration Acts must include a copy of the marking. There are provisions for cancellations of markings on the direction of the Registrar General (reg 37(2)).

3 Communication of order to Registrar General

The prescribed officer of the court is responsible for communicating every adoption order (or order authorising a foreign adoption: see chap 16) to the Registrar General, who must then comply with the directions to him which it contains (AA 1958, s 21(6)). This duty is performed by a registrar in the Family Division, the county court registrar, and in the domestic court by the justices' clerk. The rules require a copy of the order (and of any Welsh translation thereof) to be sent to the Registrar General within 7 days after it has been made (AR, r 52(4); MC(A)R, r 31(4)). The English text prevails.

With any order made in proceedings commenced after 27 May 1984, the officer of the court also sends the ADOPTION PROCEEDINGS UNIT RETURN for statistical purposes (see p 79) to the Registrar General.

When an adoption order is quashed, or an appeal against an adoption order is allowed by any court, *that* court is to give directions to the Registrar General to cancel any marking of an entry in the Registers of Births, and any entry in the Adopted Children Register which was effected in pursuance of the order (AA 1958, s 24(3)).

On amendment of an adoption order, or revocation of a direction under s 24(1), or under para 6 of Sched 5 to the 1958 Act (p 79), or on revocation under s 26, the prescribed officer of the court is to cause the amendment, or the fact of revocation, as the case may be, to be communicated to the Registrar General (s 24(2); s 26(2)).

4 Evidence of adoption and date and place of birth

A certified copy of an entry in the Adopted Children Register bearing the seal of the General Register Office is evidence:

(i) of the adoption to which the entry relates; and

(ii) where the entry contains a record of the adopted person's date of birth, country, or district and sub-district of birth, of that date or country or district or sub-district, as though it were a certified copy of an entry in the Registers of Births (AA 1958, s 20(2)).

A similar document, receivable as evidence under the adoption legislation applying in Scotland or Northern Ireland, is also receivable in England (AA 1964, s 2(1)).

Any certified copy of the entry relevant to an adoption order which has been amended, must be a copy of the entry as amended, without any note or marking being reproduced relating to the amendment or any cancelled matter (AA 1958, s 24(6)).

A copy of any entry in the Registers of Births, or the Adopted Children Register, the marking of which is cancelled on the quashing of an adoption order, on a successful appeal, or on the revocation of an order after legitimation, is to be deemed to be an accurate copy if, and only if, both the marking and the cancellation are omitted therefrom (ibid, ss 24(6) and 26(2)).

5 Inspection of register, copies, and fees

By s 20(3) of the 1958 Act, every person is entitled to search the indexes of the register at the General Register Office (part of the Office of Population Censuses and Surveys), St Catherine's House, 10 Kingsway, London WC2, and to have a certified full copy of any entry in the register on the same conditions as are applicable under the Births and Deaths Registration Act 1953, and the Registration Service Act 1953. (Registers of adopted children are not kept locally.)

The General Register Office is open for searches of the indexes from 8.30 am to 4.30 pm on Mondays to Fridays, but is closed on Saturdays. No fees are payable for searching personally in the indexes at the General Register Office. A certified copy of an entry may be obtained on personal application at a fee of £5 (£2 if applied for within 28 days of first registration). If applied for by post, the sum of £10 should be sent for each certified copy (by

crossed cheque or postal order payable to the Registrar General), and a stamped addressed envelope should be enclosed.

Section 33 of the Births and Deaths Registration Act 1953, and the regulations made thereunder (The Birth Certificate (Shortened Form) Regulations 1968: SI 1968 No 2050) provide for a shortened form of birth certificate at a fee which is now £7.50 (£2.50 on personal application). Such a certificate will include only the name and surname (see reg 6), sex, date of birth (reg 8), and place of birth (reg 9), but will *not* include any particulars relating to parentage or adoption. When application is made for a short certificate from an entry in the Adopted Children Register, the particulars given by the applicant should include the date of birth, the names and surname of the adopted person, and the adoptive parent or parents, the date of the adoption order, and the court by which it was made. The short certificate contains no details of adoption. The fee is the same as for a shortened birth certificate, but is reduced to £1.50 if applied for personally within 28 days of registration.

6 Linking documents

Certain other registers or books must be kept, in order to link the entries in the Adopted Children Register with those in the Registers of Births (AA 1958, s 20(4)). These books, however, are not open to public inspection, nor may any information contained in them be divulged to any person, except in accordance with s 20A of the 1958 Act (see chap 29), or by order of any of the courts specified in s 20(5) (see below). It is suggested that a court might make an order, for instance, if a question of the adopted person's nationality turned on natural parenthood, it not being covered by the provisions cited on p 162 because the adopter was not a British citizen or a British Dependent Territories citizen. See also *Lawson* v *Registrar General* (1956) 106 Law Journal 204 (county court), where it was the adopted person who was sought, so that a legacy could be paid to her from a godmother.

The courts in question are:
  (*i*) the High Court;
  (*ii*) Westminster County Court, or such other county court as may be prescribed (none other has so far been prescribed);
  (*iii*) the court by which an adoption order was made in respect of the person to whom the information, copy or extract relates (s 20(5)). In the case of an order made by a magis-

trates' court, this includes a court acting for the same petty sessions area (s 20(6)).

Chapter 29

Access to Birth Records

Since 1975 English law has allowed an adopted person some facilities for looking behind the screen which normally conceals the links between the Registers of Births and of Adoptions. In Scotland, disclosure of his origins had always been possible to an adopted person from the age of seventeen, by searching in official records. A person adopted in England now has similar rights when he or she comes of age. There are, however, implications which may not always be apparent, and skilled social workers acting as counsellors are available to give advice in a particular case.

1 Disclosure

The Registrar General is obliged on the application of an adopted person who has attained the age of eighteen (a record of whose birth is kept by the Registrar General), to supply that person with such information as is necessary to enable him on payment of the prescribed fee to obtain a certified copy of the record of his birth (AA 1958, s 20A(1), added by CA 1975, s 26).

Section 20A also provides for the case of an adopted person *under* the age of eighteen, whose birth record is kept by the Registrar General, and who is intending to be married in England or Wales. On application, and after payment of the prescribed fee, such a person is entitled to be informed by the Registrar General whether or not it appears from information contained in the registers of live births, or other records, that he and the person he intends to marry may be within the prohibited degrees of relationship for the purposes of the Marriage Act 1949 (s 20A(2)).

2 Application

The forms for both types of application are prescribed by the Adopted Persons (Birth Records) Regulations 1976 (SI 1976 No 1743). Under s 20A(1) two alternative forms exist, their applicability depending on whether the person was adopted before the 12, or after the 11 November 1975. This is because the Registrar General is not authorised to supply information to a person adopted before the *passing* of the CA 1975, unless that person has attended an interview with a counsellor (see below) (s 20A(6)).

Application forms for access to birth records can be obtained from the General Register Office (CA Section), Titchfield, Fareham, Hants, Box 7, PO15 5RR, and when completed should be returned to that address.

3 Counselling

Compulsory counselling in respect of a person adopted before the passing of the CA 1975 has been noted above. In other cases under s 20A(1), counselling is optional, but the Registrar General must inform the applicant that counselling services are available and where (s 20A(4)).

Counselling is not required or provided for in the case of an application under s 20A(2) (under eighteen and intending to be married).

The Registrar General, and each local authority and approved adoption society are under a duty to provide counselling for s 20A(1) applicants (s 20A(3)).

Applicants are asked to indicate on the form their choice of one of four places where they would prefer to meet a counsellor by appointment. These are:

(*i*) at the General Register Office in London; or
(*ii*) at the Social Services department of the local authority for the area in which the applicant lives; or
(*iii*) at the Social Services department of the local authority for the area where the court which made the adoption order sat; or
(*iv*) at the office of the adoption society (if approved under s 4 of the CA 1975) which arranged the adoption (s 20A(4)).

If the applicant chooses to receive counselling from a local authority or an approved adoption society, the Registrar General

must send that body the information to which the applicant is entitled (s 20A(5)).

There is no fee for counselling, but if the applicant wishes to proceed he will be charged a fee of £5 for the birth certificate. It may, however, be possible to obtain further information. Counsellors are, it is understood, able to assist the applicant to discover through which agency (if any) his adoption was arranged. The counsellor holds an authorisation to the court which, when signed by the counsellor, may lead to further information being available. The official leaflet though warns applicants that there can be no certainty that any information outside the birth certificate exists. The disclosure of the information identifying the agency that arranged the adoption would be permitted by the AR, r 53(3)(b)(ii), and MC(A)R, r 32(5)(b)(ii) (see p 8).

Part IV

Offences and Particular Prohibitions

Chapter 30

Offences and Particular Prohibitions

1 Restrictions on advertisements

It is not lawful to publish an advertisement indicating that:
  (*i*) the parent or guardian of a child wishes it to be adopted; or
  (*ii*) a person wishes to adopt a child; or
  (*iii*) any person (not being an approved adoption society or local authority) is willing to make arrangements for a child's adoption (AA 1958, s 51(1)).

No advertisement indicating that a person will undertake or arrange for the care and maintenance of a child must be published, unless it truly states that person's name and address (FCA 1980, s 15).

For the offences of contravening these provisions, see 5 below.

2 Unauthorised payments and rewards

It is unlawful to make or give to any person any payment or reward for or in consideration of:
  (*i*) the adoption by that person of a child;
  (*ii*) the grant by that person of any agreement or consent required in connection with the adoption of a child;
  (*iii*) the transfer by that person of the actual custody of a child with a view to its adoption; or
  (*iv*) the making by that person of any arrangements for the adoption of a child. (AA 1958, s 50(1))

The court must not make an adoption order in relation to a child unless it is satisfied that the applicants have not, as respects the child, contravened s 50 of the 1958 Act (CA 1975, s 22(5)).

Payments may, however, be made to an approved adoption

185

society or local authority by a parent or guardian of a child, or by an adopter, or a person who proposes to adopt a child, for expenses reasonably incurred by the society or authority in connection with the adoption (s 50(3)). The court to which an adoption application is made may authorise a payment or reward (ibid).

By s 50(3A) of the 1958 Act (added by the Criminal Law Act 1977, Sched 12), the general prohibition in s 50 is excluded in the case of payments *by* adoption agencies for:

(*i*) legal or medical expenses incurred or to be incurred by an applicant, or a person who proposes to make an application for an adoption order, in connection with the adoption;

(*ii*) placing (to another agency);

(*iii*) a contact fee to an approved voluntary organisation.

In the case of (*i*) and (*ii*), the exclusion is deemed to have applied always.

Similarly, the prohibition in s 50 of the AA 1958 does not apply to any payment made in accordance with a scheme, submitted to the Secretary of State by an approved adoption society or local authority, and approved by him, for the payment by that society or authority of *allowances* to adopters and persons proposing to adopt a child (CA 1975, s 32; which came into force on 15 February 1982). Such schemes are revocable by the Secretary of State, who must publish periodical reports on their collective operation.

For the offence of contravening s 50, see 5 below. The court may order any child in respect of whom an offence is committed to be removed to a place of safety, until he can be restored to his parents or guardian, or until other arrangements can be made for him (AA 1958, s 50(2)).

3 Restriction on arranging adoption and placing children

A person other than an adoption agency (an approved adoption society or local authority) must not make arrangements for the adoption of a child, or place a child for adoption, unless:

(*i*) the proposed adopter is a relative of the child, or

(*ii*) he is acting in pursuance of a High Court order (AA 1958, s 29(1), as substituted by CA 1975, s 28).

For the offence of contravening s 29(1), and the other offences arising out of s 29, see 5 below, and for a discussion of the provisions, see p 25.

Where a person is convicted of contravening s 29(1), the court may make a care or supervision order as if an adoption application had been refused (AA 1958, s 29(5)).

Unlike the position where s 50 of the 1958 Act has been contravened (see 2 above), the court may still make an adoption order even though there has been a breach of s 29.

4 Prohibitions on taking or sending children abroad

(a) For adoption

Section 52(1) of the AA 1958, as amended, provides that, except with the authority of an order under s 25 of the CA 1975 (see chap 16), it is not lawful for any person to take or send a child who is a Commonwealth citizen (or a citizen of the Republic of Ireland: AA 1958, s 57(3)), out of Great Britain to any place outside the UK, the Channel Islands, or the Isle of Man, with a view to the adoption of the child by any person not being its parent, guardian or relative ('relative' is defined on p 131, and for 'guardian', see below).

Section 52 does not apply to children emigrating under the authority of the Secretary of State, under s 24 of the CCA 1980 (s 24(5)).

For the offence under s 52, see 5 below.

(b) Child abduction: adoption and custodianship

By s 1(1) of the Child Abduction Act 1984, which came into force on 12 October 1984, a person connected with a child under the age of *sixteen* commits an offence if he takes or sends the child out of the UK without the appropriate consent. The section applies in the case of a child:

(i) Who is the subject of an order under s 14 of the CA 1975 freeing him for adoption; or

(ii) Who is the subject of a pending application for such an order; or

(iii) Who is the subject of a pending application for an adoption order under s 8(1) of the CA 1975; or

(iv) Who is the subject of an order under s 25 of the CA 1975, or s 53 of the AA 1958 (see chap 16), relating to adoption abroad or of a pending application for such an order; or

(v) Who is the subject of a pending application for a custodianship order (s 1(8), and Sched, para 3(1) of the 1984 Act).

References to an order or an application for an order in para 3(1) are references to one made by, or an application to, a court in England or Wales.

A person is 'connected with a child' for the purposes of s 1 if:

(a) he is a parent or guardian of the child; or
(b) there is in force a court order in England or Wales awarding custody of the child to him, whether solely or jointly with any other person; or
(c) in the case of an illegitimate child, there are reasonable grounds for believing that he is the father of the child. (1984 Act, s 1(2))

'Guardian' means a person appointed by deed or will, or by order of a court of competent jurisdiction to be guardian of a child (s 1(7)(a)).

A custody order or an order awarding custody includes an order awarding legal custody and an order awarding care and control (s 1(7)(b)). Wardship is therefore covered.

A person shall be regarded as *taking* a child if he causes or induces the child to accompany him or any other person, or causes the child to be taken (1984 Act, s 3(a)).

A person shall be regarded as sending a child if he causes the child to be sent (s 3(b)).

'Appropriate consent' in s 1(1) refers to:

(1) In the case of a child freed for adoption, the consent of the adoption agency (approved adoption society or local authority) which made the application for the order, or if the parental rights and duties in respect of the child have been transferred from that agency to another agency by an order under s 23 of the CA 1975, the consent of that other agency (Sched, para 3(2)(a)(i));
(2) In the case of a child who is the subject of a pending application for a freeing order, an adoption order, or a custodianship order, the leave of the court to which the application was made (ibid, para 3(2)(a)(ii)); and
(3) In the case of the child who is the subject of an order under s 25 of the CA 1975, or s 53 of the AA 1958, or of a pending application for such an order, the leave of the court which made the order, or as the case may be, to which the application was made (ibid, para 3(2)(a)(iii)).

References in para 3(2) to 'the court' include in any case where the court is a magistrates' court, a reference to any magistrates' court acting for the same petty sessions area as that court (1984 Act, Sched, para 5(4)).

Section 1(1) of the 1984 Act also applies in the case of a child who is *in the care of* a local authority or voluntary organisation. Where such a child, however, also falls within the provisions set out above, these provisions only apply (Sched, para 4).

For the penalties for an offence under s 1(1) of the Child Abduction Act 1984, see 5 below.

5 Table of offences and penalties

Below are summarised the offences under the AA 1958, as amended, together with some offences under the CCA 1980, the FCA 1980, and the Child Abduction Act 1984. Section 127(1) of the MCA 1980 applies on summary prosecution, so that the information must be laid within six months of the alleged commission of the offence. Proceedings may, in England and Wales, be taken by a local authority (AA 1958, s 54(2); CCA 1980 s 84; FCA 1980, s 16(5)).

It is provided by s 54(1) of the AA 1958 that, where any offence under the Act committed by a body corporate is proved to have been committed with the consent or connivance of, or to be attributable to any neglect on the part of, any director, manager, member of the committee, secretary or other officer of the body, he, as well as the body, shall be deemed to be guilty of that offence.

The penalties tabulated below are as adjusted by various paragraphs of the CA 1975, Sched 3 and are expressed in the terms enjoined by s 46 of the Criminal Justice Act 1982. Unless otherwise indicated they are penalties on summary conviction.

Statute	*Offence*	*Penalty*
AA 1958 s 29(1), (3)(*b*)	Person other than approved adoption society or local authority making arrangements for adoption of child, or placing child for adoption, unless proposed adopter is a relative of the child, or unless person is acting under High Court order.	Imprisonment not exceeding three months and/or fine not exceeding level 5 on the standard scale (see CJA 1982, s 37, and amending orders).

Statute	Offence	Penalty
s 29(3)(a)	Person taking part in management or control of body of persons which exists wholly or in part for the purpose of making arrangements for the adoption of children, and which is not an approved adoption society or local authority. For a provision as to evidence admissible in proceedings for this offence, see s 29(4).	Imprisonment not exceeding three months and/or fine not exceeding level 5.
s 29(3)(c)	Person receiving a child placed with him in contravention of s 29(1).	
s 32(2)	Contravening or failing to comply with the provisions of a regulation made under s 32(1A). (SI 1983 No 1964: see Appendix 3)	Fine not exceeding level 5.
s 34(1), (3)	Parent or guardian who has agreed to the making of an adoption order, removing the child, while the application for that order is pending, from the actual custody of the person with whom the child has his home against that person's will, without the court's leave.	Imprisonment not exceeding three months and/or fine not exceeding level 5.
s 34(2), (3)	Parent or guardian who did *not* consent to a freeing application (see chap 20) removing the child from the actual custody of the person with whom the child has his home, against that person's will, while the freeing application is pending, and the child is in the care of the applicant-agency, without the court's leave.	

Statute	Offence	Penalty
s 34A(1), (2), (6)	Any person removing a child from the actual custody of an applicant for its adoption, or of a prospective adopter who has given notice to the local authority, if the applicant or prospective adopter is the person with whom the child has had his home for the preceeding five years, against the applicant's or prospective adopter's will, except with the court's leave, or under statutory authority or on the child's arrest.	Imprisonment not exceeding three months and/or fine not exceeding level 5.
s 35(3), (6)	Proposing adopter failing to cause child to be returned to the approved adoption society or local authority which has made arrangements for its adoption, or to a suitable nominated person, within 7 days of the date of (*a*) a notice by the adopter to the society or authority of his intention not to adopt the child, or (*b*) a notice by the society or authority of its intention not to allow the child to remain in his care and possession, or (*c*) the court's refusal of or the withdrawal of an application for an adoption order in respect of the child. [Note: The court can, however, extend within limits the time allowed following a *refusal* (see p 30).	Imprisonment not exceeding three months and/or fine not exceeding level 5. As to the convicting court's power to order the return of the infant, see p 30.

Statute	Offence	Penalty
s 44(1)(*a*)	Failure to give, within the time specified, a notice required under Part IV of the Act, ie a notice required under s 40(1) by a person taking part in placing arrangements (see p 32), under s 40(4) on change of permanent address (see p 32) or under s 40(5) on death of a child (see p 32).	
	Failure to give, within a reasonable time, any information required under Part IV of the Act, ie under s 40(6) (see p 32).	
	Knowingly making or causing or procuring another to make any false or misleading statement in any such notice or information.	Imprisonment not exceeding three months and/or fine not exceeding level 5. As to the court's power to order the removal of the child, see p 32.
s 44(1)(*b*)	Refusing to allow the visiting of a protected child by a duly authorised officer of a local authority or the inspection of any premises under s 39 (see p 32).	
s 44(1)(*c*)	Keeping any child in any premises in contravention of a prohibition imposed under Part IV of the Act, ie under s 41 (see p 32).	
s 44(1)(*d*)	Refusing to comply with an order under Part IV of the Act for removal of a child, ie under s 43 (see p 32). Obstructing any person in the execution of such an order.	

Statute	Offence	Penalty
s 50(2)	Making or giving, or agreeing or offering to make or give, receiving or agreeing to receive, or attempting to obtain any payment or reward prohibited by s 50 of the Act (see p 185).	Imprisonment not exceeding three months and/or fine not exceeding level 5. As to the court's power to order the removal of the child, see p 32.
s 51(2)	Causing to be published or knowingly publishing an advertisement contravening s 51 (see p 185).	Fine not exceeding level 5.
s 52(1)	Taking or sending a child who is a Commonwealth citizen (an expression embracing British citizens) or Republic of Ireland citizen, out of Great Britain to any place outside the UK, the Channel Islands and the Isle of Man, in contravention of s 52(1), or making or taking part in any arrangements for transferring the care and possession of a child to any person for that purpose (see p 187).	Imprisonment not exceeding three months and/or a fine not exceeding level 5.
CCA 1980 s 75	Obstructing the exercise by an inspector authorised under s 74(1) of the 1980 Act of the right of entry to premises at which a protected child within AA 1958, Part IV, is being accommodated or maintained.	First offence: fine not exceeding level 1. Refusal to allow entry is deemed reasonable cause for suspicion on which a search warrant may be issued (s 75(3)).
FCA 1980 ss 15, 16	Causing to be published or knowingly publishing an advertisement in contravention of s 15 or of regulations made under it (see p 185).	Imprisonment not exceeding six months and/or fine not exceeding level 5.

Statute	Offence	Penalty
Child Abduction Act 1984 s 1(1)	A person connected with a child under sixteen, taking or sending the child out of the UK without the appropriate consent in contravention of s 1(1) (see p 187). (To be prosecuted by, or with the consent of, the DPP)	(*a*) On summary conviction, imprisonment not exceeding six months and or a fine not exceeding £1000. (*b*) On indictment imprisonment not exceeding seven years.

Appendix 1

Forms

PART II: THE MAGISTRATES' COURT PROCEEDINGS

PART I: HIGH COURT AND COUNTY COURT PROCEEDINGS

The Adoption Rules 1984

SCHEDULE I   **Rule 2(2)**

GENERAL FORMS

Form 1

Originating Process for an Order Freeing a Child for Adoption

(Heading—High Court)

In the High Court of Justice
Family Division

No   of 19

In the matter of the Adoption Act 1958 and
In the matter of the Children Act 1975 and
In the matter of   a child

Let   of   attend at the Royal Courts of Justice,
Strand, London WC2, on a date to be fixed for the hearing of the
application of   of
for an order:

1 That the said child be freed for adoption;

2 That the costs of this application be provided for;

And take notice that the grounds of the application are as follows:

(Continue as in body of the county court originating process below,
from the words 'I, an authorised officer . . .')

(Heading—County Court)

In the   County Court
Number of matter

In the matter of the Adoption Act   1958 and
In the matter of the Children Act   1975 and
In the matter of   a child

I, an authorised officer of the   of   being
an adoption agency wishing to free for adoption   ,
a child, hereby give the following further particulars in support of the
application.

1 This application is/is not made with the consent of
(and   ), the parent(s)/guardian(s) of the child.

Particulars of the child

2 **Identity etc** The child is of the   sex and is not and has
not been married. He/she was born on the   day of
        19   and is the person to whom the attached birth/
adoption certificate relates (*or*, was born on or about the day of
        19   , in   ). He/she is a   national.

3 **Parentage, etc** The child is the child of
whose last known address was

(*or* deceased) and   whose last known address was

(*or* deceased).

4 The guardian(s) of the child (other than the mother or father of the
child is/are   of   of
).)

5 **Parental agreement**. I understand that the said
(and   ) is/are willing to agree to the making of an
adoption order.)

6 I request the judge to dispense with the agreement of
on the ground(s) that   (and   ) and
there are attached hereto three copies of a statement of the facts on
which I intend to rely.)

7 **Care, etc** The child is currently living with
of   and has been living there since the
        day of   19   . (The child has been placed
with them for adoption (and they wish their identity to remain
confidential).)

(8 The child is in the care of   (who have the
powers and duties of a parent or guardian of the child) (*or* the parental
rights and duties in respect of the child).)

(9 **Maintenance**   of   is liable
by virtue of an order made by the   court at
        on the   day of   19   , (*or*
by an agreement dated the   day of   19   ),
to contribute to the maintenance of the child.)

(10 I attach hereto signed by the mother/father/guardian of the child a declaration that he/she prefers not to be involved in future questions concerning the adoption of the child.)

(11 The child is illegitimate and   of who is/claims to be the father does/does not intend to apply for the custody of the child.)

(12 No proceedings relating in whole or in part to the child have been completed or commenced in any court in England and Wales or elsewhere (except   ).)

I accordingly apply on behalf of   for an order freeing the child for adoption.

Dated this   day of   19

Notes

(**Heading**) Enter the first name(s) and surname as shown in the certificate referred to in paragraph 2; otherwise enter the first name(s) and surname by which the child is known.

If the application is made to a county court, either the child or his parent or guardian must be within the district of the county court to which the application is made.

Paragraph 2 If the child has previously been adopted, a certified copy of the entry in the Adopted Children Register should be attached and not a certified copy of the original entry in the Registers of Births. Where a certificate is not attached, enter the place, including the country, of birth if known.

Paragraph 3 If the child has previously been adopted, give the names of his adoptive parents and not those of his natural parents. If the child is illegitimate and the putative father has legal custody of the child by virtue of a court order, give details of that order under paragraph 12.

Paragraph 4 Enter particulars of any person appointed by deed or will in accordance with the provisions of the Guardianship of Infants Acts 1886 and 1925, or the GMA 1971, or by a court of competent jurisdiction to be a guardian. Do not include any person who has the custody of the child only. Delete this paragraph if the child has no guardian.

Paragraphs 5 and 6 Enter either in paragraph 5 or 6 the names of the persons mentioned in paragraphs 3 and 4, except that in the case of an illegitimate child the father of the child should be entered only if he has custody of the child by virtue of a court order. Where it is sought to dispense with parental agreement, enter in paragraph 6 one or more of the grounds set out in section 12(2) of the 1975 Act.

Paragraph 7 Enter the name and address of the person with whom the child has his home.

Paragraph 8 This paragraph should be completed where the child is in the care of a local authority or a voluntary organisation.

Paragraph 9 This paragraph should be completed where some person or body is liable to contribute to the maintenance of the child under a court order or agreement.

Paragraph 12 State the nature of the proceedings and the date and effect of any orders made.

Form 2

Agreement to an Adoption Order (Freeing Cases)

(*Heading as in Form 1*)

IF YOU ARE IN ANY DOUBT ABOUT YOUR LEGAL RIGHTS YOU SHOULD OBTAIN LEGAL ADVICE *BEFORE* SIGNING THIS FORM.

Whereas an application is to be/has been made by   for an order freeing   , a child, for adoption:

And whereas the child is the person to whom the birth certificate attached marked 'A' relates:

(And whereas the child is at least six weeks old:)

I, the undersigned   of   being a parent/guardian of the child hereby state as follows:

(1) I consent to the application of   an adoption agency, for an order freeing the child for adoption.

(2) I understand that the effect of an adoption order would be to deprive me permanently of the parental rights and duties relating to the child and to vest them in the adopters; and in particular I understand that, if and when an adoption order is made, I shall have no right to see or get in touch with the child or to have him/her returned to me.

(3) I further understand that the court cannot make an order freeing a child for adoption without the agreement of each parent or guardian of the child to the making of an adoption order, unless the court dispenses with that agreement on the ground that the person concerned—

(*a*) cannot be found or is incapable of giving agreement, or

(*b*) is withholding his agreement unreasonably, or

(*c*) has persistently failed without reasonable cause to discharge the parental duties in relation to the child, or

(*d*) has abandoned or neglected the child, or

(*e*) has persistently ill-treated the child, or

(*f*) has seriously ill-treated the child and the rehabilitation of the child within the household of the parent or guardian is unlikely.

(4) I further understand that, when the application for an order freeing the child for adoption is heard, this document may be used as evidence

of my agreement to the making of an adoption order unless I inform the court that I no longer agree.

(5) I hereby freely, and with full understanding of what is involved, agree unconditionally to the making of an adoption order.

(6) (I have been given an opportunity of making a declaration that I prefer not to be involved in future questions concerning the adoption of the child. I understand that if I make such a declaration I will not be told when the child has been adopted or whether he has been placed for adoption. I further understand that I will not be able to apply for a revocation of the order freeing the child for adoption if I make such a declaration. I hereby freely declare, with full understanding of what is involved, that I do not wish to be involved in future questions concerning the adoption of the child.)

(7) (I have been given an opportunity of making a declaration that I prefer not to be involved in future questions concerning the adoption of the child, and the effect of making such a declaration has been explained to me. I do not wish to make such a declaration.)

(8) (I have not received or given any payment or reward for, or in consideration of, the adoption of the child, for any agreement to the making of an adoption order or consent to the making of an application for an order freeing the child for adoption, for placing the child for adoption with any person or making any arrangements for the adoption of the child (other than a payment to an adoption agency for their expenses incurred in connection with the adoption).)

Signature:

This form, duly completed, was signed by the said   before
me at   on the   day of 19   .

Signature:

Address

Description

Notes

(Heading)

(*a*) Insert the name of the adoption agency applying for the order.

(*b*) Insert the first name(s) and surname of the child as known to the person giving agreement.

(*c*) If the child has previously been adopted a certified copy of the

entry in the Adopted Children Register should be attached and not a certified copy of the original entry in the Registers of Births.

(*d*) Where two or more forms of agreement are supplied to the court at the same time they may both or all refer to a certificate attached to one of the forms of agreement.

Paragraphs 6 and 7 If the parent or guardian does not make the declaration the adoption agency must, after twelve months have passed from the making of the order freeing the child for adoption, inform the parent or guardian whether an adoption order has been made in respect of the child, and, if not, whether the child has his home with a person with whom he has been placed for adoption. Further, if no adoption order has been made in respect of the child or the child does not have his home with a person with whom he has been placed for adoption, then the parent or guardian may apply to the court for revocation of the order freeing the child for adoption.

Witness Statement In England and Wales, the document should be witnessed by the reporting officer. In Scotland, it should be witnessed by a Justice of the Peace or a Sheriff, and in Northern Ireland, by a Justice of the Peace. Outside the United Kingdom it should be witnessed by a person authorised by law in the place where the document is signed to administer an oath for any judicial or legal purpose, a British consular officer, a notary public, or, if the person executing the document is serving in the regular armed forces of the Crown, an officer holding a commission in any of those forces.

Form 3

Notice of Hearing of an Application for an Order Freeing a Child for Adoption

(*Heading as in Form 1*)

To
of

Whereas an application for an order freeing for adoption   ,
a child of the   sex born on the   day of
                    19   , has been made by   of

And whereas   (and   ) was/
were appointed reporting officer(s) (and   was
appointed guardian ad litem of the child);

Take notice:

1 That the said application will be heard before the judge at
on the   day of   19   , at   o'clock
and that you may then appear and be heard on the question whether an
order freeing the child for adoption should be made.

2 That you are not obliged to attend the hearing unless you wish to
do so or the court notifies you that your attendance is necessary.

3 That while the said application is pending, if the child is in the care
of the applicant, then a parent or guardian of the child who has not
consented to the making of the application must not, except with the
leave of the court, remove the child from the actual custody of the person
with whom the child has his home against the will of that person.

(4 That the court has been requested to dispense with your agreement
to the making of an adoption order on the ground(s) that
                    and the statement of the facts on which the applicant
intends to rely is attached.)

It would assist the court if you would complete the attached form and
return it to me.

Dated the   day of   19   .

—Registrar

To the Senior Registrar of the Family Division/Registrar of the
County Court.

Number   of 19   .

I received notice of the hearing of the application on the
day of   19   .

I wish/do not wish to oppose the application.

I wish/do not wish to appear and be heard on the question whether an
order should be made.

(signature)

(address)

(date)

Notes

Preamble: Enter the first name(s) and the surname of the child as shown
in the originating process. Enter the name of the applicant agency and
the name(s) of the reporting officer(s) (and of the guardian ad litem, if
appointed).

Form 4

Application for Revocation of an Order Freeing a Child for Adoption

(*Heading as in Form 1*)

On the   day of   19   this court made an order
freeing   , a child, for adoption.

I/We   (and   ) of (address), the
former parent(s) of the child, apply for revocation of that order on the
grounds that:

1 No adoption order has been made in respect of the child, and

2 The child does not have his home with a person with whom he has
been placed for adoption, and

3 I/We wish to resume the parental rights and duties because

signed

dated

Notes

   (*a*) The application must be made to the court which made the original
      order, and not earlier than 12 months from the date of that order.

   (*b*) A parent or guardian of the child who has made a declaration
      (referred to in section 14(7) of the Children Act 1975) that he
      prefers not to be involved in future questions concerning the adop-
      tion of the child may not make application for revocation of the
      order.

   (*c*) State the reasons relied upon for the revocation of the order.

Form 5

Application for Transfer of Parental Rights and Duties Between Adoption Agencies

(Heading as in Form 1)

I, an authorised officer of the   of   ,
and I, an authorised officer of the   of   ,
both being adoption agencies, wishing to transfer the parental rights and
duties   in   respect   of   , a   child,   from
                    to   hereby give the following
further particulars in support of our application.

1 On the   day of   19   , the court made an
order freeing the child for adoption under section 14 of the Children Act
1975. A copy of that order is attached.

2 The transfer would be in the best interests of the child because

3 The administrative reasons why the transfer is desirable are

(4 The former parent(s),   of   (and
                    of   ), has/have been informed of the
making of this application.)

Dated etc

(signatures)

(addresses)

Notes

Preamble Enter the names of the two agencies concerned and enter the
name of the child as shown in the order referred to in paragraph 1.

Paragraphs 2 and 3 State concisely the reasons it is desired to transfer
the child between the agencies.

Paragraph 4 A former parent is a person as defined in section 15(1) of
the Children Act 1975. This paragraph should be deleted only if there
are no former parents.

Form 6

Originating Process for an Adoption Order/Order Authorising a Proposed Foreign Adoption

(*Heading as in Form 1*)

I/We, the undersigned,   (and   ,) wishing to adopt   , a child, hereby give the following further particulars in support of my/our application.

PART 1

Particulars of the applicant(s)

   1 *Name and address etc*

Name of (first) applicant in full

Address

Occupation

Date of Birth

Relationship (if any) to the child

(Name of (second) applicant in full

Address

Occupation

Date of Birth

Relationship (if any) to the child   )

   2 *Domicile*

I am/we are/one of us (namely   ) is domiciled in England and Wales/Scotland/Northern Ireland/the Channel Islands/the Isle of Man.

   3 *Status*

We are married to each other and our marriage certificate (or other evidence of marriage) is attached (*or* I am unmarried/a widow/a widower/a divorcee) (*or* I am applying alone as a married person and can satisfy the court that   ).

(4 I am applying alone for an adoption order in respect of my own child and can satisfy the court that the other natural parent   .)

(5 *Health*

A report on my/our health, made by a registered medical practitioner on the   day of   19   , is attached.)

Notes

Heading Enter the first name(s) and surname of the child as shown in any certificate referred to in paragraph 6 below; otherwise enter the first name(s) and surname by which the child was known before being placed for adoption.

If the application is made to the county court, either the child must be within the district of the county court to which the application is made or it must be the divorce county court in which a declaration has been made under section 41 of the Matrimonial Causes Act 1973.

Paragraph 1 Insert the address where the applicant has his home and the place (if different) where documents may be served upon him.

Paragraph 2 May be deleted if the application is for an order authorising a proposed foreign adoption.

Paragraph 3 Documentary evidence of marital status should be supplied. A married applicant can apply alone if he or she can satisfy the court that his or her spouse cannot be found, or that they have separated and are living apart and that the separation is likely to be permanent, or that by reason of physical or mental ill health the spouse is incapable of making an application for an adoption order. Any documentary evidence on which the applicant proposes to rely should be attached to the application. The name and address (if known) of the spouse should be supplied, and the marriage certificate (or other evidence of marriage) should be attached.

Paragraph 4 State the reason to be relied upon e.g. that the other natural parent is dead, or cannot be found, or that there is some other reason, which should be specified, justifying his or her exclusion. Documentary evidence, e.g. a death certificate, should be supplied where appropriate.

Paragraph 5 A separate health report is required in respect of each applicant, and the report must have been made during the period of three months before the date of the application. No report is required, however, if the child was placed for adoption with applicant by an adoption agency, or if he is the child of the applicant or either of them.

PART 2

Particulars of the child

6 Identity etc

The child is of the   sex and is not and has not been married. He/she was born on the   day of   19 and is the person to whom the attached birth/adoption certificate relates (*or* was born on or about the   day of   19   , in   ). He/she is a   national.

(7 Health

A report on the health of the child, made by a registered medical practitioner on the   day of   19   , is attached.)

(8 The child is free for adoption pursuant to section 14 of the Children Act 1975, and I/we attach hereto the order of the   court, dated   , to that effect. The parental rights and duties relating to the child were thereby vested in   (and were transferred to   by order of the   court under section 23 of the Children Act 1975 on   19   ).)

(9 Parentage, etc

The child is the child of   whose last known address was

(*or* deceased) and   whose last known address was

(*or* deceased).)

10 The guardian(s) of the child (other than the mother or the father of the child) is/are   of

(and   of

).)

(11 Parental agreement

I/We understand that the said   (and   ) is/are willing to agree to the making of an adoption order in pursuance of my/our application.)

(12 I/we request the judge to dispense with the agreement of   (and   ) on the ground(s) that   (and   ) and there are attached hereto three copies of a statement of the facts upon which I/we intend to rely.)

(13 **Care etc**

The child is in the care of   (who have the powers and
duties of a parent or guardian of the child) (*or* the parental rights and
duties in respect of the child).)

(14 **Maintenance**

                           of   is liable by
virtue of an order made by the   court
at   on the   day of   19   ,
(*or* by an agreement dated the   day of   19   )
to contribute to the maintenance of the child.)

15 **Proposed names**

If an adoption order is made in pursuance of this application, the child
is to be known by the following names:

Surname

Other names

Notes

Paragraph 6 If the child has previously been adopted a certified copy of
the entry in the Adopted Children Register should be attached and not
a certified copy of the original entry in the Registers of Births. Where a
certificate is not attached, enter the place (including the country) of birth
if known.

Paragraph 7 The report must have been made during the period of three
months before the date of the application. No report is required,
however, if the child was placed for adoption with the applicant by an
adoption agency, or if he is the child of the applicant or either of them.

Paragraph 8 The order made by the court freeing the child for adoption
and any order made under section 23 should be attached

Paragraph 9 This paragraph and paragraphs 10 to 14 only apply if the
child is not free for adoption. If the child has previously been adopted,
give the names of his adoptive parents and not those of his natural
parents. If the child is illegitimate, and the putative father has legal
custody of the child by virtue of a court order, give details of that order
under paragraph 19.

Paragraph 10 Enter particulars of any person appointed by deed or will
in accordance with the provisions of the Guardianship of Infants Acts
1886 and 1925, or the Guardianship of Minors Act 1971 or by a court of
competent jurisdiction to be a guardian. Do not include any person who

has the custody of the child only. Delete this paragraph if the child has no guardian.

Paragraphs 11 and 12 Enter either in paragraph 11 or 12 the names of the persons mentioned in paragraphs 9 and 10, except that in the case of an illegitimate child the father of the child should be entered only if he has custody of the child by virtue of a court order. Where it is sought to dispense with parental agreement, enter in paragraph 12 one or more of the grounds set out in section 12(2) of the 1975 Act.

Paragraph 13 This paragraph should be completed where the child is in the care of a local authority or a voluntary organisation.

Paragraph 14 This paragraph should be completed where some person or body is liable to contribute to the maintenance of the child under a court order of agreement.

PART 3

General

16 The child has lived with me/us continuously since the day of
        19   (and has accordingly had his home with me/us for the five years preceding the date of this application).

17 The child was (placed with me/us for adoption on the
day of   19   by   , an adoption agency) (*or* received into my/our actual custody in the following circumstances:
).

(18 I/we notified the   Council on the   day of
        19   , of my/our intention to apply for an adoption order in respect of the child.)

19 No proceedings relating in whole or in part to the child other than as stated in paragraph 8 have been completed or commenced in any court in England and Wales or elsewhere (except   .)

20 I/we have not received or given any payment or reward for, or in consideration of, the adoption of the child, for any agreement to the making of an adoption order, the transfer of the actual custody of the child with a view to adoption or the making of any arrangements for adoption (except as follows:

).

21 As far as I/we know, the only person(s) or bod(y)ies) who have taken part in the arrangements for the child's adoption are

(22 For the purpose of this application reference may be made to
                of   .)

23 I/we desire that my/our identity should be kept confidential, and
the serial number of this application is   .)

(24 I/we intend to adopt the child under the law of or within
                which is the country of my/our domicile, and evidence as
to the law of adoption in that country is filed with this process.)

(25 I/we desire to remove the child from the British Isles for the
purpose of adoption.)

I/we accordingly apply for an adoption order/an order authorising a
proposed foreign adoption in respect of the child.

Dated this   day of   19   .

                                        Signature(s)

Notes

Paragraphs 16 and 17 Under section 9 of the 1975 Act, an adoption order
cannot be made unless the child has had his home with the applicants or
one of them:—

(*a*) for at least 13 weeks if the applicant or one of them is a parent,
   step-parent or relative of the child or if the child was placed with
   the applicant by an adoption agency or in pursuance of an order
   of the High Court.
(*b*) for at least 12 months in any other case.

Paragraph 18 Notice does not have to be given if the child was placed
with the applicant by an adoption agency. Where notice does not have
to be given, no order can be made until the expiration of three months
from the date of the notice.

Paragraph 19 The nature of the proceedings and the date and effect of
any orders made should be stated. The court cannot proceed with the
application if a previous application made by the same applicant in
relation to the child was refused, unless one of the conditions in section
22(4) of the 1975 Act is satisfied. The court must dismiss the application
if it considers that, where the application is made by a married couple
of whom one is a parent and the other a step-parent of the child, or by
a step-parent of the child alone, the matter would be better dealt with
under section 42 (orders for custody etc. in matrimonial proceedings) of
the Matrimonial Causes Act 1973.

Paragraph 21 Enter the name and address of the adoption agency or

individual who took part in the arrangements for placing the child for adoption in the actual custody of the applicant.

Paragraph 22 Where the applicant or one of the applicants is a parent of the child, or a relative as defined by section 57(1) of the Adoption Act 1958 (as amended) or the child was placed with the applicant by an adoption agency, no referee need be named.

Paragraph 23 If the applicant wishes his identity to be kept confidential, the serial number obtained under rule 14 should be given.

See p 228 for additional paragraphs in Convention proceedings.

Form 7

Agreement to an Adoption Order/Proposed Foreign Adoption

(*Heading as in Form 1*)

IF YOU ARE IN ANY DOUBT ABOUT YOUR LEGAL RIGHTS YOU SHOULD OBTAIN LEGAL ADVICE *BEFORE* SIGNING THIS FORM.

Whereas an application is to be/has been made by   and
                    (*or* under serial No.   ), for an adoption order
or order authorising a proposed foreign adoption in respect of a child;

And whereas the child is the person to whom the birth certificate attached marked 'A' relates:

(And whereas the child is at least six weeks old:)

I, the undersigned   of
being a parent/guardian of the child hereby state as follows:

(1) I understand that the effect of an adoption order/an order authorising a proposed foreign adoption will be to deprive me permanently of the parental rights and duties relating to the child and to vest them in the applicant(s); and in particular I understand that, if an order is made, I shall have no right to see or get in touch with the child or to have him/her returned to me.

(2) I further understand that the court cannot make an adoption order/an order authorising the proposed foreign adoption of the child without the agreement of each parent or guardian of the child unless the court dispenses with an agreement on the ground that the person concerned–

(*a*) cannot be found or is incapable of giving agreement, or

(*b*) is withholding his agreement unreasonably, or

(*c*) has persistently failed without reasonable cause to discharge the parental duties in relation to the child, or

(*d*) has abandoned or neglected the child, or

(*e*) has persistently ill-treated the child, or

(*f*) has seriously ill-treated the child and the rehabilitation of the child within the household of the parent or guardian is unlikely.

(3) I further understand that when the application for an adoption order/order authorising the proposed foreign adoption of the child is

heard, this document may be used as evidence of my agreement to the making of the order unless I inform the court that I no longer agree.

(4) I hereby freely, and with full understanding of what is involved, agree unconditionally to the making of an adoption order/an order authorising the proposed foreign adoption of the child in pursuance of the application.

(5) As far as I know, the only person(s) or body(ies) who has/have taken part in the arrangements for the child's adoption is/are
(and   ).

(6) I have not received or given any payment or reward for, or in consideration of, the adoption of the child, for any agreement to the making of an adoption order or placing the child for adoption with any person or making arrangements for the adoption of the child (other than payment to an adoption agency for their expenses incurred in connection with the adoption).

Signature:

This form, duly completed, was signed by the said   before me at   on the   day of   19   .

Signature:

Address:

Description:

Notes

Preamble Insert either the name(s) of the applicant(s) or the serial No. assigned to the applicant(s) for the purposes of the application.

Insert the first name(s) and surname of the child as known to the person giving agreement.

If the child has previously been adopted a certified copy of the entry in the Adopted Children Register should be attached and not a certified copy of the original entry in the Registers of Births.

Where two or more forms of agreement are supplied to the court at the same time they may both or all refer to a certificate attached to one of the forms of agreement.

The father of an illegitimate child is not a parent for this purpose, but is a guardian if he has custody of the child by virtue of a court order;

"guardian" also means a person appointed by deed or will in accordance with the provisions of the Guardianship of Infants Acts 1886 and 1925 or the Guardianship of Minors Act 1971, or by a court of competent jurisdiction to be the guardian of the child.

Paragraph 3 Notice will be given of the hearing of the application and of the court by which it is to be heard. After the making of the application a parent or guardian who has agreed cannot remove the child from the actual custody of the applicant(s) except with the leave of the court.

Paragraph 5 Enter the name and address of the adoption agency or individual who took part in the arrangements for placing the child in the actual custody of the applicant(s).

Witness statement In England and Wales the document should be witnessed by the reporting officer. In Scotland, it should be witnessed by a Justice of the Peace or a Sheriff, and in Northern Ireland by a Justice of the Peace. Outside the United Kingdom it should be witnessed by a person authorised by law in the place where the document is signed to administer an oath for any judicial or legal purpose, a British consular officer, a notary public, or, if the person executing the document is serving in the regular armed forces of the Crown, an officer holding a commission in any of those forces.

Form 8

Notice of Hearing of an Application for an Adoption Order/an Order Authorising a Proposed Foreign Adoption

(*Heading as in Form 1*)

To   of

Whereas an application for an adoption order/an order authorising a proposed foreign adoption in respect of   , a child of the   sex born on the   day of   19 , has been made (by   (and   ) of   ) (*or* under the serial number   ) and whereas   (and   ) was/were appointed reporting officer(s) (and   was appointed guardian ad litem of the child);

Take Notice

(1 That the said application will be heard before the judge at   on the   day of   19 , at   o'clock and that you may then appear and be heard on the question whether an adoption order/an order authorising a proposed foreign adoption should be made.)

(2 That if you wish to appear and be heard on the question whether an adoption order/an order authorising a proposed foreign adoption should be made, you should give notice to the court on or before the   day of   19 , in order that a time may be fixed for your appearance.)

3 That you are not obliged to attend the hearing unless you wish to do so or the court notifies you that your attendance is necessary.

4 That while the application is pending, a parent or guardian of the child who has agreed to the making of an order must not, except with the leave of the court, remove the child from the actual custody of the applicant.

(5 That the application states that the child has had his home with the applicant for the five years preceding the application and accordingly, if that is correct, no person is entitled, against the will of the applicant, to remove the child from the applicant's actual custody except with the leave of the court or under authority conferred by an enactment or on the arrest of the child.)

(6 That the court has been requested to dispense with your agreement to the making of an order on the ground(s) that

and a statement of the facts on which the applicant intends to rely is attached.)

It would assist the court if you would complete the attached form and return it to me.

Dated the   day of   19   .

                                                                    Registrar

----

To the Senior Registrar of the Principal Registry of the Family Division/
Registrar of the   county court.

                                                                    No

I received the notice of the hearing of the application on the
day of   19   .

I wish/do not wish to oppose the application.

I wish/do not wish to appear and be heard on the question whether an order should be made.

                                                                    (signature)

                                                                    (address)

                                                                    (date)

Notes

Paragraph numbers in these notes refer to the appropriate paragraph in the form.

When this form is used under rule 25(2) to give notice of a further hearing of an application it is to be amended so as to refer to a further hearing and so as to give particulars of the interim order.

Preamble Enter the name(s) and surname of the child as shown in the originating process. Enter the name of the applicant(s) unless the applicant has obtained a serial number, in which case the second part in brackets should be completed.

Paragraphs 1 and 2 Paragraph 1 should be completed and paragraph 2 struck out where the notice is addressed to any respondent where the applicant does not wish his identity to be kept confidential. When a serial number has been assigned to the applicant and the notice is addressed

to an individual respondent other than the spouse of the applicant, paragraph 1 should be struck out and paragraph 2 completed.

Paragraph 5 This paragraph should be deleted except where it appears from the originating process that the child has had his home with the applicant for five years.

Paragraph 6 Unless deleted, this paragraph should contain the grounds specified in the originating application.

Form 9

Originating Process for the Annulment or Revocation of an
Adoption

In the High Court
Family Division   No   of 19

In the Matter of

and

In the Matter of the Adoption Act 1968

Let   of
attend at the Royal Courts of Justice, Strand, London WC2A 2LL on a
date to be fixed for the hearing of the application of
                    for an order:

1 That the adoption which was authorised on the   day of
          19   at   , by which
          (and   )was (*or* were) authorised to
adopt the said   be annulled (*or* revoked).

(2 That the leave of the court be granted for the purpose of making
this application out of time.)

3 That the costs of this application be provided for.

Dated this   day of   19 .

This summons was taken out by   of
          , solicitor for the above named   .

Notes

This form is for use when the adoption is to be annulled or revoked
under section 6(1) or (2) of the Adoption Act 1968. An application may
not be made unless either the adopter or both adopters, as the case may
be. or the adopted person habitually resides in Great Britain immediately
before the application is made.

Preamble Enter the full names by which the adopted person has been
known since the adoption.

Paragraph 1 Enter the description and address of the authority by which
the adoption was authorised.

Paragraph 2 Except with the leave of the court, an application to annul
an adoption may not be made later than two years after the date of the
adoption to which it relates.

Form 10

Originating Process for an Order that an Overseas Adoption or a Determination Cease to be Valid or that a Determination has been Affected by a Subsequent Determination

(*Heading as in Form 9*)

Let   of
attend at the Royal Courts of Justice, Strand, London WC2A 2LL on a
date to be fixed for the hearing of the application of
of   for:

(1 An order that an overseas adoption which was authorised on the
day of   19   at   , by which
(and   ) was (*or* were) authorised to adopt the said
do cease to be valid in Great Britain;)

(2 An order that a determination made by an authority of a Convention
country (*or* a specified country) to authorise (*or* review the authorisation
of) a Convention adoption (*or* an adoption order made under any enactment in force in a specified country and corresponding to sections 8(1)
and 24 of the Children Act 1975) do cease to be valid in Great Britain;)

(3 An order that a determination made by an authority of a Convention
country (*or* a specified country) to give (*or* review) a decision revoking
(or annulling) a Convention adoption (*or* an adoption order made under
any enactment in force in a specified country and corresponding to
sections 8(1) and 24 of the Children Act 1975) (*or* an order made under
section 8 of the Children Act 1975 as a Convention adoption order) do
cease to be valid in Great Britain;)

(4 A decision as to the extent, if any, to which a determination
mentioned in paragraph 2 (*or* 3) above has been affected by a subsequent
determination;)

(5 An order that the costs of this application be provided for.)

Dated this   day of   19 .

This summons was taken out by   of
            solicitor for the above named   .

Notes

This form is principally for use if the applicant claims that the adoption
or determination is contrary to public policy or that the authority which
purported to authorise the adoption or make the determination was

not competent to entertain the case. The applicant should delete the paragraphs which are not relevant.

Paragraph 1 An overseas adoption is one specified in an order made under section 4(3) of the Adoption Act 1968; a Convention adoption is an overseas adoption of a description designated in such an order as that of an adoption regulated by the Hague Convention on the Adoption of Children 1965.

Paragraphs 2 and 3 A Convention country means a country designated by an order of the Secretary of State as a country in which the Hague Convention on the Adoption of Children 1965 is in force (section 107(1) of the 1975 Act). A specified country means Northern Ireland, the Channel Islands, the Isle of Man or a colony, unless this meaning is modified by an order of the Secretary of State (section 11(1) of the 1968 Act).

Form 11

Affidavit in Support of Application under Section 6 of the Adoption Act 1968

(*Heading as in Form 9*)

I/ we   of
hereby make oath and say that the particulars set out in this affidavit are
true.

   1 Name of (first) adopter in full
     Address

   (2 Name of second adopter in full
     Address   )

   3 Name of adopted person in full

   (4 The said   (and the said   )
habitually reside(s) in Great Britain.)

   5 The adopted person is of the   sex, is a national of
and was born at   on the   day of   19   .

   6 On the   day of   19   the said
(and   ) was (*or* were) authorised to adopt the said
         by   at   and those persons are the
persons to whom the certified copy of an entry in a public register (or
other evidence of adoption) which is exhibited to this affidavit relates.

   (7 At the time at which the adoption was authorised the said
         was a national of   and resided in
         (the   said   was a
national of   and resided in   ) and
the adopted person was a national of   and
resided in   ).

or

   (7 *For other applications details of the marriage or, as appropriate, of
the determination or determinations should be given and any necessary
documentary evidence relating thereto supplied.*)

   (8 A statement of the facts is exhibited to this affidavit.)

Sworn, etc

   This affidavit is filed on behalf of the applicant(s).

Notes

Paragraph 3 Enter the name(s) by which the adopted person has been known since the adoption.

Paragraph 4 This paragraph is not required for applications made under section 6(3) of the Adoption Act 1968. Where this paragraph is required, no application may be made to the court unless the adopter or, as the case may be, both adopters or the adopted person habitually reside in Great Britain immediately before the application is made. Therefore, the name(s) of either the adopter(s) or the adopted person should be entered.

Paragraph 6 Enter the description and the full address of the authority which authorised the adoption. Evidence of the adoption may be given either by a certified copy of an entry in a public register relating to adoptions or by a certificate that the adoption has been effected signed by a person who is authorised by the law of the country concerned to do so.

Paragraph 7 This paragraph should be completed where the application is made under section 6(1) of the Adoption Act 1968. Enter the name of the first adopter and of the second adopter, if applicable.

Paragraph 8 A statement of facts is not required for an application to revoke a convention adoption under section 6(2) of the Adoption Act 1968. Expert evidence as to notified provisions may be necessary. In that or any other case where the applicant intends to rely on any provision of foreign law relating to adoption, any accompanying affidavit thereon must be sworn by a person who is suitably qualified on account of his knowledge or experience to give evidence as to the law concerned.

Form 12

Order Freeing a Child for Adoption

(*Heading as in Form 1*)

Whereas an application has been made by   of
, being an adoption agency, for an order freeing for adoption
, a child of the   sex, the child of   (and
);

It is ordered that the child be freed for adoption and that the parental rights and duties relating to the child be vested in the applicant;

(and as regards costs it is ordered that   ;)

(and whereas the precise date of the child's birth has not been proved to the satisfaction of the court but the court has determined the probable date of his/her birth to be the   day of   19   ;)

(and whereas it has been proved to the satisfaction of the court that the child was born in   (country);)

(and whereas the place of birth of the child has not been proved to the satisfaction of the court (but it appears probable that the child was born in the United Kingdom, the Channel Islands or the Isle of Man, the child is treated as having been born in the registration district of and sub-district of   in the county of   );)

(and whereas it has been proved to the satisfaction of the court that the child is identical with   to whom the entry numbered   made on the   day of   19   , in the Register of Births for the registration district of   and sub-district of   in the county of   relates (*or* with   to whom the entry numbered   and dated the   day of   19   , in the Adopted Children Register relates);)

It is directed that this order is sufficient proof of the above particulars for the purposes of any future adoption application in respect of the child.

And it is further recorded that   (and
) being a parent or guardian of the child made a declaration under section 14(7) of the 1975 Act that he/she prefers not to be involved in future questions concerning the adoption of the child.

Dated this   day of   19   .

Form 13

Order Revoking an Order Freeing a Child for Adoption/
Dismissing an Application to Revoke an Order Freeing a Child
for Adoption

(*Heading as in Form 1*)

Whereas an application has been made by   of
(and   of   )
for an order revoking an order freeing for adoption   ,
a child of the   sex, the child of   (and
), such order having been made by the
court on the   day of   19;

It is ordered that the said order be revoked and that the parental rights
and duties relating to the child be vested in   (and   );

(and it is ordered that   of   do make
periodical payments to the child in the sum of £   payable
;)

(It is ordered that the application be dismissed (and that the appli-
cant(s) shall not make further application under section 16 of the Children
Act 1975);)

(and it is ordered that   , the adoption agency which
obtained the order under section 14 of the Children Act 1975, is released
from the duty of complying further with section 15(3) of that Act as
respects the applicant(s).)

(And as regards costs is ordered that
.)

Dated this   day of   19   .

Form 14

Interim Order

(Heading as in Form 1)

Whereas an application has been made by   of
            (and   ) for an adoption order in respect of
        a child of the   sex, the child/adopted child of
            (and   );

It is ordered that the determination of the application be postponed
and that the applicant(s) do have the legal custody of the child until the
            day of   19   , by way of a probationary period
(*or* that the determination of the application be postponed to the
            day of   19   , and that the applicant(s) do have
the legal custody of the child until that day by way of a probationary
period) (upon the following terms, namely   );

(and as regards cost it is ordered that   ;)

(and it is ordered that the application be further heard before the judge
at on the   day of   19   , at   o'clock.)

Dated this   day of   19   .

Form 15

(Convention) Adoption Order/Order Authorising a Proposed Foreign Adoption

(*Heading as in Form 1*)

Whereas an application has been made by
of   whose occupation is   (and
                             whose occupation is   ) for an
adoption order/an order authorising a proposed foreign adoption/a
Convention adoption order in respect of   , a child of
the   sex, the child/adopted child of   (and
                 );

It is ordered that (the applicant(s) do adopt the child) (*or* the appli-
cant(s) be authorised to remove the child from Great Britain for the
purpose of adopting him/her under the law of or within the country in
which the applicant is/applicants are domiciled, and that the parental
rights and duties relating to the child (including the legal custody of the
child) be vested in the applicant(s).

(And as regards costs, it is ordered that   ;)

(And it is recorded that the   , being an adoption
agency, placed the child for adoption with the applicant(s)/the
              Council was notified of the applicant(s) intention to adopt
the child;)

(And whereas the child was freed for adoption by the
court on the   day of   19   ;)

(And whereas the precise date of the child's birth has not been proved
to the satisfaction of the court but the court has determined the probable
date of his/her birth to be the   day of   19   ;)

(And whereas it has been proved to the satisfaction of the court that
the child was born in   (country);)

(And whereas the place of birth of the child has not been proved to
the satisfaction of the court (but it appears probable that the child was
born in the United Kingdom, the Channel Islands or the Isle of Man,
the child is treated as having been born in the registration district of
              and sub-district of   in the county of   );)

(And whereas it has been proved to the satisfaction of the court that
the child was born on the   day of   19   (and is
identical with   to whom the entry numbered   made

on the   day of   19   , in the Register of Births
for the registration district of   and sub-district of
in the county of   relates) (*or* with   to 19   , in the
Adopted Children Register relates);)

(And whereas the name or names and surname stated in,the application
as those by which the child is to be known are

;)

It is directed that the Registrar General shall make in the Adopted
Children Register an entry in the form specified by regulations made by
him recording the particulars set out in this order (and that the entry be
marked with the words 'Convention order');

(And it is further directed that the aforesaid entry in the Register of
Births/Adopted Children Register be marked with the words 'adopted'/
'readopted'/'proposed foreign adoption'/'proposed foreign readoption').

Dated this   day of   19   .

MODIFICATION TO FORM 6 FOR THE PURPOSES OF CONVENTION PROCEEDINGS

Form 6 shall contain the following additional paragraphs after paragraph 25:

Part IV

Additional Information Required for a Convention Adoption Application

26 **The Child**
The child—
    (*a*) is a United Kingdom national (*or* a national of
        which is a Convention country) and
    (*b*) habitually resides at   which is in British territory
        (*or* a Convention country).

27 **The Applicants**
We are applying together, in reliance on section 24(4)(*a*) of the 1975 Act, and the first applicant is a United Kingdom national (*or* a national of   which is a Convention country) and the second applicant is a United Kingdom national (*or* a national of   which is a Convention country) and we habitually reside at   which is in Great Britain.

(*or*

27 **The Applicants**
We are applying together in reliance on section 24(4)(*b*) of the 1975 Act, and are both United Kingdom nationals, and we are habitually resident at   which is in British territory (*or* a Convention country).)

(*or*

27 **The Applicant**
I am applying alone in reliance on section 24(5)(*a*) of the 1975 Act, and am a United Kingdom national (*or* a national of   which is a Convention country) and habitually reside at   which is in Great Britain.)

(*or*

27 **The Applicant**
I am applying alone in reliance on section 24(5)(*b*) of the 1975 Act, and am a United Kingdom national and habitually reside at   which is in British territory (*or* a Convention country).)

28 **Specified Provisions**

We are both (*or* I am), accordingly, nationals of the same (*or* a national of a) Convention country, namely   and there are no specified provisions in respect of that country (*or* there are no relevant specified provisions in respect of that country because   ).)

Notes

Paragraphs 26 and 27 Documentary evidence of nationality should be exhibited. Where a child or an applicant is a national of a Convention country, evidence as to the law of the country relating to nationality applicable to that person should be supplied. Where the child is not a United Kingdom national, evidence as to the provisions relating to consents and consultations of the internal law relating to adoption of the Convention country of which the child is a national should be supplied. Any affidavit on foreign law must be sworn by a person who is suitably qualified on account of his knowledge or experience to give evidence as to the law concerned. British territory is defined in section 107(1) of the 1975 Act.

Paragraph 28 'specified provision' is defined in section 24(8) of the 1975 Act. Expert evidence as to specified provisions may be necessary; if so any affidavit on foreign law must be sworn by a person who is suitably qualified on account of his knowledge or experience to give evidence as to the law concerned.

The Magistrates' Courts (Adoption) Rules 1984

SCHEDULE I   **Rule 2(4)**

Form 1

Application for an Order Freeing a Child for Adoption

To the   Domestic Court

I, an authorised officer

[The form continues as in Form 1 in Part 1 of this Appendix]
[The notes to the form begin:
    An application to a domestic court must be made to a court within the area in which either the child or his parent or guardian is.
Introduction: Enter the first name(s) and surname as shown in the certificate referred to in paragraph 2; otherwise enter the first name(s) and surname by which the child is known. The notes proceed with the note to paragraph 2.]

Form 2

Agreement to an Adoption Order (Freeing Cases)

[This form corresponds with Form 2 in Part 1 of this Appendix except that it contains a Note to Paragraph 8 as follows:
    Any such payment or reward is illegal, except payment to an adoption agency in respect of their expenses incurred in connection with the adoption.]

Form 3

Notice of Hearing of an Application for an Order Freeing a Child for Adoption

[This form corresponds with Form 3 in Part 1 of this Appendix except that it is signed by the Justices' Clerk, to whom the attached slip is also addressed.]

Form 4

Application for Revocation of an Order Freeing a Child for Adoption

[This form corresponds, mutatis mutandis, with Form 4 in Part 1 of this Appendix.]

Form 5

Application for Transfer of Parental Rights and Duties between Adoption Agencies

[Corresponds with Form 5 in Part 1 of this Appendix.]

Form 6

Application for an Adoption Order

[Corresponds, mutatis mutandis, with Form 6 in Part 1 of this Appendix.
The Notes begin:
   The application must be made to a domestic court within whose area
   the child is.
   The reference to county court districts is omitted.
   Paragraphs 24 and 25 are omitted.]

Form 7

Agreement to an Adoption Order

[Corresponds exactly with Form 7 in Part 1 of this Appendix]

Form 8

Notice of Hearing of an Application for an Adoption Order

[Corresponds, mutatis mutandis, with Form 8 in Part 1 of this Appendix]

Form 9   **Rule 28(1)**

Application to Amend or Revoke Adoption Order

To the   Domestic Court

1 Identification of the adoption order to be amended or revoked
   Name of adopters:
   Date of adoption order:
   Name of child adopted:

2 Particulars of the applicant
   Name:
   Address:
   Relationship (if any) to the child (*or* if no such relationship, state reason for application):

If application is made under section 24 of the Adoption Act 1958, state the amendments desired and the facts relied on in support of the application.

If application is made under section 26 of the Adoption Act 1958 or section 1(1) of the Adoption Act 1960, state the facts relied on in support of the application:

I apply for the adoption order to be amended or revoked in accordance with this application.

Dated this   day of   19   .

                                                      Signature

Form 10   **Rule 31(1)**

Order Freeing a Child for Adoption

[Corresponds with Form 12 in Part 1 of this Appendix]

Form 11   **Rule 31(1)**

Order Revoking an Order Freeing a Child for Adoption/ Dismissing an Application to Revoke an Order Freeing a Child for Adoption

[Corresponds with Form 13 in Part 1 of this Appendix]

Form 12   **Rule 31(1)**

Interim Order

[Corresponds with Form 14 in Part 1 of this Appendix]

Form 13   Rule 31(1)

Adoption Order

[Corresponds, mutatis mutandis, with Form 15 in Part 1 of this Appendix]

Form 14   Rule 32(1)

Register of Adoptions

Appendix 2

Contents of Reports in Adoption Proceedings (AR and MC(A)R)

MATTERS TO BE COVERED IN REPORTS SUPPLIED UNDER RULES 4(4), 22(1) or 22(2)

So far as is practicable, the report supplied by the adoption agency or, in the case of a report supplied under rule 22(2), the local authority shall include all the following particulars:

1 **The Child**

(*a*) Name, sex, date and place of birth and address;

(*b*) whether legitimate or illegitimate at birth and, if illegitimate, whether subsequently legitimated;

(*c*) nationality;

(*d*) physical description;

(*e*) personality and social development;

(*f*) religion, including details of baptism, confirmation or equivalent ceremonies;

(*g*) details of any wardship proceedings and of any court orders or local authority resolutions relating to the parental rights and duties in respect of the child or to his custody and maintenance;

(*h*) details of any brothers and sisters, including dates of birth, arrangements in respect of care and custody and whether any brother or sister is the subject of a parallel application;

(*i*) extent of access to members of the child's natural family and, if the child is illegitimate, his father, and in each case the nature of the relationship enjoyed;

(*j*) if the child has been in the care of a local authority or voluntary organisation, details (including dates) of any placements with

foster parents, or other arrangements in respect of the care of the child, including particulars of the persons with whom the child has had his home and observations on the care provided;

(k)   date and circumstances of placement with prospective adopter;

(l)   names, addresses and types of schools attended, with dates, and educational attainments;

(m) any special needs in relation to the child's health (whether physical or mental) and his emotional and behavioural development and whether he is subject to a statement under the Education Act 1981(**a**);

(n)   what, if any, rights to or interest in property or any claim to damages, under the Fatal Accidents Act 1976(**b**) or otherwise, the child stands to retain or lose if adopted;

(o)   wishes and feelings in relation to adoption and the application, including any wishes in respect of religious and cultural upbringing; and

(p)   any other relevant information which might assist the court.

2 Each Natural Parent, including where appropriate the father of an illegitimate child

(a)   Name, date and place of birth and address;

(b)   marital status and date and place of marriage (if any);

(c)   past and present relationship (if any) with the other natural parent, including comments on its stability;

(d)   physical description;

(e)   personality;

(f)   religion;

(g)   educational attainments;

(h)   past and present occupations and interests;

(i)   so far as available, names and brief details of the personal circumstances of the parents and any brothers and sisters of the natural parent, with their ages or ages at death;

(j)   wishes and feelings in relation to adoption and the application, including any wishes in respect of the child's religious and cultural upbringing;

(k)   reasons why any of the above information is unavailable; and

(l)   any other relevant information which might assist the court.

3 Guardian(s)

Give the details required under paragraph 2(a), (f), (j) and (l).

4 **Prospective Adopter(s)**

    (*a*)   Name, date and place of birth and address;

    (*b*)   relationship (if any) to the child;

    (*c*)   marital status, date and place of marriage (if any) and comments on stability of relationship;

    (*d*)   details of any previous marriage;

    (*e*)   if a parent and step-parent are applying, the reasons why they prefer adoption to an order relating to the custody of the child;

    (*f*)   if a natural parent is applying alone, the reasons for the exclusion of the other parent;

    (*g*)   if a married person is applying alone, the reasons for this;

    (*h*)   physical description;

    (*i*)   personality;

    (*j*)   religion, and whether willing to follow any wishes of the child or his parents or guardian in respect of the child's religious and cultural upbringing;

    (*k*)   educational attainments;

    (*l*)   past and present occupations and interests;

    (*m*) particulars of the home and living conditions (and particulars of any home where the prospective adopter proposes to live with the child, if different);

    (*n*)   details of income and comments on the living standards of the household;

    (*o*)   details of other members of the household (including any children of the prospective adopter even if not resident in the household);

    (*p*)   details of the parents and any brothers or sisters of the prospective adopter, with their ages or ages at death;

    (*q*)   attitudes to the proposed adoption of such other members of the prospective adopter's household and family as the adoption agency or, as the case may be, the local authority considers appropriate;

    (*r*)   previous experience of caring for children as step-parent, foster parent, child-minder or prospective adopter and assessment of ability in this respect, together where appropriate with assessment of ability in bringing up the prospective adopter's own children;

(s) reasons for wishing to adopt the child and extent of understanding of the nature and effect of adoption;

(t) any hopes and expectations for the child's future;

(u) assessment of ability to bring up the child throughout his childhood;

(v) details of any adoption allowance payable;

(w) confirmation that any referees have been interviewed, with a report of their views and opinion of the weight to be placed thereon; and

(x) any other relevant information which might assist the court.

5 Actions of the adoption agency or local authority supplying the report

(a) Reports under rules 4(4) or 22(1):

    (i) brief account of the agency's actions in the case, with particulars and dates of all written information and notices given to the child, his natural parents and the prospective adopter;

    (ii) details of alternatives to adoption considered;

    (iii) reasons for considering that adoption would be in the child's best interests (with date of relevant decision); and

    (iv) reasons for considering that the prospective adopter would be suitable to be an adoptive parent and that he would be suitable for this child (with dates of relevant decisions) or, if the child has not yet been placed for adoption, reasons for considering that he is likely to be so placed.

OR

(b) Reports under rule 22(2);

    (i) confirmation that notice was given under section 18 of the 1975 Act, with the date of that notice;

    (ii) brief account of the local authority's actions in the case; and

    (iii) account of investigations whether child was placed in contravention of section 29 of the 1958 Act.

6 Generally

(a) Whether any respondent appears to be under the age of majority or under a mental disability; and

(b) whether, in the opinion of the body supplying the report, any other person should be made a respondent (for example, a person claiming to be the father of an illegitimate child, a spouse or ex-spouse of a natural parent, a relative of a deceased parent, or a person with any of the parental rights and duties).

7 **Conclusions**

(This part of the report should contain more than a simple synopsis of the information above. As far as possible, the court should be given a fuller picture of the child, his natural parents and, where appropriate, the prospective adopter.)

   (*a*) Except where the applicant or one of them is a parent of the child, a summary by the medical adviser to the body supplying the report, of the health history and state of health of the child, his natural parents and, if appropriate, the prospective adopter, with comments on the implications for the order sought and on how any special health needs of the child might be met;

   (*b*) opinion on whether making the order sought would be in the child's best long-term interests, and on how any special emotional, behavioural and educational needs of the child might be met;

   (*c*) opinion on the effect on the child's natural parents of making the order sought;

   (*d*) if the child has been placed for adoption, opinion on the likelihood of full integration of the child into the household, family and community of the prospective adopter, and on whether the proposed adoption would be in the best long-term interests of the prospective adopter;

   (*e*) opinion, if appropriate, on the relative merits of adoption and custody; and

   (*f*) final conclusions and recommendations whether the order sought should be made (and, if not, alternative proposals).

SCHEDULE 3   **Rule 15(4)**

REPORTS ON THE HEALTH OF THE CHILD AND OF THE APPLICANT(S)

This information is required for reports on the health of a child and of his prospective adopter(s). Its purpose is to build up a full picture of their health history and current state of health, including strengths and weaknesses. This will enable the local authority's medical adviser to base his advice to the court on the fullest possible information, when commenting on the health implications of the proposed adoption. The reports made by the examining doctor should cover, as far as practicable, the following matters.

1 The Child

Name, date of birth, sex, weight and height.

A A health history of each natural parent, so far as is possible, including:

  (*i*) name, date of birth, sex, weight and height;

  (*ii*) a family health history, covering the parents, the brothers and sisters and the other children of the natural parent, with details of any serious physical or mental illness and inherited and congenital disease;

  (*iii*) past health history, including details of any serious physical or mental illness, disability, accident, hospital admission or attendance at an out-patient department, and in each case any treatment given;

  (*iv*) a full obstetric history of the mother, including any problems in the ante-natal, labour and post-natal periods, with the results of any tests carried out during or immediately after pregnancy;

  (*v*) details of any present illness including treatment and prognosis;

  (*vi*) any other relevant information which might assist the medical adviser; and

  (*vii*) the name and address of any doctor(s) who might be able to provide further information about any of the above matters.

B A neo-natal report on the child, including:

  (*i*)   details of the birth, and any complications;

  (*ii*) results of a physical examination and screening tests;

  (*iii*) details of any treatment given;

  (*iv*) details of any problem in management and feeding;

  (*v*) any other relevant information which might assist the medical adviser; and

  (*vi*) the name and address of any doctor(s) who might be able to provide further information about any of the above matters.

C A full health history and examination of the child, including:

  (*i*) details of any serious illness, disability, accident, hospital admission or attendance at an out-patient department, and in each case any treatment given;

  (*ii*) details and dates of immunisations;

  (*iii*) a physical and developmental assessment according to age, including an assessment of vision and hearing and of neurological, speech and language development and any evidence of emotional disorder;

(*iv*) for a child over five years of age, the school health history (if available);

(*v*) any other relevant information which might assist the medical adviser; and

(*vi*) the name and address of any doctor(s) who might be able to provide further information about any of the above matters.

D The signature, name, address and qualifications of the registered medical practitioner who prepared the report, and the date of the report and of the examinations carried out.

2 The Applicant

(If there is more than one applicant, a report on each applicant should be supplied covering all the matters listed below.)

A (*i*) name, date of birth, sex, weight and height;

(*ii*) a family health history, covering the parents, the brothers and sisters and the children of the applicant, with details of any serious physical or mental illness and inherited and congenital disease;

(*iii*) marital history, including (if applicable) reasons for inability to have children;

(*iv*) past health history, including details of any serious physical or mental illness, disability, accident, hospital admission or attendance at an out-patient department, and in each case any treatment given;

(*v*) obstetric history (if applicable);

(*vi*) details of any present illness, including treatment and prognosis;

(*vii*) a full medical examination;

(*viii*)details of any daily consumption of alcohol, tobacco and habit-forming drugs;

(*ix*) any other relevant information which might assist the medical adviser; and

(*x*) the name and address of any doctor(s) who might be able to provide further information about any of the above matters.

B The signature, name, address and qualifications of the registered medical practitioner who prepared the report, and the date of the report and of the examinations carried out.

Appendix 3

The Adoption Agencies Regulations 1983

Citation, commencement, extent and interpretation

1 (1) These regulations may be cited as the Adoption Agencies Regulations 1983 and shall come into operation on 27th May 1984.

(2) These regulations shall not apply to Scotland.

(3) In these regulations, unless the context otherwise requires:
'the Act' *means* the Adoption Act 1958;
'the 1975 Act' *means* the Children Act 1975;
'adoption agency' *means* an approved adoption society or local authority;
'adoption panel' *means* a panel established in accordance with regulation 5;
'prospective adopter' *means* a person who proposes to adopt a child.

(4) Any reference in these regulations to any provision made by or contained in any enactment or instrument shall, except insofar as the context otherwise requires, be construed as including a reference to any provision which may re-enact or replace it, with or without modification.

(5) Any reference in these regulations to a numbered regulation or the Schedule is to the regulation bearing that number in or the Schedule to these regulations and any reference in a regulation or the Schedule to a numbered paragraph is a reference to the paragraph bearing that number in that regulation or the Schedule.

Approval of adoption societies

2 (1) An application to the Secretary of State under section 4 of the 1975 Act (approval of adoption societies) shall be made in writing on a form supplied by the Secretary of State.

(2) An unincorporated body of persons shall not apply for approval under section 4 of the 1975 Act.

244

Annual reports and information to be provided by approved adoption societies

3 Every approved adoption society shall:

(*a*) furnish the Secretary of State with two copies of the society's annual report as soon as is reasonably practicable after the issue thereof and with such other information as and when the Secretary of State may from time to time require;

(*b*) notify the Secretary of State in writing of any change in the society's name or in the address of its registered or head office within one month after such change;

(*c*) where the society proposes to cease, or expects to cease, to act as an adoption society, so notify the Secretary of State in writing not less than one month, or as soon as is reasonably practicable, before the date when the society will cease, or expects to cease, so to act; and

(*d*) where the society has ceased to act as an adoption society, notify the Secretary of State in writing that it has ceased so to act as soon thereafter as is reasonably practicable.

Application of regulations to certain adoption agencies

4 Where an adoption agency operates only for the purpose of putting persons into contact with other adoption agencies and for the purpose of putting such agencies into contact with each other or for either of such purposes, regulation 5 and, to the extent that it requires consultation with the adoption panel and the making of arrangements for the exercise of the panel's functions, regulation 6, shall not apply to such an agency.

Establishment of adoption panel and appointment of members

5 (1) An adoption agency shall forthwith establish at least one adoption panel and shall appoint the persons referred to in paragraphs (2) and (3) to be members of such a panel, so however that no more than 10 members shall be appointed to a panel and the persons appointed to a panel shall include at least one man and one woman.

(2) The adoption agency shall appoint as chairman of an adoption panel a person who has such experience in adoption work as the agency considers appropriate.

(3) In addition to the chairman the persons to be appointed shall include:

(*a*) two of the social workers in the employment of the adoption agency,

(b) at least one member of the adoption agency's management committee where the agency is an approved adoption society or, where the agency is a local authority, at least one member of that authority's social services committee,

(c) the person nominated as the medical adviser to the adoption agency under regulation 6(4) (or one of them if more than one are appointed), and

(d) at least two other persons not being members or employees of the adoption agency or elected members where the agency is a local authority.

(4) A person appointed to an adoption panel shall hold office subject to such conditions as to the period of his membership and otherwise as may be determined by the adoption agency.

(5) An adoption panel shall make the recommendations specified in regulation 10 only when at least five of its members meet as a panel and one of those is a social worker in the employment of the adoption agency.

(6) An adoption panel shall keep a written record of any of the recommendations specified in regulation 10 which it makes.

Adoption agency arrangements for adoption work

6 (1) An adoption agency shall, in consultation with the adoption panel and to the extent specified in paragraph (5) with the adoption agency's medical adviser, make arrangements which shall be set out in writing to govern the exercise of the agency's and the panel's functions and such arrangements shall be reviewed by the agency not less than once every three years.

(2) Subject to regulations 14 and 15, the arrangements referred to in paragraph (1) shall include provision:

(a) for maintaining the confidentiality and safekeeping of adoption information, case records and the indexes to them,

(b) for authorising access to such records and indexes or disclosure of information by virtue of regulation 15, and

(c) for ensuring that those for whom access is provided or to whom disclosure is made by virtue of regulation 15(2)(a) agree in writing before such authorisation is given that such records, indexes and information will remain confidential, so however that a child who is placed for adoption or who has been adopted and his prospective adopter or adoptive parent shall not be required to give such agreement in respect of that child's adoption.

(3) The adoption agency shall satisfy itself that social work staff employed on the agency's work have had such experience and hold such qualifications as the adoption agency considers appropriate to that work.

(4) The adoption agency shall nominate at least one registered medical practitioner to be the agency's medical adviser.

(5) The adoption agency's medical adviser shall be consulted in relation to the arrangements for access to and disclosure of health information which is required or permitted by virtue of regulation 15.

Adoption agency's duties in respect of a child and his parents or guardian

7 (1) When an adoption agency is considering adoption for a child it shall either:

(*a*) in respect of the child, having regard to his age and under-standing, and as the case may be his parents or guardian, so far as is reasonably practicable:

(i) provide a counselling service for them,

(ii) explain to them the legal implications of and procedures in relation to adoption and freeing for adoption, and

(iii) provide them with written information about the matters referred to in head (ii), or

(*b*) satisfy itself that the requirements of sub-paragraph (*a*) have been carried out by another adoption agency.

(2) Where, following the procedure referred to in paragraph (1), an adoption agency is considering adoption for a child, the agency shall:

(*a*) set up a case record in respect of the child and place on it any information obtained by virtue of this regulation,

(*b*) obtain, so far as is reasonably practicable, such particulars of the parents or guardian and having regard to his age and under-standing the child as are referred to in Parts I and III to V of the Schedule together with any other relevant information which may be requested by the adoption panel,

(*c*) arrange and obtain a written report by a registered medical practitioner on the child's health which shall deal with the matters specified in Part II of the Schedule, unless such a report has been made within six months before the setting up of the case record under sub-paragraph (*a*) and is available to the agency,

(*d*) arrange such other examinations and screening procedures of and tests on the child and, so far as is reasonably practicable, his parents, as are recommended by the adoption agency's medical

adviser, and obtain a copy of the written report of such examinations, screening procedures and tests, and

(e) prepare a written report containing the agency's observations on the matters referred to in this regulation, which shall be passed together with all information obtained by it by virtue of this regulation to the adoption panel or to another adoption agency.

(3) Where the identity of the father of an illegitimate child is known to the adoption agency, it shall so far as it considers reasonably practicable and in the interests of the child:

(a) carry out in respect of the father the requirements of paragraph (1)(a) as if they applied to him unless the agency is satisfied that another adoption agency has so complied with those requirements,

(b) obtain the particulars of him referred to in Parts III and IV of the Schedule together with any other relevant information which may be requested by the adoption panel, and arrange and obtain a copy of the written report of such examinations, screening procedures and tests on him as are recommended by the adoption agency's medical adviser, and

(c) ascertain so far as possible whether he intends to apply for custody of the child.

Adoption agency's duties in respect of a prospective adopter

8 (1) When an adoptive agency is considering whether a person may be suitable to be an adoptive parent, either:

(a) it shall:

(i) provide a counselling service for him,

(ii) explain to him the legal implications of and procedures in relation to adoption, and

(iii) provide him with written information about the matters referred to in head (ii), or

(b) it shall satisfy itself that the requirements of sub-paragraph (a) have been carried out in respect of him by another adoption agency.

(2) Where, following the procedure referred to in paragraph (1), an adoption agency considers that a person may be suitable to be an adoptive parent, it shall:

(a) set up a case record in respect of him and place on it any information obtained by virtue of this regulation,

(b) obtain such particulars as are referred to in Part VI of the

Schedule together with, so far as is reasonably practicable, any other relevant information which may be requested by the adoption panel,

(c) obtain a written report by a registered medical practitioner on the prospective adopter's health which shall deal with the matters specified in Part VII of the Schedule, unless such a report has been made within six months before the setting up of the case record under sub-paragraph (a) and is available to the agency,

(d) obtain a written report in respect of any premises which that person intends to use as his home if he adopts a child,

(e) obtain written reports of the interviews with two persons nominated by the prospective adopter to provide personal references for him,

(f) obtain a written report from the prospective adopter's local authority in relation to him, and

(g) prepare a written report containing the agency's observations on the matters referred to in this regulation, which shall be passed together with all information obtained by it by virtue of this regulation to the adoption panel or to another adoption agency.

Adoption agency's duties in respect of proposed placement

9 (1) Subject to paragraph (2), an adoption agency shall refer its proposal to place a particular child for adoption with a prospective adopter, which it considers may be appropriate, together with a written report containing its observations on the proposal and any information relevant to the proposed placement, to its adoption panel.

(2) An adoption agency shall refer its proposal to place a child for adoption to the adoption panel only if:

(a) any other adoption agency which has made a decision in accordance with regulation 11(1) that adoption is in the best interests of the child or that the prospective adopter is suitable to be an adoptive parent, has been consulted concerning the proposal, and

(b) any local authority or voluntary organisation which has parental rights and duties in respect of the child by virtue of section 14 or 23 of the 1975 Act (freeing child for adoption and transfer of parental rights and duties) or in whose care the child is, has been consulted and agrees with the proposal.

(3) An adoption agency which has a proposal to place a particular child for adoption with a prospective adopter shall set up case records in respect of them to the extent that it has not already set up such records

and place on the appropriate record any information, reports and decisions referred to it by another adoption agency together with any information to be passed to the adoption panel by virtue of this regulation in respect of them.

(4) An adoption agency shall obtain, so far as is reasonably practicable, any other relevant information which may be requested by the adoption panel in connection with the proposed placement.

Adoption panel functions

10 (1) Subject to paragraphs (2) and (3), an adoption panel shall consider the case of every child, prospective adopter and proposed placement referred to it by the adoption agency and shall make one or more of the recommendations to the agency, as the case may be, as to:

   (*a*) whether adoption is in the best interests of a child and, if the panel recommends that it is, whether an application under section 14 of the 1975 Act (freeing child for adoption) should be made to free the child for adoption,

   (*b*) whether a prospective adopter is suitable to be an adoptive parent, and

   (*c*) whether a prospective adopter would be a suitable adoptive parent for a particular child.

(2) An adoption panel may make the recommendations specified in paragraph (1) at the same time or at different times, so however that it shall make the recommendation specified in paragraph (1)(*c*) in respect of a particular child and prospective adopter only if:

   (*a*) that recommendation is to be made at the same meeting of the panel at which a recommendation has been made that adoption is in the best interests of the child, or

   (*b*) an adoption agency decision has been made in accordance with regulation 11(1) that adoption is in the best interests of the child, and

   (*c*) in either case:

      (i) the recommendation specified in paragraph (1)(*c*) is to be made at the same meeting of the panel at which a recommendation has been made that the prospective adopter is suitable to be an adoptive parent, or

      (ii) an adoption agency decision has been made in accordance with regulation 11(1) that the prospective adopter is suitable to be an adoptive parent.

(3) In considering what recommendations to make the panel shall have

regard to the duties imposed upon the adoption agency by sections 3 and 13 of the 1975 Act (duty to promote welfare of child and religious upbringing of adopted child) and shall, as the case may be:

   (a) consider and take into account all the information and reports passed to it by virtue of regulations 7(2)(e), 8(2)(g) and 9(1),

   (b) request the adoption agency to obtain any other relevant information which the panel considers necessary,

   (c) obtain legal advice in relation to each case together with advice on an application for an adoption order or, as the case may be, an application to free a child for adoption.

Adoption agency decisions and notifications

11 (1) An adoption agency shall make a decision on a matter referred to in regulation 10(1)(a), (b) or (c) only after taking into account the recommendation of the adoption panel made by virtue of that regulation on such matter.

(2) As soon as possible after making such a decision the adoption agency shall, as the case may be, notify in writing:

   (a) the parents of the child, including the father of an illegitimate child where the agency considers this to be in the child's interests, or the guardian of the child, if their whereabouts are known to the agency, of its decision as to whether it considers adoption to be in the best interests of the child,

   (b) the persons to be notified under sub-paragraph (a), if it considers adoption to be in the best interests of the child, of its decision as to whether an application under section 14 of the 1975 Act (freeing child for adoption) should be made to free the child for adoption,

   (c) the prospective adopter of its decision as to whether it considers him to be suitable to be an adoptive parent, and

   (d) the prospective adopter of its decision that he would be suitable as such for a particular child.

Placement for adoption

12 (1) Where an adoption agency has decided in accordance with regulation 11(1) that a prospective adopter would be a suitable adoptive parent for a particular child it shall provide the prospective adopter with written information about the child, his personal history and background, including his religious and cultural background, his health history and current state of health, together with the adoption agency's written proposals in respect of the adoption, including proposals as to the date of placement for adoption with the prospective adopter.

(2) If the prospective adopter accepts the adoption agency's proposals the agency shall:

> (*a*) inform the child of the proposed placement for adoption with the prospective adopter where the child is capable of understanding the proposal,
>
> (*b*) send a written report of the child's health history and current state of health to the prospective adopter's registered medical practitioner, if any, before the proposed placement, together with particulars of the proposed placement,
>
> (*c*) notify the local authority and the district health authority in whose area the prospective adopter resides in writing before the placement with particulars of the proposed placement,
>
> (*d*) notify the local education authority in whose area the prospective adopter resides in writing before the placement with particulars of the proposed placement if the child is of compulsory school age within the meaning of section 35 of the Education Act 1944(**a**) or the adoption agency's medical adviser considers the child to be handicapped,
>
> (*e*) place the child with the prospective adopter, so however that where the child already has his home with the prospective adopter the agency shall notify the prospective adopter in writing of the date the child is placed with him by the agency for adoption,
>
> (*f*) notify in writing the parents of the child, including the father of an illegitimate child where the agency considers this to be in the child's interests, or the guardian of the child, if their whereabouts are known to the agency, that the child has been placed for adoption, so however that no such notification shall be given to a person who has made a declaration under section 14(7) or 15(4) of the 1975 Act (declaration as to no further involvement with child),
>
> (*g*) ensure that the child is visited within one week of the placement and on such other occasions as the adoption agency considers necessary in order to supervise the child's well-being,
>
> (*h*) ensure that written reports are obtained of such visits,
>
> (*i*) provide such advice and assistance to the prospective adopter as the agency considers necessary,
>
> (*j*) monitor the child's health during the placement to the extent that the adoption agency's medical adviser considers necessary, and
>
> (*k*) review the placement of the child if an application for an adoption order has not been made within three months of the place-

ment, and on such other occasions as the adoption agency considers necessary.

Review of case where no placement made within six months of freeing for adoption

13 (1) Where a child has been freed for adoption by virtue of an order under section 14 of the 1975 Act (freeing child for adoption) and six months have elapsed since the making of that order and the child does not have his home with a prospective adopter, the adoption agency in which parental rights and duties are then vested by virtue of section 14 or 23 of the 1975 Act shall review that child's case to determine why no placement has been made and what action if any should be taken to safeguard and promote his welfare.

(2) A case to which paragraph (1) applies shall be subject to such a review at intervals of not more than six months.

Confidentiality and preservation of case records

14 (1) Subject to regulation 15, any information obtained or recommendations or decisions made by virtue of these regulations shall be treated by the adoption agency as confidential.

(2) Where a case record has been set up by an adoption agency under regulations 7(2)(*a*), 8(2)(*a*) or 9(3) in respect of a child or a prospective adopter, any report, recommendation or decision made by that agency by virtue of these regulations in respect of that child or that prospective adopter shall be placed on the case record relating to that child or, as the case may be, that prospective adopter, and any case records set up by the agency together with the indexes to them shall be kept in a place of special security.

(3) Subject to regulation 16(2), an adoption agency shall preserve the indexes to all its case records and the case records in respect of those cases in which an adoption order is made in a place of special security for at least 75 years and shall preserve other case records in a place of special security for so long as it considers appropriate, so however that any case records and indexes may be so preserved on microfilm or such other system as reproduces the total contents of any such record or index.

Access to case records and disclosure of information

15 (1) Subject to paragraph (3), an adoption agency shall provide such access to its case records and the indexes to them and disclose such information in its possession, as may be required:

   (*a*) to those holding an inquiry under section 76 of the Child Care Act 1980 (**a**) (inquiries), for the purposes of such an inquiry,

(*b*) to the Secretary of State,

(*c*) subject to the provisions of sections 29(7) and 32(3) of the Local Government Act 1974(**b**) (investigations and disclosure), to a Local Commissioner, appointed under section 23 of that Act (Commissioners for Local Administration), for the purposes of any investigation conducted in accordance with Part III of that Act,

(*d*) to the persons and authorities referred to in regulations 11 and 12 to the extent specified in those regulations,

(*e*) to a guardian ad litem or reporting officer appointed under rules made pursuant to section 20 of the 1975 Act (guardian ad litem and reporting officer) for the purposes of the discharge of his duties in that behalf, and

(*f*) to a court having power to make an order under the Act, the Adoption Act 1968(**a**) or Part I of the 1975 Act for the purposes of the discharge of its duties in that behalf.

(2) Subject to paragraph (3), an adoption agency may provide such access to its case records and the indexes to them and disclose such information in its possession, as it thinks fit:

(*a*) for the purposes of carrying out its functions as an adoption agency, and

(*b*) to a person who is authorised in writing by the Secretary of State to obtain information for the purposes of research.

(3) A written record shall be kept by an adoption agency of any access provided or disclosure made by virtue of this regulation.

Transfer of case records

16 (1) Subject to paragraphs (2) and (3), an adoption agency may transfer a copy of a case record (or part thereof) to another adoption agency when it considers this to be in the interests of a child or prospective adopter to whom the record relates, and a written record shall be kept of any such transfer.

(2) An approved adoption society which intends to cease to act or exist as such shall forthwith either transfer its case records to another adoption agency having first obtained the Secretary of State's approval for such transfer, or transfer its case records:

(*a*) to the local authority in whose area the society's head office is situated, or

(*b*) in the case of a society which amalgamates with another

approved adoption society to form a new approved adoption society, to the new society.

(3) An adoption agency to which case records are transferred by virtue of paragraph (2)(*a*) or (*b*) shall notify the Secretary of State in writing of such transfer.

Progress reports under section 15 of the 1975 Act

17 Where parental rights and duties relating to a child who is in Great Britain have been transferred from one adoption agency to another by virtue of an order under section 23 of the 1975 Act, the agency in which those rights and duties are vested shall provide such information as the agency which obtained the order under section 14 of the 1975 Act considers necessary for it to comply with its duty under section 15(2) and (3) of the 1975 Act (progress reports to former parent).

Revocations

18 The Adoption Agencies Regulations 1976(**a**) and The Adoption Agencies (Amendment) Regulations 1981(**b**) are hereby revoked.

Regulations 7(2)(*b*) and (*c*)
and (3)(*b*), and 8(2)(*b*) and (*c*)

SCHEDULE

PART I

PARTICULARS RELATING TO THE CHILD

1 Name, sex, date and place of birth and address.

2 Whether legitimate or illegitimate at birth and, if illegitimate whether subsequently legitimated.

3 Nationality.

4 Physical description.

5 Personality and social development.

6 Religion, including details of baptism, confirmation or equivalent ceremonies.

7 Details of any wardship proceedings and of any court orders or

local authority resolutions relating to the parental rights and duties in respect of the child or to his custody and maintenance.

8 Details of any brothers and sisters, including dates of birth, arrangements in respect of care and custody and whether any brother or sister is also being considered for adoption.

9 Extent of access to members of the child's natural family and, if the child is illegitimate, his father, and in each case the nature of the relationship enjoyed.

10 If the child has been in the care of a local authority or voluntary organisation, details (including dates) of any placements with foster parents, or other arrangements in respect of the care of the child, including particulars of the persons with whom the child has had his home and observations on the care provided.

11 Names, addresses and types of schools attended, with dates and educational attainments.

12 Any special needs in relation to the child's health (whether physical or mental) and his emotional and behavioural development and whether he is subject to a statement under the Education Act 1981(**a**).

13 What, if any, rights to or interest in property or any claim to damages, under the Fatal Accidents Act 1976 (**b**) or otherwise, the child stands to retain or lose if adopted.

14 Wishes and feelings in relation to adoption and, as the case may be, an application under section 14 of the 1975 Act, including any wishes in respect of religious and cultural upbringing.

15 Any other relevant information which the agency considers may assist the panel.

PART II

MATTERS TO BE COVERED IN REPORT ON THE CHILD'S HEALTH

1 Name, date of birth, sex, weight and height.

2 A neo-natal report on the child, including:

   (*a*) details of the birth, and any complications.

   (*b*) results of a physical examination and screening tests,

   (*c*) details of any treatment given,

(*d*) details of any problem in management and feeding,

(*e*) any other relevant information which may assist the panel,

(*f*) the name and address of any doctor who may be able to provide further information about any of the above matters.

3 A full health history and examination of the child, including:

(*a*) details of any serious illness, disability, accident, hospital admission or attendance at an out-patient department, and in each case any treatment given,

(*b*) details and dates of immunisations,

(*c*) a physical and developmental assessment according to age, including an assessment of vision and hearing and of neurological, speech and language development and any evidence of emotional disorder,

(*d*) for a child over five years of age, the school health history (if available),

(*e*) any other relevant information which may assist the panel.

4 The signature, name, address and qualifications of the registered medical practitioner who prepared the report, the date of the report and of the examinations carried out together with the name and address of any doctor (if different) who may be able to provide further information about any of the above matters.

PART III

PARTICULARS RELATING TO EACH NATURAL PARENT, INCLUDING WHERE APPROPRIATE THE FATHER OF AN ILLEGITIMATE CHILD

1 Name, date and place of birth and address.

2 Marital status and date and place of marriage (if any).

3 Past and present relationship (if any) with the other natural parent, including comments on its stability.

4 Physical description.

5 Personality.

6 Religion.

7 Educational attainments.

8 Past and present occupations and interests.

9 Names and brief details of the personal circumstances of the parents and any brothers and sisters of the natural parent, with their ages or ages at death.

10 Wishes and feelings in relation to adoption and, as the case may be, an application under section 14 of the 1975 Act, including any wishes in respect of the child's religious and cultural upbringing.

11 Any other relevant information which the agency considers may assist the panel.

Part IV

Particulars Relating to the Health of each Natural Parent including where appropriate the Father of an Illegitimate Child

1 Name, date of birth, sex, weight and height.

2 A family health history, covering the parents, the brothers and sisters (if any) and the other children (if any) of the natural parent with details of any serious physical or mental illness and inherited and congenital disease.

3 Past health history, including details of any serious physical or mental illness, disability, accident, hospital admission or attendance at an out-patient department, and in each case any treatment given.

4 A full obstetric history of the mother, including any problems in the ante-natal, labour and post-natal periods, with the results of any tests carried out during or immediately after pregnancy.

5 Details of any present illness, including treatment and prognosis.

6 Any other relevant information which the agency considers may assist the panel.

7 The signature, name, address and qualifications of any registered medical practitioner who supplied any of the information in this Part together with the name and address of any doctor (if different) who may be able to provide further information about any of the above matters.

Part V

Particulars Relating to a Guardian

1 Particulars referred to in paragraphs 1, 6, 10 and 11 of Part III.

PART VI

PARTICULARS RELATING TO THE PROSPECTIVE ADOPTER

1 Name, date and place of birth and address.

2 Domicile.

3 Marital status, date and place of marriage (if any) and comments on stability of relationship.

4 Details of any previous marriage.

5 If a married person proposes to adopt a child alone, the reasons for this.

6 Physical description.

7 Personality.

8 Religion, and whether willing to follow any wishes of a child or his natural parents or guardian in respect of the child's religious and cultural upbringing.

9 Educational attainments.

10 Past and present occupations and interests.

11 Details of income and comments on the living standards of the household.

12 Details of other members of the prospective adopter's household (including any children of the prospective adopter even if not resident in the household).

13 Details of the parents and any brothers or sisters of the prospective adopter, with their ages or ages at death.

14 Attitudes to adoption of such other members of the prospective adopter's household and family as the agency considers appropriate.

15 Previous experience of caring for children as step-parent, foster parent, child-minder or prospective adopter and assessment of ability in this respect, together where appropriate with assessment of ability in bringing up the prospective adopter's own children.

16 Reasons for wishing to adopt a child and extent of understanding of the nature and effect of adoption.

17 Assessment of ability to bring up an adopted child throughout his childhood.

18 Details of any adoption allowance payable.

19 Names and addresses of two referees who will give personal references on the prospective adopter.

20 Name and address of the prospective adopter's registered medical practitioner, if any.

21 Any other relevant information which the agency considers may assist the panel.

Part VII

Matters to be Covered in Report on Health of the Prospective Adopter

1 Name, date of birth, sex, weight and height.

2 A family health history, covering the parents, the brothers and sisters (if any) and the children (if any) of the prospective adopter, with details of any serious physical or mental illness and inherited and congenital disease.

3 Marital history, including (if applicable) reasons for inability to have children.

4 Past health history, including details of any serious physical or mental illness, disability, accident, hospital admission or attendance at an out-patient department, and in each case any treatment given.

5 Obstetric history (if applicable).

6 Details of any present illness, including treatment and prognosis.

7 A full medical examination.

8 Details of any daily consumption of alcohol, tobacco and habit-forming drugs.

9 Any other relevant information which the agency considers may assist the panel.

10 The signature, name, address and qualifications of the registered medical practitioner who prepared the report, the date of the report

and of the examinations carried out together with the name and address of any doctor (if different) who may be able to provide further information about any of the above matters.

EXPLANATORY NOTE

(This Note is not part of the Regulations.)

These Regulations supersede and replace with amendments the Adoption Agencies Regulations 1976. The amendments take account of the bringing into operation on 27th May 1984 of the provisions specified in the Children Act 1975 and the Adoption Act 1976 (Commencement) Order 1983/S.I. 1983/1946), in particular section 14 of the Children Act 1975 (Freeing child for adoption).

The Regulations make provision for the approval of adoption societies and for annual reports and information to be provided by such societies (regulations 2 and 3). They provide for the establishment of adoption panels by adoption agencies and for arrangements to be made by agencies in relation to their adoption work (regulations 4, 5 and 6). They specify the procedures to be followed before and after a child is placed for adoption (regulations 7–13). They make provision for the confidentiality and preservation of case records and for access to case records and disclosure of information (regulations 14 and 15). They also make provision in respect of the transfer of case records between adoption agencies and progress reports to former parents of children who have been freed for adoption (regulations 16 and 17).

Appendix 4

Table of Corresponding Provisions (AA 1976)

AA 1958	AA 1976	AA 1958	AA 1976
s 20	s 50(1)–(6)	s 47	s 37(4)
s 20A	s 51	s 48	s 37(3)
s 21(1), (4)–(6)	Sch 1, para 1(1), (3)–(5)	s 50	s 57, s 67(3)
		s 51	s 58
s 24(1)–(3)	Sch 1, para 4(1)–(3)	s 52	s 56(1), (2)
		s 54(1)	s 68
s 24(4)	Sch 1, para 2(1)	s 55	s 69
s 24(6), (7)	Sch 1, para 4(4), (6)	s 56	s 67
		s 57	s 72(1), (3), (4), s 56(3)
s 26(1)	s 52(1)		
s 26(2)	Sch 1, para 6	Sch 5, paras 5–7, 10	Sch 2, paras 4, 5, 8
s 26(3)	s 52(4)	**AA 1960**	
s 27	Sch 1, para 5(1)	s 1(1), (3)	s 52(2), (4)
s 28(1)	s 72(1)	**AA 1964**	
s 29(1)	s 11(1)	s 1(5)	s 59(3)
s 29(2A)	s 11(2)	s 2(1)	s 60
s 29(3)–(5)	s 11(3)–(5)	s 3	Sch 1, para 2
s 32(1), (1A), (2), (3)	s 9	**AA 1968**	
s 32(4)	s 67(5)	s 4(3)	s 72(2)
s 34	s 27	s 5(1)	s 59(1)
s 34A	s 28, s 67(1), (3)	s 6(1), 3–(5)	s 53(1)–(5)
s 35	s 30	s 6(2)	s 52(3)
s 36(1), (2)	s 31	s 7	s 54
s 36(3)	s 22(4)	s 8	Sch 1, paras 1, 3–5
s 37	s 32		
s 38	s 33(1)	s 9	s 70
s 39	s 33(2)	s 10(1)	s 71(2)
s 40(4)–(6)	s 35	s 11	s 71(1), s 72
s 43	s 34	s 12(1)	s 66(1)
s 44	s 36	s 12(2)–(4)	s 67
s 45	s 37(1)		
s 46	s 37(2)		

CA 1975	AA 1976	CA 1975	AA 1976
s 1	s 1	s 25	s 55
s 2	s 2	s 30	s 29
s 3	s 6	s 100	s 62
s 4	s 3	s 101	s 63
s 5	s 4	s 102	s 61
s 6	s 5	s 106	s 67(1), (2), (4),
s 7	s 8		(5)
s 8(1)–(5), (7),		s 107	s 72
(8)	s 12	Sch 1, paras	
s 9	s 13	1(1), (2), (4)	s 38
s 10	s 14	1(5)	s 72(1)
s 11	s 15	1(6)	s 46(3)
s 12(1)–(5)	s 16	2	s 46(1), (2)
s 13	s 7	3	s 39(1), (2),
s 14	s 18		(4)–(6)
s 15	s 19	4	s 41
s 16	s 20	5(1), (2)	Sch 2, para 6
s 17	s 26	5(3)	s 46(1)
s 18	s 22(1)–(3)	6	s 42
s 19	s 25	7	s 47
s 20(1), (2)	s 65	8	s 48
s 21	s 64	9	s 39(3)
s 22(1), (2)	s 66(3), (4)	10	s 44(1)
s 22(3)	s 23	11	s 49
s 22(4), (5)	s 24	14	s 43
s 23	s 21	15	s 45
s 24(1)–(8)	s 17, s 12(5)	16	s 44(2), (3)
s 24(8A)	s 53(1)	17	s 46(5)
s 24(9)	s 70, s 71(2)		

Index

INDEX

CAROL ELLIS has written several books for young people. Her subjects have included law in Ancient Greece, African American artists and activists, the Gilded Age, endangered species, and the martial arts. She lives in New York.